Modern European History

A Garland Series of Outstanding Dissertations

General Editor
William H. McNeill
University of Chicago

Associate Editors

Eastern Europe
Charles Jelavich
Indiana University

Great Britain
Peter Stansky
Stanford University

France
David H. Pinkney
University of Washington

Russia
Barbara Jelavich
Indiana University

Germany
Enno E. Kraehe
University of Virginia

MODERN EUROPEAN HISTORY

Bering's First Expedition

Expedition

A Re-examination Based on Eighteenth-Century
Books, Maps, and Manuscripts

Carol Louise Urness

Garland Publishing, Inc.
New York and London 1987

Library of Congress Cataloging-in-Publication Data

Urness, Carol Louise.
  Bering's first expedition.

  (Modern European history)
  Originally presented as the author's thesis
(Ph. D.)—University of Minnesota, 1982.
  Bibliography: p.
  1. Kamchatskaîa ėkspedit͡sii͡a (1st : 1725–1730)
2. Bering, Vitus Jonassen, 1681–1741. I. Title.
II. Series.
G700 1725.B47U76 1987   910'.92'4   87-7434
ISBN 0-8240-8065-3 (alk. paper)

All volumes in this series are printed on acid-free,
250-year-life paper.

Printed in the United States of America

BERING'S FIRST EXPEDITION: A RE-EXAMINATION BASED ON
EIGHTEENTH CENTURY BOOKS, MAPS, AND MANUSCRIPTS

A THESIS
SUBMITTED TO THE FACULTY OF THE GRADUATE SCHOOL
OF THE UNIVERSITY OF MINNESOTA

by

Carol Louise Urness

IN PARTIAL FULFILLMENT OF THE REQUIREMENTS
FOR THE DEGREE OF
DOCTOR OF PHILOSOPHY

June, 1982

TABLE OF CONTENTS

INTRODUCTION

This dissertation examines eighteenth century books, maps, and manuscripts relating to the First Kamchatka Expedition of Vitus Bering. Peter the Great initiated the expedition to explore northeastern Siberia, and he selected Vitus Bering, a Dane with more than twenty years of service in the Russian Navy, to lead the expedition, which lasted from 1725 to 1730. Through the examination of the sources written by contemporaries of Peter the Great and Vitus Bering, a new understanding of the First Kamchatka Expedition emerges.

From the earliest reports of the expedition to the present, most writers about the First Kamchatka Expedition assumed that Peter had sent Bering to explore the northeastern corner of the Siberian mainland, to determine whether or not it was connected to America and thus to find out if a northeast passage by sea around the eastern part of Asia was possible. Bering sailed between the Chukchi Peninsula and the North American continent through the strait that now bears his name, but he did not continue westward along the Siberian coast to a river known to the Russians, the Kolyma or Lena, and critics from his time to our own have accused him of failing to prove the possibility of a passage. Yet Bering, in his "Short Account" of his expedition, stated he had "fully and completely" satisfied the orders given to him by Peter the Great.

The idea that Peter the Great wanted Bering to explore the eastern part of Siberia as part of a northeast passage from western Europe to the Pacific Ocean was fostered in western Europe, which

had a longstanding hope of finding a northern sea route to China,
Japan, and the East Indies, either by a northeast passage or a
northwest passage through or around North America. Thus any reports
of Russian explorations received by western Europeans were liable
to be incorporated into western European hopes for discovering a
northeast passage. The first chapter of the dissertation establishes
this broad historical context.

Many western Europeans traveled or served in Russia during the
time of Peter the Great. Some of them returned to their homelands
and published books about their experiences in Russia. Chapter II
of this study is a survey of the accounts of these contemporaries
of Peter the Great as they pertain either to the interior route (by
river and overland) to China or to Russian explorations in the
northern seas. Russia had obtained trading privileges with China in
1689 by the Treaty of Nerchinsk and some writers stated that the
route to China was rapid and easy. Others reported that the route
was long and dangerous and that Peter wanted to improve it by building
canals between rivers. Some commentators believed a northeast passage
was impractical because of the difficulties of sailing in the north
and the huge "mountains of ice" in the northern seas. Russian
explorations, according to contemporaries of Peter, offered slight
hope for any northeast passage from western Europe to the Pacific
Ocean.

On maps, the hope for a possible northeast passage focussed
on the question of a land connection between Asia and America, not

on the conditions for sailing in the northern seas. Two European mapmakers, Nicolaas Witsen (1641-1717) and Guillaume Delisle (1675-1726) portrayed unclosed promontories extending from eastern Siberia toward America on their early maps of Asia. Both of these maps were influential and were copied by other cartographers; these maps helped establish the idea that the "end" of northeastern Asia was unknown and that Peter sent Bering to explore this area. But Witsen and Delisle made later maps, based on information from Peter, without any open-ended promontories. These maps, together with the commentaries of Peter's contemporaries, are good documentary evidence that Peter the Great did not send Bering to discover whether the mainland of Asia was connected to America, as part of a search for a northeast passage.

In the mid-twentieth century, a different purpose was postulated for the First Kamchatka Expedition. Manuscript maps published in an atlas edited by Aleksei V. Efimov, in 1964, show that the coast of northeastern Asia, prior to Bering's expedition, was not believed to join to America. Attention shifted to maps, since it is known that Bering received a map made in Germany with his instructions from Peter. Boris P. Polevoi, on the basis of a map of Kamchatka made by Johann Baptist Homann (1663-1724), stated that Peter wanted Bering to explore the land shown east of Kamchatka on the map. Raymond H. Fisher accepted Polevoi's identification of the land to the east as the area Peter sent Bering to explore. Fisher elaborated this thesis in Bering's Voyages: Whither and Why, published in 1977.

Expedition using eighteenth century sources--Bering's "Short Account," Peter's instructions to Bering, and Homann's maps. The result is an interpretation of the voyage which is different from either the traditional view of it or the Polevoi/Fisher interpretation.

Why did the view that Bering was looking for a northeast passage become so dominant in the literature about the expedition? This question is considered, again, in the context of the early sources. The authorship and content of the first newspaper article about the expedition, published in 1730 in St. Petersburg, are an important part of the answer to this question. The newspaper article, as indicated in Chapter VI, was incorporated into the printings of Bering's "Short Account" which appeared in western Europe. The article features the northeast passage, a subject which Bering does not mention in his own "Short Account" of the expedition. Finally, the views of Bering's contemporaries about the purpose and accomplishments of the First Kamchatka Expedition are recorded in Chapter VII.

This study does not attempt to recreate the events of the First Kamchatka Expedition. Rather, it demonstrates how the early transmission of information about the expedition affected the views of its purpose and results. The writings of contemporaries of Peter the Great and Bering, considered in the context of their publication and authorship, reveal new information about the First Kamchatka Expedition. A re-examination

of these writings leads to a new interpretation of the purpose
and results of the expedition. In addition, this re-examination
provides a rationale for the development and persistence of the
earliest interpretation of the expedition.

In my research, I have had two great advantages, I have
had the good fortune to benefit not only from Raymond H.
Fisher's publications, but by his friendship, advice,
and encouragement. Fisher based his studies of the Bering
voyages on the works of Soviet scholars, the manuscript
maps published by Efimov, contemporary publications about the
voyages in western Europe, and the writings of historians
about the Bering voyages. My own research, obviously, could
not have been undertaken without the pioneering work of Fisher
and the Soviet scholars of the Bering voyages.

I have also had the advantage of a unique library resource,
the James Ford Bell Library at the University of Minnesota. The
quality of its holdings made this study possible. The library
has a manuscript map of the First Kamchatka Expedition, the
eighteenth century printings and translations of Bering's "Short
Account"of the expedition, and nearly all of the printed
eighteenth century accounts of travelers to Russia. These are
present in various translations and editions. Whenever possible,
I have quoted from the earliest English editions or translations
of these sources after comparing the original text with all
subsequent editions and translations. Because the first printings

of Bering's "Short Account" of his expedition are rare and are important to this study, transcriptions of five of them are included as an appendix to this study.

Carol Urness

Acknowledgements

This study was completed over a number of years and I have enjoyed the help, in one form or another, of many people. I appreciate the support and interest of my family, especially my parents, Dorothy Skow Urness and Carl Urness, and friends, especially Dorothy Bohn, Arnold Fredrickson, Dorothy Lockard, Dorothy Nelson, Lois Newstrand, Karen Sheldon, and Frank Sinnen. Colleagues at the University Libraries, particularly in the James Ford Bell Library (John Parker, Jane Rasmussen, Vicki Zobel) and in the Special Collections Department (John Jenson, Austin McLean, and Kathy Tezla) offered moral support. John Jenson and Jackie Sund helped with the final typing.

I benefited by a thesis committee at the University of Minnesota at a critical time in my research (Theofanis Stavrou, chairman; Thomas Noonan, David Noble, Fred Lukermann, John Rice). Professor Stavrou, my adviser throughout, proved not only patient and understanding, but also confident in the outcome of my research, for which I am extremely grateful.

Raymond H. Fisher and John Parker provided aid in the form of supportive criticism in readings of early drafts of loosely-directed chapters. They were both relieved, undoubtedly, when I told them, "I'll wait until I finish before I let you read anything else."

Jean McGreehan helped me with more obscure eighteenth-century German passages than I care to remember, but in the process we became friends and learned the joys of joint scholarship, which I hope will bear fruit of another kind.

Most of all, I thank Jessie Richardson, my friend and fellow birdwatcher, for typing all of the text in its various preliminary drafts. She and Ben gave up many weekend walks in the woods and spring and fall birding vacations for this study. If there was reproach in their hearts, they never showed it.

Chapter I

The Historical Context: Russia and European Expansion

This dissertation has two themes: the first is how a close examination of eighteenth century books, maps, and manuscripts describing the First Kamchatka Expedition relates to the standard view of the purpose and results of the expedition; the second is an explanation of the purpose and results of the expedition, based on the examination of these sources. The earliest printed accounts of Russian geographical discoveries established the initial attitudes about the purpose of these discoveries--attitudes which have persisted to the present.

Western Europeans in the early eighteenth century found it difficult to believe that Russia had become a maritime nation. Yet Russian ships were sailing to western European ports. As one contemporary wrote of Peter the Great: "The maritime and trading Powers, from whom he learnt Navigation, Building of Ships, and so many other Arts unknown to Russia before his Reign; and of whom he borrowed so many skilful Workmen of all kinds, perceived too late, that they had raised themselves a very potent and dangerous Rival."[1] Western Europeans identified reports of Russian geographical discoveries with their own dream of finding a northern sea passage to the east.

As a historical background to western European attitudes toward Russian geographical discoveries, a very brief summary of European interest in reaching eastern lands is useful, for it was in relation to this interest that many of western Europe's initial attitudes toward Russia were formed.

Beginning in the mid-fifteenth century, European obsessions with reaching "the Indies" initiated the expansion of Europe. Reports of rich kingdoms, eastern Christians, and fabulous trading opportunities stirred Europeans to search for a sea route to eastern lands. Following their first voyages, European explorers, merchants, missionaries, and settlers went to lands far from Europe. They founded commercial empires, colonies, missions, and trading settlements that spread European influence to distant parts of the world by the eighteenth century.[2] At the outset of this period, Russia was less known to western Europe than China or India, and seemed as remote. By the eighteenth century, however, Russia had expanded its frontiers to become a full European power, and additionally, had created an eastern empire that stretched across Asia to the Pacific Ocean and to North America, where the Russian presence could lead to potential conflict with other European empires. Russia was thus involved in European expansion in two ways--initially as a little-known region on the northeastern fringe of Europe which was described in connection to Europe's obsession with reaching eastern lands, and secondly as a part of Europe which was itself expanding its territory.

Western European fascination with eastern regions had a long history--not unnatural since it was all one land mass, over which people and goods had moved for centuries. Alexander's conquests in India and Roman trade with China testify to the political and commercial interest. Early geographers--Ptolemy, Strabo, and Pliny, for example--reflect a scientific interest in the location and extent of Asia, a land to which Claudius Ptolemy's Geography (2nd century A.D.) gives no eastern boundary.

The crusades kept alive contact with eastern peoples, and pilgrimage literature reported about non-Christian and Christian nations in Asia. In the thirteenth century, traders from the Mediterranean Sea were engaged in a lively trade in the Black Sea. Ships were sent out from the Mediterranean on exploring missions down the west coast of Africa, searching for an all-water route to India. Here was an early expression of the desire to circumvent the overland route to eastern trade.

The Mongol empire, reaching from China to Europe, kept the momentum from the east moving westward to focus European attention on defense. At the same time, Mongol control of the caravan route facilitated travel and trade, and the religious tolerance of the Mongols encouraged European hopes that the Mongols might be converted to Christianity. This gave rise to diplomatic and religious initiatives in the west which produced the travels of Giovanni da Pian Carpine and Willem van Ruysbroeck in the mid-thirteenth century. Accounts of their experiences and those of other travelers in the thirteenth and fourteenth centuries were written down and widely circulated, whetting European interest in eastern lands.

The most famous travel narrative of the thirteenth century was

written by Marco Polo, a Venetian. His <u>Travels</u> became a chief
source of European knowledge of the east. Polo included a short
notice of Russia, which was at that time under Mongol dominion:
"Russia is a very large province lying towards the north. The
people are Christians and observe the Greek rite. . . . It is not
a country of much commercial wealth. It is true, however, that it
produces precious furs--sables, ermine, vair, <u>ercolin</u>, and foxes in
abundance, the best and most beautiful in the world. There are also
many silver mines, yielding no small amount of silver. But there
is nothing else worth mentioning. . . ."[3] At the outset of the age
of printing, the books of geographers, travelers, missionaries, navigators and cartographers appeared along with fabulous tales about
the riches to be found in the east. Marco Polo's <u>Travels</u> appeared
in numerous editions and translations.[4] In the many books published
in the early age of printing, little was added to the knowledge of
Russia beyond what Marco Polo had said. No printed books appeared
that described the coming of the Varangians to Russia in the ninth
century, or told of Novgorod in the north and Kiev in the south, or
described the conquest by the Mongols. No notice was taken of the
assumption of the title "Grand Prince of Moscow" by Ivan Kalita in
1328, or of the success of his descendants in adding to his power
and territory as tribute collectors for the Mongols. Russia was
still known only as a large land in the north, where the people
were Orthodox Christians and the chief wealth came from furs. European attention was focussed on lands farther to the east and on

the caravan route that led to them.

Europeans wanted to find a sea route to the eastern lands.
Some Europeans believed that this route could be found to the west.
This idea was supported by the Geography of Ptolemy and by descriptions of distances recorded by Marco Polo. The thesis was first
tested in 1492 by Christopher Columbus, and later by his successors
in exploration to the west. The search for a route to the southeast was led by Portugal. For over seventy years before Columbus
sailed for Spain, Portuguese ships had been sent in explorations
southward along the African coast, in hopes of finding a sea route
to the east. The preeminence of Portugal and Spain in exploration
was such that in 1494 the Treaty of Tordesillas, sanctioned by the
papacy in an effort to prevent conflict between the two powers,
divided the dominion of the earth between them, by a line of demar-
cation established at the longitude of 180° west of the Cape Verde
Islands. The position of this line on the other side of the globe
could only be guessed at, but the intention was clear: Portugal was
given rights to the eastern corner of South America, to Africa, India,
and to the East Indies; Spain was to have the rest. Portuguese
ships, commanded by Vasco da Gama, reached Calicut in 1498, thus
opening a sea route to trade in India. The rest of Europe was not
to be excluded so easily, however, but with the southern sea routes
claimed by Portugal and Spain, attention turned to explorations in
the north. In 1497 and 1498 John Cabot made two voyages for the English in search of a westward route in the northern hemisphere from

Bristol to Cathay.[5] Later expeditions of Danes, Dutch, French, and
Italians were sent to North America for the same purpose.

An alternative to a sea route was a different river and overland
route, and one proposal to compete with the Portuguese sea route was
made early in the sixteenth century. A Genoese merchant, Paolo Centurione, got a letter of introduction from Pope Leo X to Basil III,
Grand Prince of Moscow. Centurione wanted to open a new trade route
to India, from the valley of the Indus River over the mountains to
the Oxus River, then to the Caspian Sea, and via the Volga and Oka
rivers to Moscow, and finally overland to the Baltic. This route was
not tried, but Basil III did send an ambassador, Demetrius Gerasimov,
to Rome. Gerasimov's report on Russia was included in a book by
Paolo Giovio, De Legatione Moscovitarum, published in 1525.[6] An
ambassador from the Austrian Hapsburgs, Baron Sigismund von Herberstein, after visiting Muscovy in 1517-18 and again in 1526-27, wrote
a substantial account of Russia which was first published in the mid-
sixteenth century and appeared in many translations and editions.[7]

In the mid-sixteenth century, Russia came to England's attention
for another reason--the search for a sea route to the east. England
wanted to share in the eastern trade. In 1527 Robert Thorne, an
English merchant trading in Seville, wrote a letter to Henry VIII
stating " . . . there is left one way to discover, which is into the
North: for that of the foure partes of the worlde, it seemeth three
parts are discovered by other Princes."[8] Thorne's proposals and
arguments for easy sailing to the north went unanswered until 1553,

when the young Edward VI was on the throne. In the spring of that
year, three ships, under the command of Sir Hugh Willoughby, left
England to seek a northeastern route to Cathay. During a storm the
ships were separated, and two of them anchored on the coast of
Lapland. That winter all the men froze to death. The third ship,
under Richard Chancellor, reached the White Sea. When Ivan IV
learned of their arrival, the Englishmen were escorted to Moscow
and given a warm reception. The tsar was delighted, for Poland/
Lithuania and Sweden effectively controlled Russia's trading relations with the west. A particular concern of these western
neighbors was to prevent the entry of either goods or people who
might increase the military strength of Russia. The English presented an opportunity to circumvent this embargo by opening trade
by a direct sea route. Following this voyage, the Muscovy Company
was established in England to develop trade with Russia. England
had "discovered" Russia; commercial and diplomatic relations were
developed between them. Englishmen and Scots entered service in
Russia, and English interest in Russia, and in the lands to the
northeast of it, was heightened.[9] The search for a northeast passage
continued. In 1556 Stephen Burough sailed between Novaia Zemlia
and Vaygach Island and into the Kara Sea. In 1580 Arthur Pet and
Charles Jackman tried to cross the Kara Sea but turned back because
of ice.

The Dutch followed in the footsteps of the English, both in
trade and exploration. One of their merchants, Olivier Brunel,

had made an overland trip to the Ob River; in 1584 he sailed from Archangel in search of a northeast passage, losing his life in the attempt.   In 1594 three Dutch ships were sent out to search for the passage, one sailing north of Novaia Zemlia and the other two following the route along the Siberian coast.   Though none of these succeeded, the next year seven Dutch ships tried the Kara Sea route. In 1596 Willem Barents, a participant in the earlier expeditions, rounded the far northern tip of Novaia Zemlia, where he wintered. Barents died on the return voyage the next summer, but some of his men survived and returned home.[10]   Russians took this possible threat to their monopoly on Siberian fur trade seriously.   In 1619 foreigner were forbidden to sail east of the Iamal Peninsula.[11]

For over half a century the Dutch and English made no further voyages in search of a northeast passage, but the dream of finding a sea route to the east did not die.   One theory held that it should be possible to sail north to an open polar sea and proceed either directly across the pole or near it to reach the east.[12]   As the geography of North and South America was more fully revealed, the hope of finding an easy direct westward route faded, to be replaced by the goal of discovering a northwest passage either in the northern part of North America or around it to the north.[13]   And the idea persisted that there might be an easy northeast passage just beyond Novaia Zemlia in the east, in the seas western Europeans had not sailed.   Gerardus Mercator portrayed these ideas on a map--the ideas persisted for centuries.

Russians were establishing a distant empire at the same time,
in a great eastward movement that would give them access to two
possible routes to eastern trade. One route was by the interior--
overland and by river. It led to China. The other was the possible
northeast route by sea, which might open trade to Japan, to the East
Indies, and possibly to America as well. That the Russians came to
utilize the first route and to explore the second was no accident.
This was made possible by Russian eastward expansion, which was in
turn based on the fur trade.

Russians had obtained furs from the lands to the east for centuries. The Novgorod chronicles of the 11th and 12th centuries indicate that expeditions of tribute collectors were sent out from Novgorod to the forested regions of the northeast to collect furs, and "probably no other single factor contributed so much to the prosperity of Novgorod in the thirteenth and fourteenth centuries as the export of furs collected beyond the Dvina as tribute or obtained through trade with the natives."[14] The furs were traded for the products of the west through the merchants of the Hanse. In the 1470s, when Ivan III conquered Novgorod, the fur trade to the northeast came under control of Moscow. Ivan kept this fur trade as his private monopoly, and sold rights to the trade to Novgorod merchants. In 1552, Ivan IV captured Kazan, and afterwards the Stroganov family was given large landholdings along the Kama River. The Stroganovs sent the cossack Ermak on an expedition east of the Urals in 1581, and Ermak captured Sibir, the capital of Khan Kuchum. To hold it, Ermak sought help from Ivan, who sent his men. This was a major step in the eastward expansion.[15] By 1639 the cossack Ivan Moskvitin reached the Sea of Okhotsk. The Siberian river system which the Russians were able to control by building ostrogs (forts) at strategic points, made possible this incredibly swift expansion to the east. In eastern Siberia the advance was spearheaded by cossacks and promyshlenniki (fur hunters), with the government following after. The market for furs was in Europe, and the extension of control to reach the most accessible fur trading areas, along the

rivers, was profitable to the government and to the fur traders.[16]
Against Russians armed with guns the Siberian tribes--poorly armed
and fighting among themselves--could not offer effective and
sustained resistance.[17] The English and Dutch ships loading cargoes
at Archangel were a powerful incentive for eastward expansion.

With the movement of cossacks and promyshlenniki into the
Amur River valley, conflicts between the Russians and the Chinese
developed. At the same time, Russia had a longstanding interest in
trade with China, and sent Ivan Petlin to China in 1618-19 to
seek trade relations, and dispatched Fedor Isakovich Baikov on
the same kind of a mission in 1654-58. Both of these attempts
failed. In 1685, when the need to settle the boundary in the Amur
region became critical, Fedor Alekseevich Golovin was named the
first Russian ambassador plenipotentiary to China. His charge was
to retain rights to the river for Russians. The Chinese took the
Russian ostrog of Albazin in 1685-86, however, and in view of this
loss, in 1687 Golovin was instructed to attempt to secure trading
privileges with China if the Amur had to be given up. By provisions
of the Treaty of Nerchinsk, signed in August, 1689, the Russians
surrendered access to the Amur River but gained the right to
caravan trade with China.[18] At one stroke the Russians had trade
with China on an official basis, a privilege coveted by other
Europeans. The beginning of formal trade with China had a momentous
impact for Siberia, because of the establishment in 1669 of the
Hudson's Bay Company. That company would satisfy a major portion

of the European demand for furs with American beaver.[19] With the opening of the China trade, Siberian furs could be directed to the new market in China. Chinese trade was to be a monopoly of the Russian government, and the river and overland route to China was under Russian control.

Western Europeans stood to gain little, if any, benefit from a Russian interior route to China, but great benefit by a northeast passage route. In the 1670s the English planned an expedition to sail in search of it. Reports of Dutch and Russian voyages, published in the Philosophical Transactions of the Royal Society in 1674 and 1675, served as a catalyst for the expedition. The reports have characteristics which will recur throughout this study: they were based, supposedly, on actual voyages; they were endorsed by an individual who had experience in Russia and had obtained information from the Russians; they were buttressed by geographical theory; they touted the wealth of lands in the North Pacific and stressed secrecy surrounding the results of voyages there.

The first of the publications was a short letter by Nicolaas Witsen, a Dutchman who had been in Russia for several months in 1664-65. Witsen, born in 1641, was a member of a prominent merchant family. Witsen served many terms as burgomaster of Amsterdam. Thoug his experience in Russia was limited, his curiosity about the east was aroused, and he gathered all the information about it he could. Through the rest of his life he continued his efforts to gather information about the eastern part of Russia.[20]

Witsen, in the 1670s, believed in the possibility of a northeast passage. In his letter he states: "The Samojeds as well as
the Tartars do unanimously affirm, that passing on the back of Nova
Zembla, at a considerable distance from the shore, Navigators may
well pass as far as Japan."[21] The earlier Dutch and English attempts
to sail the northeast passage had failed because the route taken
was south of Novaia Zemlia. On the map published with Witsen's
letter, Novaia Zemlia is shown as a peninsula, attached at its
eastern end to the coast of Asia, as follows:

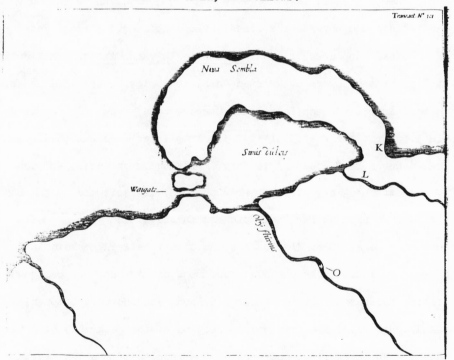

Witsen had written to Stanislav Loputsky, Tsar Alexis's icon
painter, in 1673 or 1674, asking about an expedition the tsar had
sent to Novaia Zemlia. Loputsky sent Witsen the map which appeared

with Witsen's letter, and may have deliberately misinformed Witsen
to keep state secrets, because other Russian maps of the period
represent Novaia Zemlia as an island.[22] On the Loputsky map the
unnamed river "L" (the Enisei) "runs toward China" but is "not
everywhere navigable."

Later in 1674 an article titled "A Narrative of some Observations made upon several Voyages, undertaken to find a way for sailir
about the North to the East-Indies, and for returning the same way
from thence hither; Together with Instructions given by the Dutch
East-India Company for the Discovery of the famous Land of Jesso
near Japan" appeared in the Philosophical Transactions. This articl
describes the voyage of Maerten Gerritsen Vries, who sailed under
orders from the Dutch East India Company on a voyage to the North
Pacific from the East Indies.[23] In 1643 Vries "set out to discover
the unknown East-coast of Tartary, the Kingdom of Catay, and the
West-coast of America, together with the Isles scituate to the East
of Japan, cryed up for their richess in silver and gold."[24] Because of fogs, Vries did not see the strait between Hokkaido and
Sakhalin, making both one huge land mass on his map. He calls one
of the islands he visited Staaten Eyland, and another, Compagnies
Land. His map reflects a new conception of the geography of Asia
and the North Pacific, and records the results of the last western
European exploration of the area before the late eighteenth century.[25] The map gave encouragement to the belief in the northeast
passage, since the southeast direction of the coast beyond Novaia

Map illustrating the Vries voyage.

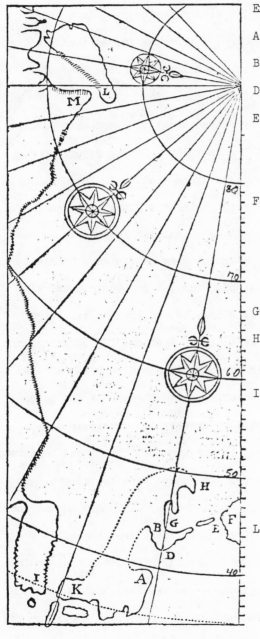

Explanation:

A. Japan

B. Capital of Jesso

D. Southeast corner of Jesso

E. Vries strait. The writer says it should be called the Strait of Anian.

F. Staaten Land. In the writer's view, it should be called the "West-corner of America."

G. Bay reached by Vries.

H. Northern point reached by Vries.

I. and K. Strait between Korea and Japan, which is "the nearest way to sail out of the East-Indies into these parts by the North. . ."

L. and M. Strait between Novaia Zemlia and the mainland.

Zemlia (now detached from Asia) would facilitate the voyage. Vries, of course, had not explored this part of the coast. In the commentary that appears with this map, the writer states that the land at "F" named "Companies Land" is actually the "West-corner of America." (See reproduction of this map.)

In 1675 another article by Witsen about the northeast passage appeared in the Philosophical Transactions. Witsen reports that merchants of Amsterdam, "some years since" sailed to the northeast, and "being advanced to the seventy-ninth or eightieth degree of Northern-latitude, they passed above an hundred leagues above Nova-zembla towards the East; And, although they gave strict charge to conceal what they had seen and observed; yet it became publickly known, that they had discover'd a Sea, beyond Nova-zembla, free from all Ice, and very convenient for Navigation."[26] The merchants, according to Witsen, were going to pursue this discovery but were prevented from doing so because of the interference of the Dutch East India Company, which wanted to preserve its monopoly on the trade. Then the merchants went to the king of Denmark and he agreed to sponsor a voyage of discovery. The ships were fitted out, but the governors of the Dutch East India Company dissuaded the mariners from making the voyage by bribing them. Therefore, the ships went to Spitsbergen on a fishing voyage instead. The Dutch East India Company then sent its own expedition--the Vries expedition--to the North Pacific from the East Indies. Witsen had great hopes for the northeast passage, by which, in his estimation, ships could sail from Europe to Japan in five, or six weeks at the most.[27] At that time, the voyage from Europe to the East Indies by the route eastward around Africa required at least nine months.

Captain John Wood led the English expedition of 1676 for the discovery of a northeast passage. Wood had studied the late sixteenth-century voyage of Willem Barents, and had noted that Barents believed that a great open sea existed between Spitsbergen and Novaia Zemlia.[28] Barents had advised future navigators to sail northeastward from North Cape in order to reach this sea and to find the passage. The publications about the Dutch and Russian voyages noted above supported this belief. They were further buttressed by the English geographer Joseph Moxon, who published A Briefe Discourse of a Passage by the North-Pole to Japan, China, &c. pleaded by three Experiments in 1674.[29] The "three experiments" of Moxon were: 1. Moxon's meeting with a Dutch sailor twenty-two years earlier, in Amsterdam in a "Drinking-house." The Dutch sailor said he had sailed to the pole and even beyond it, via an open sea. To Moxon ". . . he seem'd a plain honest and unaffectatious Person, and one who could have no design upon me." That it was warm at the pole did not surprise Moxon, since the sun shone there in the summer all the time; that there was no ice at the pole was not to be wondered at, as ice, according to the theories of the time, could only be formed on the shores of land, and no land had ever been discovered that far north. 2. The report of James Ben, an Englishman who sailed with the Dutch to Japan, and returned to

England in 1668. He claimed the Dutch ship he was on had sailed to Japan and he had gone "400 Dutch miles" or almost 27° further north where he saw only open sea, not land. 3. The report of Nicolaas Witsen published in the Philosophical Transactions, indicating ". . . the certainty of a Passage found by the Russians this last Year. . ."[30] Moxon's text is illustrated with a map, reproduced here.[31]

Wood was convinced that a northeast passage was feasible and he set out to gather support for an expedition to find it. He obtained two ships: the Speedwell belonged to the king, the Prosperous to a group of merchants. They were fitted out for trade to Japan and "Tartaria." Following the advice of Barents, Wood directed his course northeast from North Cape. Wood declared this was his first mistake. They met ice on June 22, and coasted along it hoping to find a passage to the open sea. They were unable to get north of 76°. For Wood this proved the reports of the Dutch voyages were all false, and he concluded that even if there were no land north of 80°, "the Sea is all frozen and always will be so."[32] On June 29 the ships were separated in foggy and stormy weather. The Speedwell, Wood's ship, struck submerged rocks near the northern coast of Novaia Zemlia. The ship was lost, but 68 of the 70 men on board reached shore safely. They began to prepare the longboat for sailing to Russia, but problems arose, because the longboat could carry only half the men, and no one wanted to stay on Novaia Zemlia. Captain Wood notes: "All I could do in this Exigency, was, to let the

The Moxon map.

Brandy-bottle go round, which kept them always fox'd, till the eighth of July (the ninth day after we had been ashoar) Captain Flawes came so seasonably to our relief."[33] The stranded men were able to return home with Captain Flawes in the Prosperous. Wood called the place they were shipwrecked "Point Speed-ill" and writes of Novaia Zemlia: "It is the most miserable Country that lyeth on the Foundation of the Earth; a Country most part of it covered perpetually with Snow. . . ."[34] After this voyage, the exploration of the northern Asiatic coast was left to the Russians. Western European geographers could only speculate about Russian success.

Until geographers could incorporate the results of Russian explorations on their maps, they had little other than speculation and earlier maps to guide them in their maps of northern Asia and the North Pacific. Two maps of Nicolas Sanson will serve to illustrate the widespread view of the geography of these regions. Sanson lived from 1600 to 1667, and was the preeminent French geographer of his day. Maps ascribed to him, with alterations, continued to be published after his death, as these two maps from an atlas published in 1683 were.[35] (See reproductions)

On the map of Asia, the west end of Novaia Zemlia is separated from the Asian continent by a narrow strait, and the eastern portion of it is not shown. Farther east, Sanson, like Mercator before him, depicts a promontory named "Taibin" (Tabin). This was derived by Mercator from Pliny (Gaius Plinius Secundus, 23-79 A.D.). A narrow strait separates Asia from a large land to the east called "Iesso,

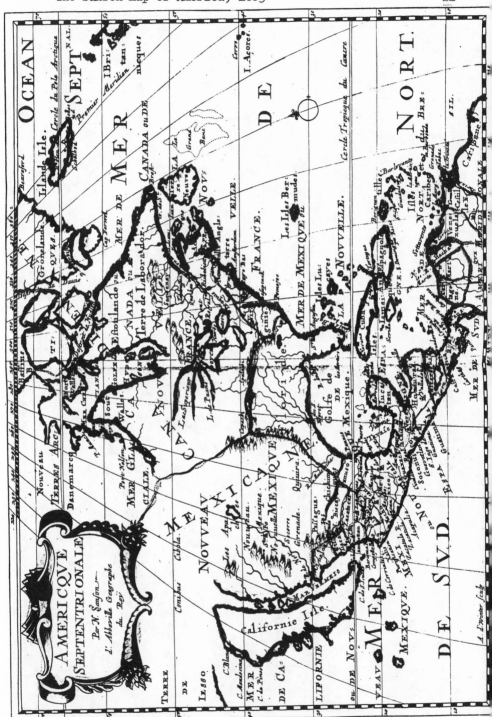

Yezo, or Sesso." The strait reflects the belief in the Strait of Anian, dating from the mid-sixteenth century.[36] Europeans had no factual information about the land of Jesso, and its location, size, and purported wealth would tempt the imagination of Europeans for decades to follow.

The Sanson map of North America in the 1683 atlas masks the paucity of information about northwestern North America by a conveniently-placed cartouche. California on this map is shown as an island.[37] Europeans had no information about the west coast of America north of Cape Mendocino and Cape Blanco. This map shows the land of Jesso with a strait between it and California. No information from the Vries expedition is included on the map.

These maps reflect the common conceptions of the geography of northern Asia, the North Pacific, and the northwest coast of America in the 1680s. These conceptions were based on speculation, not on experience. In spite of the voyage of Captain Wood and others before him, western geographers clung stubbornly to their beliefs in northern passages--a polar route, a passage by the northwest through America, or a route to the northeast along the Asian coast. Russia was claiming and exploring lands to the north and to the east. Given their own long obsession with finding a sea route to the east, it is not surprising that western Europeans saw in these Russian explorations a continuation of their own search for a northeast passage. If Russia found the passage, and monopolized it, Russia could enter the arena of trade in the Pacific with a great advantage over the rest of Europe.

Footnotes

Chapter I

1. Aubry de la Mottraye, Travels through Europe, Asia, and into
    Parts of Africa, 3 vols. (London: For the Author, 1732), III,
    145, translated from the French original of 1727. Volume three
    has the title The Voyages and Travels. . . in several Provinces
    and Places of the Kingdoms and Dukedoms of Prussia, Russia,
    Poland, etc. The author did not like this translation and
    translated the third volume himself for an edition with French
    and English versions in parallel columns, with the title:
    Voyages en anglois et en francois d'A. de La Motraye, en divers
    provinces et places de la Prusse ducale et royale, de la Russie,
    de la Pologne &c. (The Hague: l'Auteur, 1732). La Mottraye
    was in Russia as a visitor in 1714 and again in 1726.

2. There are many studies of this general subject. My own favorite
    is the work of Robert L. Reynolds, Europe Emerges: Transition
    toward an Industrial World-wide Society, 600-1750 (Madison:
    University of Wisconsin Press, 1961). Reynolds notes the common
    tendency to omit the expansion of Russia and states "The ex-
    pansion of the Europeans has often been told before, but to
    leave out the Muscovites of Great Russia has always seemed to me
    a feat comparable to erecting the Empire State Building with a
    complete gap where the fourth floor belongs." (p. viii).

3. Marco Polo, The Travels of Marco Polo, translated by Ronald

Latham (London: The Folio Society, 1968), p. 284. "Vair" refers to squirrel; "ercolin" was not identified but may refer to marten. After making this statement, Polo goes on to report that it is so cold in Russia that the people there can barely survive the climate.

4. Marco Polo's Travels continues to be one of the most popular books ever written. The National Union Catalog (pre-1956) lists twelve pages of editions and translations of this book. The best edition in English, with commentary on the printed and manuscript versions of the Travels, is the following: Sir Henry Yule, ed., The Book of Ser Marco Polo, 2 vols. (London: John Murray, 1926).

5. On Cabot, see Henry Harrisse, John Cabot, the Discoverer of North-America, and Sebastian, his Son (London: B. F. Stevens, 1896); James A. Williamson, The Cabot Voyages and Bristol Discovery under Henry VII, Hakluyt Society, Works, 2d series, CXX (Cambridge: Hakluyt Society, 1962).

6. For an interesting discussion of early theories and sources for the river route, see James D. Tracy, ed., True Ocean Found: Paludanus's Letters on Dutch Voyages to the Kara Sea, 1595-1596 (Minneapolis: University of Minnesota Press, 1980).

7. For an evaluation of this work and its impact on the western view of Russia, see Sigismund von Herberstein, Notes upon Russia, translated and edited by R. H. Major, 2 vols., Hakluyt Society, Works, 1st series, X (London: Hakluyt Society, 1851);

XII (London: Hakluyt Society, 1852).

8. Richard Hakluyt, Voyages, 2 vols. (London: J. M. Dent, 1907),
    I, 214.

9. M. S. Anderson, Britain's Discovery of Russia, 1553-1815
    (London: St. Martin's Press, 1958). On the development of the
    Russia Company, see T. S. Willan, The Early History of the
    Russia Company, 1553-1603 (Manchester: Manchester University
    Press, 1956).

10. On Barents, see Gerrit de Veer, The Three Voyages of William
    Barents to the Arctic Regions (1594, 1595, 1596), 2d ed.,
    Hakluyt Society, Works, 1st series, XLIV (London: Hakluyt
    Society, 1876).

11. Raymond H. Fisher, The Russian Fur Trade, 1550-1700 (Berkeley;
    Los Angeles: University of California Press, 1943), p. 78.

12. John K. Wright, "The Open Polar Sea," Geographical Review,
    XLIII (1953), pp. 338-65; E. L. Towle, "The Myth of the Open
    North Polar Sea," Actes du Dixième Congrès Internationale
    d'Histoire des Sciences, II (1964), pp. 1037-41.

13. For a general history of this subject, see Ernest S. Dodge,
    Northwest by Sea (New York: Oxford University Press, 1961).

14. George V. Lantzeff and Richard A. Pierce, Eastward to Empire:
    Exploration and Conquest on the Russian Open Frontier, to 1750
    (Montreal: McGill-Queen's University Press, 1973), p. 34.

15. On Ermak see Terence Armstrong, ed., Yermak's Campaign in
    Siberia: A Selection of Documents, Hakluyt Society, Works,

2d series, CXLVI (London: Hakluyt Society, 1975).

16. See Fisher, Russian Fur Trade. James R. Gibson, Feeding the Russian Fur Trade: Provisionment of the Okhotsk Seaboard and the Kamchatka Peninsula, 1639-1856 (Madison: University of Wisconsin Press, 1969) contains an excellent summary of the historical background of Russian eastward expansion on pages 3-34. For a general account see John A. Harrison, The Founding of the Russian Empire in Asia and America (Coral Gables: University of Miami Press, 1951).

17. Peter I. Liashchenko, History of the National Economy of Russia to the 1917 Revolution, translated by L. M. Herman (New York: Macmillan Company, 1949), pp. 237-42. In 1662 the population of Siberia was estimated to be 288,000 persons, of whom about 70,000 were Russians. (p. 242).

18. A detailed study of the caravan trade is Clifford M. Foust, Muscovite and Mandarin: Russia's Trade with China and Its Setting, 1727-1805 (Chapel Hill: University of North Carolina Press, 1969). Foust notes "The Russians preferred the real and concrete advantages of Peking trade to the uncertain benefits of trapping in the Amur basin and sailing the river's waters to an unknown sea." (p. 7). By the treaty Russia gained official trade relations, rather than the sporadic trade opportunities that had existed previously.

19. In the late seventeenth and early eighteenth centuries, furs coming from North America were greatly increased in numbers,

threatening a glut of the market. See E. E. Rich, "Russia and the Colonial Fur Trade," in The Economic History Review, second series, VII, No. 3 (April, 1955), pp. 307-28.

20. For general information about Witsen, see Johannes Keuning "Nicolaas Witsen as a Cartographer," in Imago Mundi, XI (Leiden: E. Brill, 1954), pp. 95-110. For further studies of Witsen and Peter the Great, see the following chapter and the bibliography.

21. [Nicolaas Corneliszoon Witsen] "A Letter, not long since written to the Publisher by an Experienced Person residing at Amsterdam, containing a true Discription of Nova Zembla, together with an Intimation of the Advantage of its Shape and Position," Philosophical Transactions, X, No. 101 (London, 1674), 3.

22. Leo Bagrow, A History of Russian Cartography up to 1800, edited by Henry W. Castner (Wolfe Island, Ontario: The Walker Press, 1975), pp. 75-76.

23. "A Narrative of some Observations made upon several Voyages, Undertaken to Find a Way for Sailing about the North to the East-Indies, and for Returning the same Way from thence Hither; Together with Instructions Given by the Dutch East-India Company for the Discovery of the Famous Land of Jesso near Japan," Philosophical Transactions, X, No. 109 (London, 1674), pp. 197-207. The map published with the article is reproduced here. This article is a translation from Dirck

Rembrantsz van Nierop, <u>Tweede</u> <u>deel</u> <u>van</u> <u>Enige</u> Oefeningen. . . .
(Amsterdam: A. S. van der Storck, 1674).

24. <u>Ibid.</u>, p. 198.

25. George Alexander Lensen, <u>The</u> <u>Russian</u> <u>Push</u> <u>toward</u> <u>Japan:</u>
<u>Russo-Japanese</u> <u>Relations,</u> <u>1697-1875</u> (Princeton: Princeton
University Press, 1959), p. 23.

26. [Nicolaas Corneliszoon Witsen] "A Summary Relation of what
hath been hitherto discovered in the Matter of the North-
East Passage; Communicated by a good Hand," <u>Philosophical</u>
<u>Transactions</u>, XI, No. 118 (London, 1675), pp. 418-19.

27. <u>Ibid.</u>, p. 424. The "fishing trip" the Danish ship went on
was probably a whaling voyage. Henry Hudson had sighted
whales near the west coast of Spitsbergen in 1607. Following
this, hundreds of Dutch and English--and later Danish--ships
went there for whales. In the two decades after Hudson's
voyage, "something like 16,000 men engaged in the slaughter
of whales around Spitsbergen." See Terence Wise, <u>Polar</u>
<u>Exploration</u> (London: Almark Publishing Co., 1973), p. 11·

28. <u>An</u> <u>Account</u> <u>of</u> <u>several</u> <u>late</u> <u>Voyages</u> & <u>Discoveries</u> <u>to</u> <u>the</u> <u>South</u>
<u>and</u> <u>North</u>. . . . (London: S. Smith and B. Walford, 1694).
Wood's report on his voyages is found on pages 143-96.
Wood thought that the Barents voyages were made in 1606 and
1607, rather than in the late 1590s. Of the seven reasons
given by Wood for undertaking his voyage, Barents's opinion
that there was an open sea between Greenland and Novaia

Zemlia is given first.

29. Joseph Moxon, A Briefe Discourse of a Passage by the North-Pole to Japan, China &c. . . . (London: J. Moxon, 1674). The same text was printed in John Harris, Navigantium atque Itinerantium Bibliotheca: Or, A Compleat Collection of Voyages and Travels, 2 vols. (London: Thomas Bennet, etc., 1705), pp. 616-33.

30. Harris, Navigantium, I, 616-17.

31. The reproduction of this map is from Joseph Moxon, Ein kurtzer Discours von der Schiff-Fahrt bey dem Nord-Pol nach Japan, China, und so weiter (Hamburg: Johan Nauman und Georg Wolff, 1676).

32. Harris, Navigantium, I, 615. This is another printing of Wood's own commentary on the voyage, with some textual differences from his report cited above in footnote 28.

33. Ibid.

34. An Account of several late Voyages, p. 193.

35. Nicolas Sanson, l'Europe en plusieurs cartes, et en divers traittés de geographie et d'histoire (Paris: Chez l'Autheur, 1683). The map of Asia appears in Part II, l'Asie, preceding page 3. The map of America is in Part IV, l'Amerique, precedin page 3.

36. Godfrey Sykes, "The Mythical Straits of Anian," Bulletin of the American Geographical Society, 47, No. 3 (1915), 167-71. Henry R. Wagner, The Cartography of the Northwest Coast of

America to the Year 1800, 2 vols. (Berkeley: University of California Press, 1937), I, 53-67.

37. Wagner, Cartography, I, 144-47.

Chapter II

Peter the Great and Routes to the East: The Contemporary
View from the West

During the reign of Peter the Great, a new image of Russia
emerged in the west. Military actions in 1695 brought an early
awareness of Russia to western Europe, when Peter began a campaign
against the Turks in support of his ally Jan Sobieski of Poland.
That summer Peter directed a siege against Azov, which failed because the Russians could not cut off aid to Azov by sea. The
following winter, at Voronezh, Peter directed the building of a
fleet of ships--twenty-five galleys and 1300 river barges. The
next summer Azov capitulated, and the news rocked Europe. On the
heels of this victory Peter announced his intention of building a
fleet for the Black Sea, for centuries the "private lake" of the
Turks.[1]

Next, Peter did something no Russian ruler before him had
done--he traveled to western Europe with Russia's Great Embassy. The
stated purpose of the 1697-98 embassy was to seek military alliances
against the Turks, and "Peter Mikhailov" was a member of it. This
alias was only a thin disguise for a very tall tsar. It served as
a convenience for Peter, sparing him the need to participate in
formal diplomatic relations. The attention of western Europe was
focussed on the ruler and on his country.[2]

Peter, in this year and a half away from Russia, had extended visits in Holland and England. With insatiable curiosity and immense energy he collected experience, knowledge, and ideas to take back with him to Russia. He also sent home shiploads of books, maps, tools, navigation equipment, and guns, and he hired nearly 1000 foreigners to serve in Russia. Here was a further pipeline of information about Russia, which had ceased to seem so remote from the west.

Peter's plans for a navy on the Black Sea failed, because Russia's allies in war against the Turks wanted peace, and Russia could not carry on the war alone. So the Russian fleet of ships was useless, though one ship carried the Russian ambassador, Emilian Ukraintsev, to the peace negotiations in 1699. For the first time in centuries, a Russian vessel sailed the Black Sea to Constantinople. Ukraintsev reported that other European diplomats-- Austrian, Venetian, English, Dutch, and French--were anxious to prevent close relations between the Ottoman Empire and Russia. Ukraintsev reported further: "The English and Dutch ministers range themselves beside the Turks and have better intentions toward them than they have towards you, Sire. They hate you and envy you because you have begun to build ships and have inaugurated navigation at Azov as well as at Archangel. They fear this will hamper their maritime trade."[3] On 3 July 1700 a thirty-year truce with the Turks was signed. Peter received the news on August 8, and the day after the formal announcement of the peace was made, Peter declared war on Sweden.

The Great Northern War, as it was called, pitted Peter against the young Charles XII of Sweden. At issue was dominance of the north; the fighting lasted until 1719. When the war ended, Sweden was eclipsed as a northern power, and Russia emerged to fill the void. At the beginning of the war Russia's prospects seemed bleak. The Russians besieged the Swedish fortress of Narva in October 1700. Peter directed the operations at Narva until November 19, when he left the fortress. The following day Charles XII, with an army of some 10,500 men attacked the Russian army of some 40,000 and routed them completely. The victory supported Charles in his belief that he was invincible in battle and that the Russians could not fight. For Peter, the defeat strengthened his resolve to build Russian military forces. For western Europe, the glory that Peter had won in battle against the Turks quickly dissipated. Nine years later, at Poltava, the tables were turned. Charles was the defeated one; Peter was the victor. Western Europe was jolted into the realization that Russia had become a major European power.

Russia was developing a navy also. In 1702 a rumor circulated that the Swedes were planning a naval assault on Archangel, Russia's only port for trade with the west. Peter went to Archangel to direct the building of ships to protect it. No attack materialized, but Peter's determination to have a port on the Baltic led to the taking of Nöteborg (renamed Schlüsselburg), a small Swedish fort

on the Neva River, that summer. The following year Russia took
Nyenskans, a small Swedish settlement on the Neva near the Gulf
of Finland. Peter immediately began building a port on the Baltic
and building ships to protect it. When peace came at last, St.
Petersburg, like Russia, was rising in northern Europe.

In the eyes of western Europe, Russia had indeed changed.
The Russian army had to be respected. The navy, though in its
infancy, was growing, and Russian ships sailed to European ports.
Peter the Great seemed to be transforming Russia into a new country,
a western European country. Russia would never again seem distant
from the rest of Europe. And with the heightened awareness of
Russia came interest in Russia as a link between western Europe and
lands to the east.

Western Europeans wanted information about Russian routes
to eastern lands, and during the reign of Peter the Great, several
writers commented on these routes in the books they wrote about
Russia. The writers based their commentaries on experience in
Russia, or on information they obtained from Russia. Some of them
traveled to China for the Russian government; others had employment
in Russia that afforded them access to firsthand information about
the routes to the east. The commentaries of these writers reveal
diverse opinions about the feasibility of Russian routes to the east.
In this chapter, these commentaries will be considered in two
categories: comments on the interior route (river and overland) and
comments on the northeast passage.[4]

The Interior Route

Nicolaas Witsen published a large, detailed map of Russia
dated 1687.[5] It was the earliest printed map showing the river
and overland route to China and the first to provide western
Europeans with knowledge of the vast river system of Siberia.[6]
Though Witsen's map was issued in only a few copies, for distri-
bution to friends, it had a profound influence on later European
maps of Siberia.[7] In preparing his map, Witsen had access to
many Russian sources. During his visit to Russia in 1664-65,
Witsen obtained a copy of the report made by Baikov on his mission
to China in 1654-58. After he returned to Amsterdam, Witsen
received a copy of Petlin's account of his 1618-19 mission to
China. Witsen corresponded with individuals in Russia, Siberia,
and China and drew upon many maps made by inhabitants of Siberia
in preparing his map. The Secretary of the Siberian Department,
Andreas A. Vinius, corresponded with Witsen and sent him maps which
Vinius had collected for publication.[8] In addition, Witsen studied
the reports and maps of Jesuits who had been in China. Because of
his access to information from these various sources, Witsen was
in a unique position to incorporate firsthand information from
Russian sources with material from western sources, and in this
way he was able to produce the most detailed map of northeastern
Asia made to its time.

When Evert Izbrandszoon Ides was named to undertake a commercial and diplomatic mission to China for Peter the Great, he wrote to Witsen asking for a copy of Witsen's map.[9] Ides, a "German" who had lived in Russia since 1677, traveled to China in 1692-95.[10] He took a copy of Witsen's map with him and followed it as a guide in his journey. Witsen's map was a model for the map published with his account of the embassy.

The first published account Europeans had of Ides' embassy was written by Adam Brand, secretary to the embassy. Brand published his book in German in 1698, and it was translated for an English edition the same year; in 1699 it appeared in Dutch and French editions.[11] The book is little more than a chronicle of the route taken, and this rapid publication of it indicates the interest of Europeans in the regions through which the embassy passed and the paucity of information about this part of the world. When the embassy left Moscow in March, 1692, Brand reports it consisted of only twenty-one men. At Nerchinsk a caravan formed with over 400 men, and "There were abundance of Gentlemen and Merchants belonging to our Caravan who traveled with Furrs to China."[12] This swelling of the number of participants suggested the Russian trade to China was lucrative. Though the journey was long--nearly three years--Brand describes the river and overland route to China without stressing its difficulties.

In 1704 an account of the embassy, ascribed to Ides, appeared in Amsterdam. About this book Witsen writes: "The description of Isbrandts is composed by me, as it was published from papers that

were very confusedly written in Hamburgish or Lower-Saxon. He was
my friend and is now deceased."[13] The similarities between this
book and the Brand text indicate the same sources were used for
part of it, though the Ides' text is much expanded. The book
was dedicated to Peter the Great, with his approval. The book
features the seas and rivers of Russia, which Ides (or Witsen)
advises Peter are ready "to welcome the Sons of Neptune, fitted
out by your Czarish Majesty's unwearied care, as being rare and
uncommon guests."[14] The book was translated for editions in other
languages and received wide circulation in Europe.[15]

The route taken by the embassy was not a direct one, and
Ides reports that by another route, travel from Tomsk to China for
trade was "very expeditious," and it was "practicable to go thither
in 12 weeks and return back in as short a time."[16] This trade
route was used by the Bukharians. The route, Ides admits, is
difficult, since all supplies, even wood and water, have to be
carried by camel. Even so, the short time required for the journey
to China was appealing, since the embassy needed months to make its
journey to Peking. Ides reports: "But it is utterly impossible for
Russians or other Nations to travel this Road, by reason that it
is infested with several Robbers, which set on the Passengers, and
very often deprive them of all that they have gained by so tedious
and fatiguing a Journey."[17]

Philippe Avril, a French Jesuit, describes several routes to
China, including the caravan route noted by Ides. Avril left

Marseilles in 1686, and traveled a southern route to the Caspian
Sea, then to the Volga River, and on to Moscow with a group of
merchants. Avril asked permission to travel from Moscow to China
with a caravan, but permission was denied him. He returned to
France and in 1691 published a book about his travels.[18] Avril
states the distance to China was much overestimated by geographers.
On the basis of information he received, Avril had no doubt that
if the Russians would allow the journey from France to China via
Archangel and Tobolsk, it could be made in six months, at the
most.[19] His book has an accompanying map, copied from a map in
Moscow, on which several routes to China are shown. Avril reports
the Russians "have so levell'd and remov'd all Difficulties, that
they make no more of going to China, than of travelling to Arch-Angel
or Astrakan."[20] A man named "Mouchim Pouchkim," the governor of
Smolensk, told Avril the Russians believed America had been popu-
lated from a "very well peopled" island near the mouth of the
"Kawoina River."[21] Avril said the man was afraid of getting into
trouble with the Russian court by revealing too much information.
In explaining why the Russians did not use the northeastern rivers
and seas to trade to China and Japan, Avril cites the Russians'
lack of experience in "Sea Affairs" and the great difficulties of
sailing at the mouths of the rivers in the north and east, and he
maintains "of all the ways that lead to that flourishing Empire,
that which the Muscovites make choice of now-a days, is both the
safest and the shortest."[22] A similar statement appears in an

Map of Philippe Avril, 1692.

English book by Jodocus Crull, published in 1698. Crull, a physician who never visited Russia, compiled his text from sources he considered trustworthy. He records the eastward expansion of Russian fur traders and notes "it is easie to be imagined, that the Muscovites, after they had hunted out these so far distant Countries, did not acquiesce here, but left no Stone unturned till they had made themselves an easie Passage through those Tartarian Countries to the Empires of China and Japan."[23] It is noteworthy that Crull believed Russians had an easy route not only to China, but to Japan as well.

In the eighteenth century, commentators on the interior route describe it as lengthy and difficult, and they suggest that Peter the Great wanted to find an alternate route or shorten the existing route by building canals. Peter's interest in improving Russian trade through the building of canals is well known.[24] In 1704 a very beautiful book on the river system of Russia, with canal sites indicated, was printed for Peter by the Doncker publishing firm in Amsterdam.[25]

A statement that the interior route to China was long and dangerous appears in a book by Friedrich Christian Weber, a foreign minister from Hanover who served in Russia from 1714 to 1720. At the time, Hanover was allied with Russia against Sweden in the Great Northern War and Weber was close to Peter and the court. Weber talked with two priests who had made the caravan journey to China, and reports the journey was "one of the most fatiguing that can

be undertaken" and requires at least sixteen months one way. Weber
holds "it would be difficult to find Persons to undertake it, was
not the Trouble so amply recompensed by the great Gains."[26] Two
merchants had proposed a project to make a "communication" between
several lakes and rivers, Weber notes, so that goods could go from
Archangel to the east for trade with Japan and the East Indies. The
project involved building canals between rivers in Siberia and using
the Amur River.[27] Even if the Amur had been held by the Russians,
this would have been an incredibly difficult project. The concern
to improve the interior route, writes Weber, is because the finding
of a northeast passage "has been hitherto found impracticable."[28]

The Northeast Passage

As noted earlier, in the 1670s Nicolaas Witsen was an ardent
believer in the northeast passage. By 1687, the date given on his
first map, Witsen was clearly less certain that the passage was
possible. In the northeast part of his map, Witsen portrays two
open-ended peninsulas, Cape Tabin and Ice Cape. At the end of the
latter is the phrase: "Ice Cape. The end of this head is unknown."
This conception of northeastern Asia is similar to the one on a
map of Andreas Vinius, dated sometime between 1678 and 1683, a map
which Witsen presumably received from Vinius himself.[29] In com-
menting about his map in 1691, Witsen states he was "yet in suspense
about northeast Asia and whether or not it had a connection with
America. He further notes the receipt of new information from

Witsen's map of 1687.

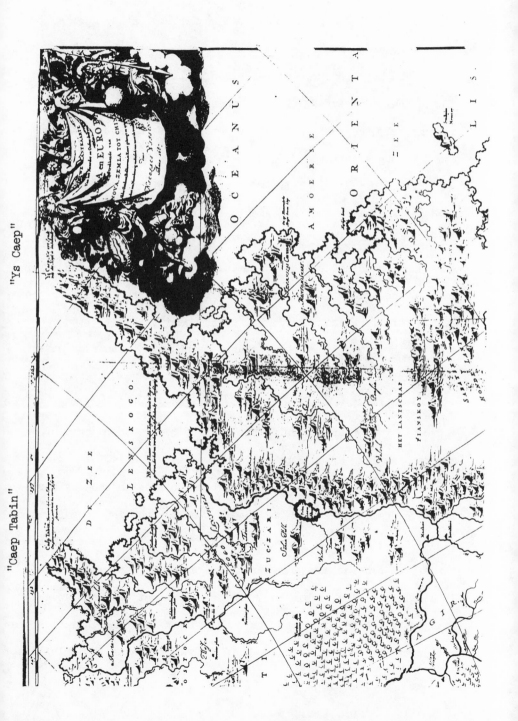

Russia, indicating that Novaia Zemlia was an island.[30]

In 1692 Witsen published, as a commentary on his map and the area it covered, his Noord en Oost Tartarye. This book describes the geography, economy, natural history, peoples, and languages of "North and East Tartary" in more than 600 folio pages. It was unquestionably the most informative work on this area to its time--and for long afterward.[31] Witsen comments on the northeastern part of his map: "Some believe that this section is attached to land and connected to North America; but this is uncertain, as neither water nor land have been tested there and the end of the same section is unknown. Fishermen, or others who sail the river Lena in the summertime, come sometimes to this remote section and search for fish teeth there; but on the eastern bank, or on the side of the river Amur, the entrance is unknown, either by water or by land."[32] Though in this portion of his text Witsen states the geographical relationship between Asia and America is not known, in two other places in his text he refers to reports of mariners sailing around the northeast corner of Asia.[33]

Witsen hosted Peter the Great when the Russian embassy was in Amsterdam in 1697. At the time Witsen was working on a revision of his map, and during this visit Peter told Witsen the northeastern corner of Asia was not joined to America in the Cape Tabin area.[34] In a later edition of his map, Witsen places dotted lines at the ends of both Cape Tabin and Ice Cape, though he still indicates the extent of Ice Cape is unknown. Did Witsen, or Peter, at this time, believe a northeast passage from Archangel to the Pacific was a

possibility? Did the question of a northeast passage revolve

around the presence or absence of a land connection between Asia

and America?

The relationship of Witsen to Ides' book provides possible

answers to these questions. According to the Ides' text, the

barrier to the northeast passage is not land, but ice. The pertinent

passage reads:

> A great deal hath been said concerning the Weygats,
> by English, Danes, and Hollanders, who with Ships have
> endeavoured to bore through this Icy Channel, which hath
> been done indeed once or twice, but then those who did it,
> were repulsed, and forced to return to their own Country,
> by the Vehement Current of Ice in the South or Icy-Sea; of
> which Mr. Nicholas Witsen, Burger-master of Amsterdam,
> treats at large, that Gentleman having obtained an exact
> account of whatever is remarkable, from several Persons
> who have been there; all which Observations he hath
> incomparably well digested in his Chart of Weygats and the
> Sea-Coasts, to the River Oby, by which it plainly appears,
> that from Weygats to the Icy or Holy Cape, the Sea is
> utterly unnavigable with Ships, and should a second Christo-
> pher Columbus appear, and point out the course of the Heavens,
> he could not yet drive away these Mountains of Ice: For God
> and Nature have so invincibly fenced the Sea side of Siberia
> with Ice, that no Ship can come to the River Jenisea, much
> less can they come farther Northwards into the Sea. Not to
> mention the Voyage from the Icy or Holy Cape, round Japan
> and Jedzo, I shall only insert what I have collected from
> the informations of the Russians, who several times have
> sailed through the Streights of Weygats to the Oby.[35]

The text goes on to report the difficulties of sailing in the

northern regions.

The content of this passage suggests it was written by Witsen,

not by Ides. The reference to earlier voyages of Europeans to

find a northeast passage reflects Witsen's interest. Peter the

Great gave Ides permission to print his book, but at the time it was not published in Russia. The date of Ides' death is unknown; because Witsen stated the book was not ready for publication when he received it, Witsen may well have received the Ides account of his embassy from Peter for publication.[36]

When Peter the Great visited England in 1698, he hired John Perry for service in Russia as a civil engineer. Perry, a naval officer who had been court-martialled because of his actions in a battle with two French privateers, accepted the offer eagerly and went with Peter to Holland. Perry continued on from there ahead of the embassy and arrived in Russia in the summer of 1698. His first assignment was to construct a canal between the Don and Volga rivers to join the Black and Caspian seas. A German, Colonel Breckell, had begun a canal for this purpose in 1693 but abandoned it because of lack of supplies, workmen, and because of the opposition of Prince Boris Alexeevich Golitsyn, the governor of Astrakhan. In 1699 Perry began a canal at a new site. He encountered the same problems his predecessor had. In 1701 the project was abandoned, temporarily, because of the war with Sweden.[37]

Perry remained in Russia, working on other river projects, and in 1711 he planned a canal to connect St. Petersburg with the Volga River. After further troubles, including heated exchanges with Admiral Fedor M. Apraksin over his pay, Perry sought the assistance of Sir Charles Whitworth, the British ambassador to Russia. Perry returned home the next year under Whitworth's

protection. He blamed his difficulties in Russia on Peter's
associates, not on Peter.[38]

Once home, Perry began writing a book describing his work
in Russia. He "was prevailed upon by the Persuasions of some
Friends" to enlarge the subject of his book to include Peter's
plans for maritime discoveries in the north and accounts of the
trade to China.[39] About the latter Perry reports the trade is
difficult, "the whole Way perform'd by Land Carriage, which
requires many Horses and Men, and is both very tedious and charge-
able."[40] In spite of this the trade is "beneficial;" Russians
trade furs to China, primarily. At the time Perry was writing,
the Samoyeds who lived on the northern coast of Siberia, where
the best furs came from, were not subject to the tsar. Perry
states the tsar will extend his rule to the area "when there is
a Time for it."[41]

Perry's statement: "I have often heard the Czar say, that he
intends to . . . search out whether it is possible for Ships to
pass by the way of Nova Zembla into the Tartarian Sea" has been
cited as contemporary evidence that Peter believed a northeast
passage was feasible and he hoped to find it.[42] But Perry goes on.
He reports Peter planned to find some place east of the Ob River
to build a port for trade "to China, Japan, &c."[43] If some of the
seas east of Novaia Zemlia could be used by ships, another port
would be built west of the Ob River area, somewhere between Archangel and Novaia Zemlia, at which European ships could get goods

from the east. In the winter, these goods would be brought from the port east of the Ob River area to the second port by sled, "the easiest Land Carriage in the World."[44]

Peter had sent people from Tobolsk to explore to the mouth of the Ob River, Perry reports, but they were unsuccessful because of the hostility of the Samoyeds.[45] Peter considered sending explorers to Novaia Zemlia to search for a possible sea passage around it: "But he is notwithstanding of the Opinion that there is none; and says, that he believes his Country joins here to America, and that that Part of the World was first peopled this way, when there was not such vast Quantities of Ice, and the Cold had not so strongly possess'd the Parts near the Pole."[46] This concept of northern geography Perry attributes to Peter is reflected on some Russian maps of the time.[47]

Perry, however, was writing a book for an English audience with a strong interest in a possible northeast passage. Perry notes the warmth of the climate in the north during the summer, when the wind blows from the sea. He maintains that if the English sailors of Sir Hugh Willoughby's expedition, when they were caught in the northern winter, had gone to land and built a hut "in the ground" they could have passed the winter safely and continued their voyage the next summer.[48] On the map accompanying Perry's book, there is no land connection between Novaia Zemlia and the Siberian coast and no eastward-jutting peninsula to prevent ships from rounding the northeastern corner of Asia. For many readers,

John Perry's map of 1716, by Herman Moll.

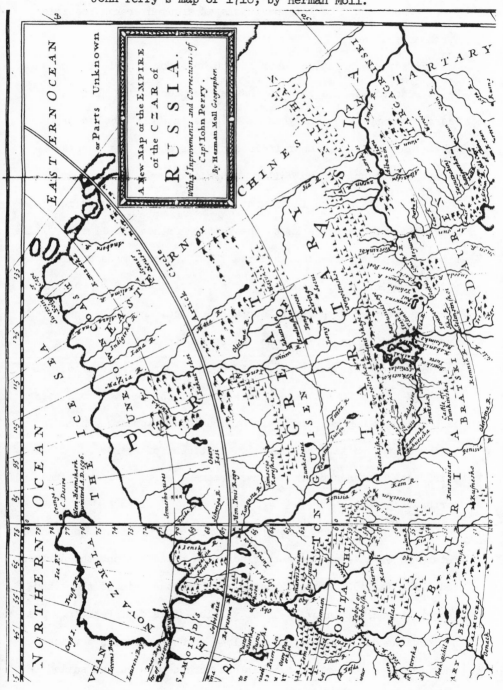

Perry's book could be interpreted as an argument for a possible northeast passage.

Friedrich Christian Weber saw no hope for a northeast passage. He says Novaia Zemlia is a peninsula, "consequently there is no Passage through the Straights of Waigats into the Icy Sea or Tartarian Ocean."[49] Weber includes in his account of Russia the report of Johann Bernard Müller, a Swede who was captured at the Battle of Poltava, and later went to Siberia and assisted in the conversion of the Ostiacks to the Russian Orthodox religion. Müller's report on his experiences is dated 1716. An anonymous Russian writer, Müller says, describes the mouth of the Ob River as an area "surrounded with great Mountains of Ice, that have subsisted from ancient Times . . . those Places are inaccessible, consequently altogether unknown."[50] Even if it were possible to sail north of Novaia Zemlia, there is a barrier in the east to a passage, as on Weber's map a long "chain of mountains" appears "which is believed to joyn with the Northern Continent of America." In this case, Witsen's peninsula has become a solid barrier to the northeast passage.[51]

Peter Henry Bruce also provides contemporary testimony that Peter the Great's attempts to find a sea passage along the northern coast had failed. Bruce's grandfather was a cousin to the grandfather of General Iakov V. Bruis, a close friend of Peter's. The two cousins had left Scotland in 1647 to enter foreign service. They intended to remain together but were separated and sailed on

Weber's map, from the English edition of 1723.

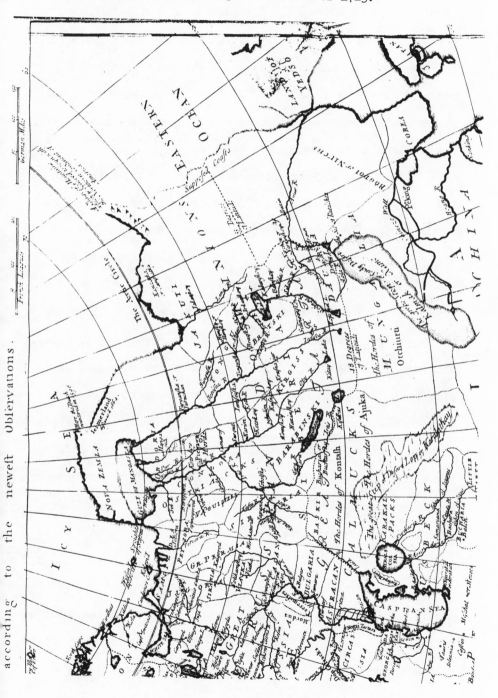

different ships. One cousin joined Russian service and the other
Prussian. In 1710, at the invitation of Iakov Bruis, Peter Bruce
left the Prussian army and joined the Russian military forces. He
remained in Russia until 1724. Just how close Peter Bruce was to
his eminent relative at Peter's court is not known, but Iakov Bruis
was involved in explorations of Siberia.[52]

In his Memoirs, Peter Bruce says "various attempts" have been
made, at the tsar's orders, to find a sea passage from Archangel
to the East Indies, "but that was found impracticable, by reason
of the many large shoals of ice, like islands, floating upon
those seas."[53] In 1697 Peter sent a man knowledgeable in mathe-
matics to explore the Lena River to its mouth and to discover
whether or not the seas north and east of it continued to China.
This expedition reached 70° north on the river, where the expedition
halted, as "the prince of that country would neither accept his
presents, nor suffer him to proceed down the river, but threatened
if he did not return from whence he came, he would give orders to
cut him and his men to pieces; this put an end to his farther progres
and discoveries, and he was obliged to return."[54] According to
Bruce, no further explorations of this area could be made while
the people there were so hostile.

What patterns have emerged from these commentaries? The interior route to China, initially thought to be easy, was admitted
to be a very long and difficult one. Proposals to make the route
more convenient through the building of canals had not been

implemented. Though the interior route provided Russia with access to trade with China, the access was limited because of the length of the route. Russia had tried to find a northeast passage by sea but Russian explorations from Archangel eastward in search of a passage were not successful. The longstanding question about whether or not Novaia Zemlia was attached to the mainland of Siberia was still debated, but the position of Novaia Zemlia was not the only obstacle to a possible northeast passage. Instead, the "mountains" of ice in the Ob River region blocked the passage, making navigation there impossible, or nearly so. The seas to the east of the Ob River were little-known because of the hostility of the people living on the coast. To this point, Russian explorations along the northern coasts offered slight hope for any northeast passage from Archangel to the Pacific Ocean. The best that might be hoped for, according to John Perry's record of Peter's view, would be a partial northeast passage somewhere east of the Ob River region. But Russian maritime explorations were not limited to a search for a northeast passage, as will be seen in the following chapter.

Footnotes

Chapter II

1. For a general commentary, see M. S. Anderson, Peter the Great
   (London: Thames and Hudson, 1978), pp. 36-50. Russian rela-
   tions with the Turks are described in Benedict H. Sumner,
   Peter the Great and the Ottoman Empire (London: Basil Blackwell
   & Mott, Ltd., 1949).

2. Reinhold Wittram, "Peters des Grossen erste Reise in den
   Westen," in Jahrbücher für Geschichte Osteuropas, neue Folge,
   III:4 (1955), pp. 373-403; N. A. Baklanova, "Velikoe posol'stvo
   za granitsei v 1697-1698 gg." in Petr Velikii: Sbornik statei,
   edited by A. I. Andreev (Moscow and Leningrad: AN SSSR, 1947),
   pp. 3-62.

3. Robert K. Massie, Peter the Great: His Life and World (New
   York: Alfred A. Knopf, 1980), p. 285. The translation is from
   Constantin de Grunwald, La Russie de Pierre le Grand (Paris:
   Hachette, 1953), p. 127.

4. The reference here to one "interior route" is a matter of convenience, as there were of course a number of possible routes to
   China. The goal would have been to find the one route that was
   the fastest and most convenient. The "northeast passage"
   refers to any route predominantly by sea along the north coast
   of Siberia, but includes river routes to the northern seas,
   and in the Ob River region, a possible land portage as well.

5. The map, titled Nieuwe lantkaarte van het noorder en ooster deel van Asia en Europa strekkende van Nova Zemla tot China, is dated 1687 but may have been printed as late as 1690. See Boris P. Polevoi, "O kartax severnoi Azii N. K. Vitsena" in Izvestiia AN SSSR, Seriia geograficheskaia (Moscow) No. 2 (1973), pp. 124-33; Johannes Keuning, "Nicolaas Witsen as a Cartographer," in Imago Mundi, XI (1954), pp. 95-110.

6. The emphasis placed on the configuration of the northeastern portion of Witsen's map often obscures its importance in this respect. See The James Ford Bell Library: An Annotated Catalog of Original Source Materials Relating to the History of European Expansion, 1400-1800 (Boston: G. K. Hall & Co., 1981), p. 489.

7. Keuning, "Nicolaas Witsen," pp. 98, 108-9.

8. Polevoi, "O kartax severnoi Azii," p. 125.

9. Evert Ysbrandszoon Ides, Three Years Travels from Moscow Over-land to China (London: W. Freeman, etc., 1706), p. 90.

10. Ides was born in Holstein in 1660. His parents were Dutch, apparently. See his biography by Friedrich Ratzel in Allgemeine Deutsche Biographie, XIII, 747-49. A contemporary, John Perry, stated that Ides was a native of Denmark. Ides writes that he was "the first German that ever went through this vast Country to, and returned from China." Ides, Three Years Travels, p. 90.

11. The book first appeared as: Adam Brand, Beschreibung der

chinesischen Reise (Hamburg: F. C. Greflingern, 1698). It was translated as follows: Adam Brand, A Journal of an Embassy from their Majesties John and Peter Alexowits, Emperors of Muscovy, &c. into China (London: D. Brown and T. Goodwin, 1698; Relation du voyage de Mr Evert Isbrand . . . a l'empereur de la Chine (Amsterdam: J. L. de Lorme, 1699); Seer aenmercklijcke land- en water-reyse . . . uyt Muscouw na China (Tyel: Jan van Leeuwen, etc., 1699).

12. Brand, Journal, p. 90.

13. Keuning, "Nicolaas Witsen," p. 107. Keuning translated this passage from a letter written in 1709 by Witsen to Gijsbert Cuper, the burgomaster of Deventer.

14. Ides, Three Years Travels, sig. A3^r. Besides the obvious reference, the writer may be adding another meaning, for at this time the "Society of Neptune," a group interested in science, was meeting secretly in Moscow. Peter was a member of it. See Valentin Boss, Newton and Russia: The Early Influence, 1698-1796 (Cambridge: Harvard University Press, 1972), p. 16.

15. The Dutch edition is Evert Ysbrandszoon Ides, Drei-jarige reize naar China (Amsterdam: F. Halma, 1704); a second Dutch edition was printed in 1710. The work was translated as follows: The Three Years Travels of His Excellency E Ysbrant Ides from Mosco to China (London, 1705); Three Years Travels from Moscow Over-land to China (London: W. Freeman, etc., 1706);

57

57

*Dreyjährige Reise nach China von Moscau ab zu lande durch gros
Ustiga, Siriania, Permia, Sibirien, Daour und die grosse
Tartarey* (Frankfurt: T. Fritsch, 1707). It was published in
French in Jean Frederic Bernard, *Recueil de voiages au nord*,
10 vols. (Amsterdam, 1725-38), VIII, 1-217.

16. Ides, *Three Years Travels*, p. 100.

17. *Ibid.* See also Clifford M. Foust, *Muscovite and Mandarin:
Russia's Trade with China and Its Setting, 1727-1805* (Chapel
Hill, University of North Carolina Press, 1969), p. 15.

18. Philippe Avril, *Voyage en divers etats d'Europe et d'Asie,
entrepris pour decouvrir un nouveau chemin a la Chine* (Paris:
C. Barbin, etc., 1692). A second French edition was published in 1693, and the book was translated into English
as *Travels into Divers Parts of Europe and Asia, Undertaken
. . . to Discover a New Way by Land into China* (London: T.
Goodwin, 1693).

19. Avril, *Travels*, sig. A3^V. Avril is especially critical of
the geographer Isaac Vossius.

20. *Ibid.*, p. 135.

21. *Ibid.*, pp. 176-79. According to this man, hunters going after
"the Behemot" (walrus) were sometimes caught in a thaw and
were carried out to sea on huge pieces of ice. He believed
that this was how people first reached America, which was
"not far off from that part of Asia which juts out into the
Sea of Tartary." The name "Kawoina" may refer to the Kolyma
River, but since he states the Lena flows into it, this is

uncertain. "Mouchim Pouchim" is Matvei Pushkin, a member of an old boyar family. He and his family did get into trouble, when his son Fedor was implicated in the streltsy conspiracy against Peter in 1697. Matvei Pushkin died in exile in Eniseisk in 1706. See V. Korsakova, "Matvei Stephanovich Pushkin," in Russkii biograficheskii slovar, XV, 318-19.

22. Avril, Travels, pp. 170-71.

23. Jodocus Crull, The Antient and Present State of Muscovy, 2 vols. (London: A. Roper and A. Bosvile, 1698), I, 73. Crull repeats the passage from Avril (see footnote 21) about the proximity of America to Asia in the north and the hunters being carried out to sea, possibly to America, on huge pieces of ice.

24. On Peter's interest in canals, both between rivers and in St. Petersburg, see Massie, Peter the Great, pp. 606-08; 778-80. Interest in canals for improving river transport was widespread at the time. An example is the work of the French engineer, Bouillet, Traite des moyens de rendre les rivieres navigable (Paris: E. Michallet, 1693).

25. Cornelius Cruys, Nieuw pas-kaart boek . . . (Amsterdam: H. Doncker ₍1704₎). Cruys was a Dutchman hired during Peter's visit to Holland in 1697. The title page of the book is in Dutch and Russian; there is an engraving showing Peter the Great. The introduction is in Dutch; the map inscriptions are in Russian.

26. Friedrich Christian Weber, The Present State of Russia, 2
    vols. (London: W. Taylor, 1723), I, 172. The work first emerged
    as Das veränderte Russland, 2 vols. (Frankfurt: N. Förster,
    1721). It was published in French as Memoires pour servir
    a l'histoire de l'empire russien, 2 vols. (The Hague: T.
    Johnson and J. van Duren, 1725) and in another French edition
    published in Paris that year.

27. Weber, Present State, pp. 177-78. The route was to follow the
    Dvina, Vychegda, Tavda, Irtish, Ob, Ket, Enisei, and Angara
    rivers to Lake Baikal. From there it would go to the Shilka
    River by an unnamed river, and from the Shilka to the Amur
    River and thence to the sea.

28. Ibid., p. 178.

29. Polevoi, "O kartax severnoi Azii," p. 125; Keuning, "Nicolaas
    Witsen," p. 99, notes that Witsen nowhere in his work admits
    that he received maps from Vinius.

30. See the letter of Witsen to Robert Southwell, president of
    the Royal Society, in the Philosophical Transactions, XVII,
    No. 193 (London, 1691), pp. 492-94.

31. Nicolaas Corneliszoon Witsen, Noord en oost Tartarye, 2 vols.
    (Amsterdam, 1692). The book, like the map, was published in
    few copies, and was very rare from the time of its publication.
    Perhaps also because of its length, this work was not translated
    from Dutch into other European languages.

32. Witsen, Ibid., II, 542-43. The "fish teeth" referred to in

this passage are walrus tusks.

33. Ibid., II, 36, 468.

34. Polevoi, "O kartax severnoi Azii," p. 130.

35. Ides, Three Years Travels, p. 93.

36. Ratzel, "Evert Izbrandszoon Ides," p. 748.

37. Charles Whitworth, An Account of Russia as It was in the Year 1710 (n.p., Strawberry Hill, 1758), pp. 151-52; John Perry, The State of Russia, under the Present Czar (London: Benjamin Tooke, 1716), sig. B2^r; G. P. Moriarty, "John Perry," in Dictionary of National Biography, XLV, 35-6.

38. Perry, State of Russia, sig. A3^r-A3^v. Perry states he held Peter in the highest personal esteem, and would have been happy to serve Peter all his life, except for the interference of Peter's associates.

39. Ibid., sig. A3^r. This enlarged scope, naturally, would have greater appeal to book buyers as well.

40. Ibid., p. 62.

41. Ibid., pp. 77, 80.

42. Ibid., p. 61. See Glynn Barratt, Russia in Pacific Waters, 1715-1825: A Survey of the Origins of Russia's Naval Presence in the North and South Pacific (Vancouver: University of British Columbia Press, 1981), p. 1, for an example of this use of Perry's quotation.

43. Ibid., p. 61.

44. Ibid. This idea was not so farfetched as it might appear to be

at first. A. E. Nordenskiöld, in The Voyage of the Vega

round Asia and Europe, translated by Alexander Leslie (New

York: Macmillan and Co., 1882) notes the Russians carried

on an active trade in the Arctic Ocean long before the Eng-

lish or Dutch explored there and Russians sometimes sailed

around the Iamal Peninsula, though they more often used land

transport across the peninsula. (p. 205).

45. Ibid., p. 77

46. Ibid., p. 70.

47. Atlas geograficheskikh otkrytii v Sibiri i v severo-zapadnoi

Amerike XVII-XVIII vv., edited by A. V. Efimov (Moscow:

Nauka, 1964), maps 32, 34, 48. See also the following chapter.

48. Perry, State of Russia, p. 68.

49. Weber, Present State of Russia, I, sig. A5^r.

50. Ibid., p. 47.

51. This supposed connection between Asia and America will be dis-

cussed in more detail later. Guillaume Delisle's 1706 map,

based on Witsen's map, bears a statement about a chain of

mountains, noting that whether or not this chain joins America

is not known. Weber believed it was connected to America.

52. Iakov Bruis is discussed at some length in Valentin Boss, Newton

and Russia. The relationship to Peter Henry Bruce is on pages

15-16.

53. Peter Henry Bruce, Memoirs of Peter Henry Bruce, Esq. (London:

For the Author's Widow, 1782), p. 175.

54. Ibid., pp. 174-75.

Chapter III

Peter the Great and Russian Explorations in the East:
The View from the West

During the reign of Peter the Great, Russians explored the
eastern limits of Siberia. Russians discovered a sea route to
Kamchatka, across the Sea of Okhotsk. They mapped Kamchatka and
explored its nearby seas. Russians sailed to the Kurile Islands.
They tried to find a route to Japan and attempted to determine
the geographical relationship between Siberia and America. How
much information about these explorations reached contemporaries
in western Europe? How was the information published in western
Europe and what effect did the manner of publication have on the
western European view of the purpose of Russian explorations?
This chapter will focus on these questions, specifically as they
relate to information supplied by Peter the Great to individuals
in western Europe.

When Peter visited Amsterdam in 1697, he greeted Nicolaas
Witsen as a friend. Though Witsen was in Russia only once, before
Peter was born, Witsen had maintained correspondence with Russians
and sustained an interest in Russia. Witsen knew of Peter's love
of ships; when Peter wanted a Dutch frigate for use in the White
Sea, Witsen sent him a specially-furnished ship, the Holy Prophecy,
in 1694. Burgomaster Witsen and the young tsar of Russia shared
a deep interest in ships. In 1671 Witsen had published a massive

volume on shipbuilding, containing just the kind of information
Peter hoped to gather in person through work in the shipyards of
the Dutch East India Company.[1] Peter was in Amsterdam for four
months during the late summer and early fall of 1697 and he saw
Witsen frequently during that time.

Witsen was revising his map of northeastern Asia, extending
it eastward to include lands beyond the Asian mainland. European
maps had commonly shown land very near to the eastern part of
Asia, land thought to extend to, or be a portion of, North America.
But Europeans had little factual information about the North Pacific
area. Witsen had studied the 1643-45 voyage of Maerten Gerritsen
Vries, the cartography of which was recorded on a number of maps
published not long before Peter's visit to Amsterdam. The land of
"Jesso" was discovered during this voyage. This land appears on
the 1693 map of the Italian geographer Vincenzo Coronelli, and on
a map made for the French by the Italian Jacques Cassini in 1696.
(See reproductions).[2] A map in a collection of voyages edited by
Melchisédech Thévenot, published in Amsterdam in 1696, shows not
only Jesso but land further east, called "Da Gama Land."[3] This
latter refers to the purported discovery of João da Gama, a Portuguese who sailed a northern route from Macao to China in 1589 or
1590. Little was known about this voyage, as Spanish officials
confiscated Da Gama's records.[4]

These lands--or rumored lands--were supposedly rich and were
ripe for traders who could discover routes to them. Even the

65

Portion of a map by Vincenzo Coronelli, published in
Epitome cosmografica in 1693.

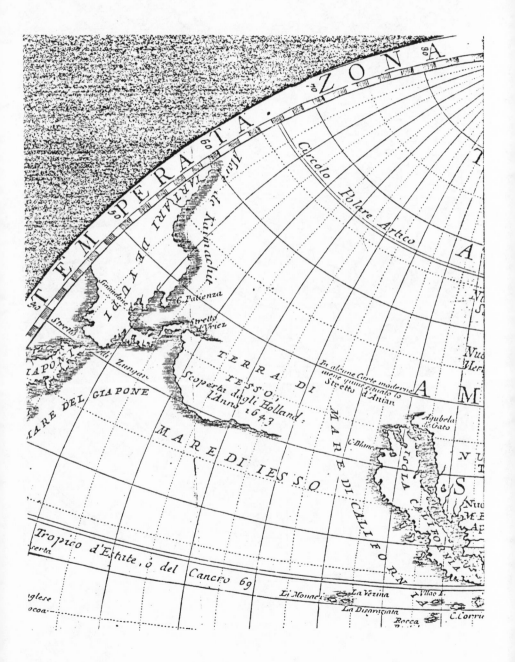

Portion of a world map by Jacques Cassini, 1696.

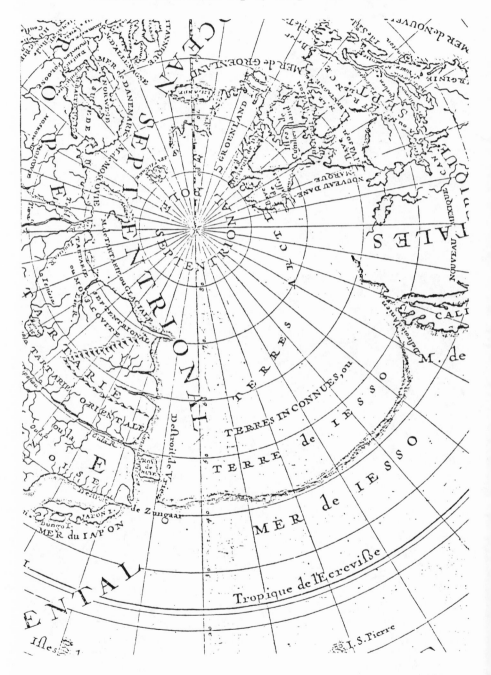

Map from Thévenot, published in 1696, showing "Iezo" and Da Gama Land.

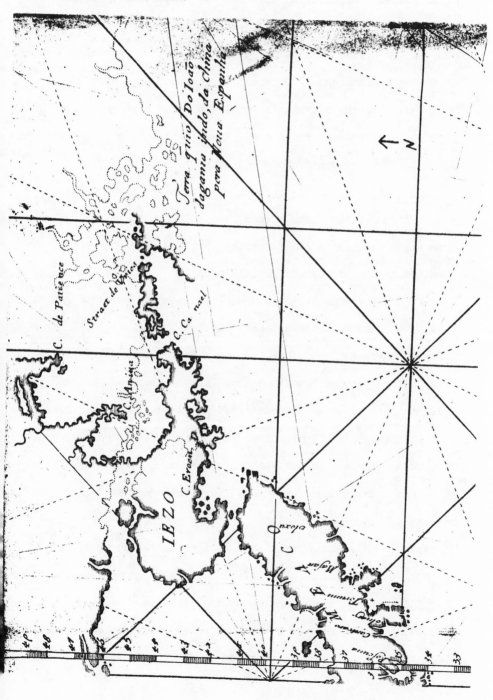

geographical configuration of Japan was conjectural; on some maps
Japan was portrayed as an island, on others it was part of the
much larger island, Jesso, and on others it was a peninsula attached
to the Asian mainland.[5] The confusion on the maps gave a clear
message: Europeans had little knowledge of an area which held great
promise for discovery and trade. Russia was in a good position to
undertake the exploration of this area.

As noted earlier, Peter shared information about Russian discoveries in the east with Witsen, and told him there was no land
connection between Asia and America in the Cape Tabin region. The
question of the open-ended peninsula called "Ice Cape" remained.
Following discussions with Witsen, Peter sent an order to Andrei
Vinius, in Moscow, to investigate the feasibility of sending a
party of cossacks to explore the mouth of the Lena River, to determine if a passage from it to the Pacific Ocean was possible.[6]
This has been cited as evidence that Peter hoped to discover a
northeast passage.[7] The failure of this expedition was referred
to by James Bruce, and may rather be seen as a reflection of the
statement made by John Perry that Peter intended, if a northeast
passage from European Russia to the east was not possible, to try
to discover a passage from the Lena River eastward around the
northern tip of Asia to the Pacific Ocean.[8]

Information from Russia about the area near Ice Cape was
included in the Ides text Witsen edited for publication in 1704.
About the area near Ice Cape the text reports: "The farther out

The northeastern corner of Asia, from the Dutch edition of Ides,
    published in 1704.

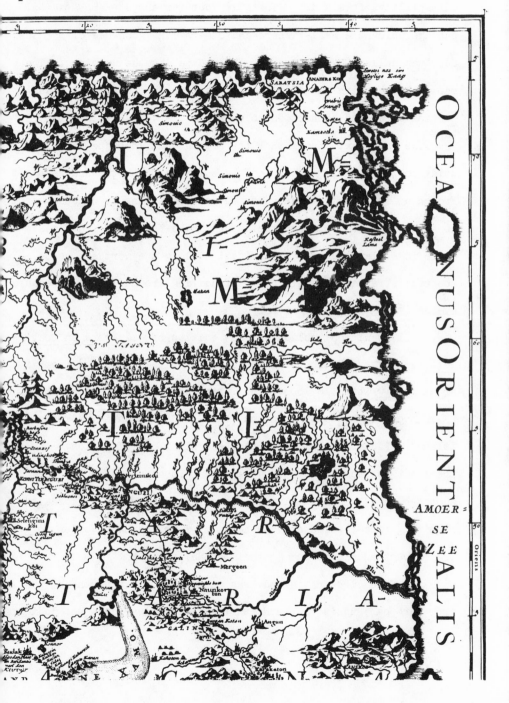

we sail, the course of the Sea is still the more interrupted by the
multiplicity of Islands." There is "not far above" Kamchatka "a
passage which the Seal-Fishers and others make good use of."[9] Ice
Cape was called "Sweitoinos" or "Holy Cape" by the Russians. The
map published with the Ides text shows this cape without any sug-
gestion of a land connection to America.[10]

The Ides text states that the area around Ice Cape is very
cold, so that sometimes the ice there was so thick the sea was
frozen up for two or three years in succession, as it had been from
1694 until 1697.[11] Though the map with the Ides text indicates
there is no land barrier to navigation along the northern coast,
the text stresses the difficulty of sailing around Ice Cape because
of ice.[12]

In 1705 Witsen published a new edition of his Noord en Oost
Tartarye. This edition includes a letter Witsen received from
Archangel, written in 1698. The letter includes the statement:

"According to many opinions, the Ice-Cape ends in broken
islands. Fishermen come down the Lena River, sailing along
the coast (as some wish to do), around this cape and to the sea-
shores by the Kamchatka River. There they slay whales and seals,
requiring three, three and one half, or four months in order to
travel back and forth and do their trade."[13]
With Ice Cape circumnavigated, was there hope for a northeast passage
from European Russia to the North Pacific? Witsen does not indicate
any in his book.

Map of Nicolaas Witsen, published in 1785.

Map of Nicolaas Witsen, published in 1785.

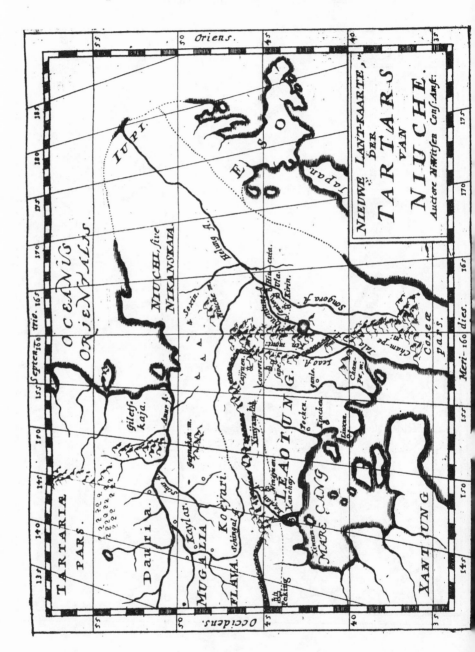

Witsen was working on a large map which included lands east
of the Asian mainland. In a letter of 1705 he writes to a friend:
"Please God Almighty to give me yet a year or two strength and
health, Your honour will see the great map extends further to the
east, as far as Japan and Yeso and near to America."[14] By 1707
part of this large map was engraved, but "I grow old and my strength
decreases every day. . . . I hope, however, it will be ready next
winter; as the Tsar has seen it, I can publish it."[15] This large
version of the map, apparently, was not completed.[16] Two of Witsen's
later maps, reproduced here, show lands in the North Pacific. These
lands, derived from the Vries and Da Gama voyages, may have been
the cartography which Witsen intended to include in his unfinished
large map.[17] In the map showing the northern part of Asia, Witsen
has closed off the two peninsulas with dotted lines, showing that
he did not believe that Asia was joined to America by land.

When Witsen died in 1717, western Europe lost its most ardent
student of northeastern Asia. Witsen's lasting imprint on the
maps of his contemporaries was the inclusion on maps of an arm of
land jutting out into the sea, a postulation of a land connection
to America.[18] His later maps had little influence. The maps reproduced here were not published until 1785, years after his death.[19]
Thus Witsen's early work gave support to the thesis that Russians
did not know the geography of northeastern Asia and were exploring
the seas near Kamchatka to determine whether or not a land connection existed between Asia and America.

In the 1705 edition of Noord en Oost Tartarye, Witsen states that sailors had gone around Ice Cape and that Cape Tabin did not join to America. But the editions of Noord en Oost Tartarye were published in very few copies. Witsen's massive volumes in Dutch about northeastern Asia were neither translated nor widely circulated.[20] Russian explorations, according to the Ides text which Witsen edited, revealed that what prevented a northeast passage was not a land barrier, but the ice of the northern seas. Unlike his own book, the Ides text was translated and published in several European languages in the eighteenth century. Why was the description of the northeast passage overlooked? The Ides book is a description of an embassy to China, not a treatise on northern Asia. The information about Russian explorations is only part of a much larger text.[21] Further, the relationship of Witsen to this text was not clear and scholars of Witsen did not recognize the importance of the Ides text as a record of Witsen's views about a possible northeast passage.[22]

Peter the Great discussed the geography of eastern Asia with the famous French geographer, Guillaume Delisle, in 1717. Peter visited Paris that year on his second journey to western Europe. In the years since his first visit, Peter had received information concerning Russian explorations in eastern Asia, including some information about Japan. In 1696 the cossack Vladimir Atlasov became prikazchik (commander) of the Anadyr ostrog. Under his orders, the cossack Luka Morozko led an expedition southward into

western Kamchatka. Atlasov, in the years 1697 to 1699, explored
and conquered western Kamchatka, almost to its southern tip.
While on his expedition, Atlasov met Dembei, a Japanese castaway.
Dembei had sailed from his native Osaka in 1695 with a fleet of
ships carrying goods for trade to Edo. During a typhoon, Dembei's
ship was separated from the rest. It reached Kamchatka, where the
Japanese were taken prisoners. Though Atlasov did not recognize
Dembei was Japanese, he took him along with him to Iakutsk, from
whence both went to Moscow. They met Peter early in 1702.[23]

In Moscow, officials of the Siberian Department identified
Dembei as a Japanese, on the basis of a German book describing
Japan. This book, presumably, was a collection of travels compiled
by Christoph Arnold, Wahrhaftige Beschreibungen dreyer mächtigen
Königreiche, Japan, Siam, und Corea, published in Nuremberg in
1672. It included an illustrated account of Japan written by the
French Jesuit François Caron, and was accompanied by a map showing
Japan as a peninsula of Asia.[24] Dembei recognized the illustrations
in a book as pictures of his homeland. The impression that Japan
was part of Asia was further bolstered by Dembei, who apparently
did not understand that the Russian word "Kitai" meant China,
confusing it with the Japanese city of Akita, on the northwestern
coast of Japan. Dembei told the Russians he had gone to this place
by sea and by land. He stressed the great wealth of his country
and the potential for trade there.[25]

From Atlasov, Peter received assurances that Japan was close

Map of Japan in Arnold, <u>Wahrhaftige</u> <u>Beschreibungen</u>, 1672.

to Kamchatka, for the Kamchadals, Atlasov asserted, had goods--
china, crockery, and fabrics--which they did not make themselves.
The goods were identified as Japanese in origin. What Atlasov did
not know was that these goods were traded to the Kamchadals via
the Kurile Islanders, who acted as middlemen in the trade.[26]

Atlasov went back to Kamchatka in 1706 and was murdered there
in 1711 by mutineers. To excape punishment two of the mutineers,
Danilo Antsiferov and Ivan Kozyrevskii, crossed from Kamchatka
to Shimshu, the northernmost of the Kurile Islands. On the strength
of information they received from the Ainu, they were able to
prepare a map showing several of the islands. They offered to find
a route to Japan in order to dissuade Peter from punishing them
for their part in the murder of Atlasov, and in 1713 they sailed
further southward in the Kurile Islands.[27] In 1714 two explorers
had gone from Okhotsk along the coast in search of a route to
Japan and they sighted land to the east. They sailed to an island,
but died before they could make any reports on their discoveries.[28]
Peter received maps and reports of the discoveries in the east
from Atlasov and others, and when he visited Delisle in 1717 Peter
showed him some Russian manuscript maps.[29]

Delisle had published, in 1706, a "Carte de Tartarie." This
map was based, largely, on Witsen's first map.[30] In northern Asia,
in Delisle's map, a mountainous, open-ended peninsula is shown,
with the notation that whether or not the end of this joins with
some other continent is unknown. To the east of the "Amour" river

The Delisle map of 1706. The legend on the promontory reads:
"On ne sait pas ou se termine cette Chaine de montagnes, et si
elle ne va pas joindre quelque autre continent."

is Jesso, just visible within the frame of the map. This map

helped to establish Delisle's reputation as the foremost French

cartographer of his time.[31] In 1714 Delisle published another map

of the same area. The open-ended promontory of land in the north-

east remains. This map incorporates material from the Vries voy-

age. In it, Delisle joins Japan and Jesso into one large island.

Whether or not Japan connected to Jesso was a subject of interest

to Delisle, who wrote an article on the subject.[32]

Delisle made a map, unfortunately undated, which he states in

the cartouche was formed on the basis of information he received

from the tsar. In this map, Japan appears as a separate island,

not connected to Jesso. The land of Jesso appears as part of the

Asian mainland. In the northeast, where the earlier notation

near the promontory indicated "end unknown" is a cape, with five

islands in the sea beyond it.[33] In his 1714 map Novaia Zemlia

is shown as a peninsula; in the later map it is not, though its

southern coast is not depicted. The claim Delisle makes to

having information from Russia is well substantiated in the pre-

sentation of Novaia Zemlia and Ice Cape.[34]

Delisle made another map, bearing the date 1720, which is

very similar to the undated map made using information from Peter.

Presumably this map was made after the undated one, for on it

Ice Cape is still further reduced; many islands are depicted in

the sea beyond it.[35] The series of Delisle maps supports the

thesis that Peter the Great did not believe a promontory in the

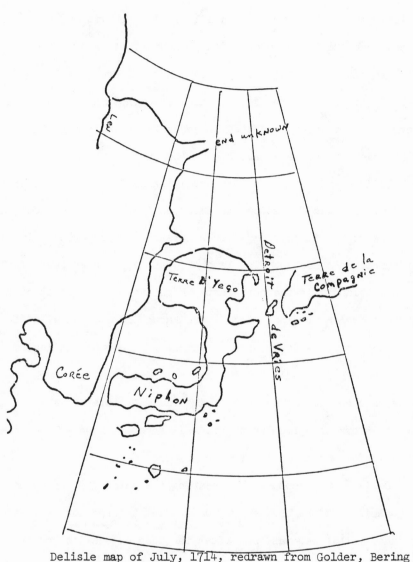

Delisle map of July, 1714, redrawn from Golder, Bering's Voyages, I, facing page two.

Undated Delisle map.

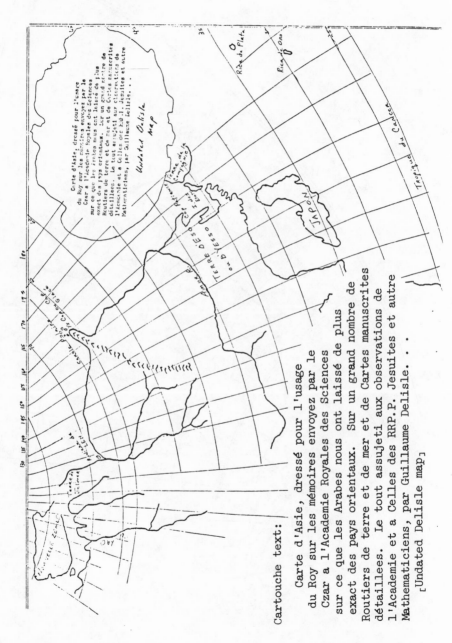

Cartouche text:

Carte d'Asie, dressé pour l'usage
du Roy sur les mémoires envoyez par le
Czar a l'Academie Royales des Sciences
sur ce que les Arabes nous ont laissé de plus
exact des pays orientaux. Sur un grand nombre de
Routiers de terre et de mer et de Cartes manuscrites
détaillees. Le tout assujeti aux observations de
l'Academie et a Celles des RRP.P. Jesuites et autre
Mathematiciens, par Guillaume Delisle...

[Undated Delisle map]

82

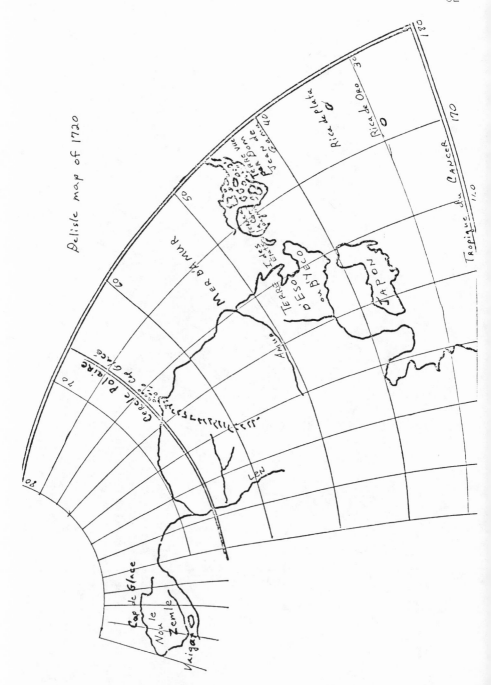

Delisle map of 1720

The Nicolas Bion map of Asia

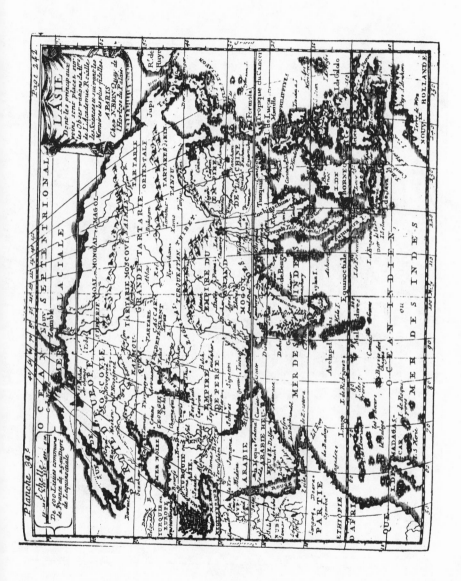

The Nicolas Bion map of America.

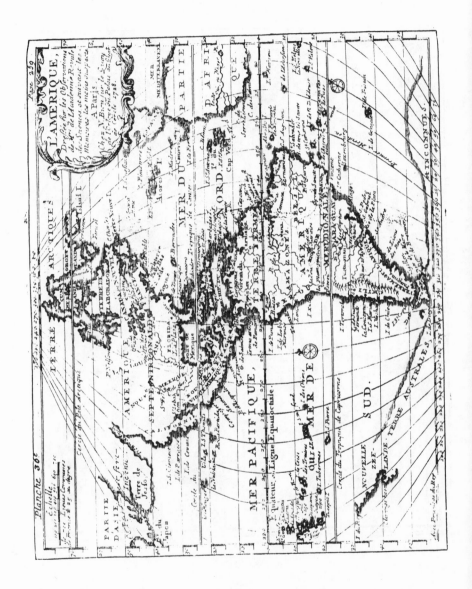

northeast connected Asia with America. He shared this information
with Delisle, who incorporated it in his maps. While Delisle's
first map was widely copied by other European cartographers, his
later maps were not.[36] Thus, Delisle, like Witsen, helped to foster
the belief that Russian explorations were directed toward deter-
mining whether or not a land connection between Asia and America
existed in the north, even though Delisle's later maps indicated
that there was none.

At the time Peter visited Paris, the idea that America was
close to Asia was evident on many European maps. For example,
Peter may well have obtained a copy of a book by Nicolas Bion,
published in 1717. Bion had the title "King's engineer for mathe-
matical instruments" and specialized in nautical instruments.
With Peter's known interest in maritime matters, it is likely
Bion's book describing their use would have appealed to him. The
book contains maps showing land close to Asia--land believed to be
part of America.[37]

The results of Russian explorations indicated there was no
land connection between Asia and America in the north, but southeastern Kamchatka had not been explored. In May, 1718, Peter decided to send an expedition to explore southeastern Kamchatka.
A map made that year by Iakov A. Elchin, governor of Iakutsk, is
believed to be the one Peter used in drafting the instructions
for this expedition.[38] The map shows a large bulge of land going
southeastward from Kamchatka in the direction of America.

The Elchin map, 1718.

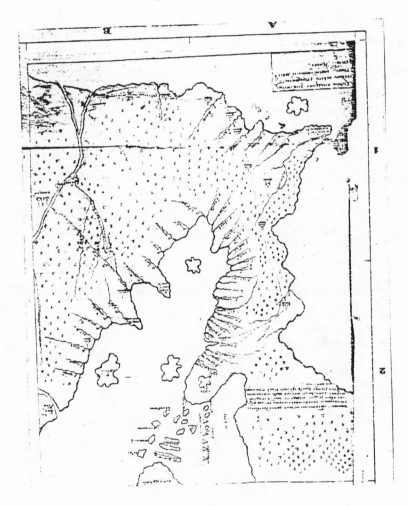

Map of Evreinov and Luzhin, 1722.

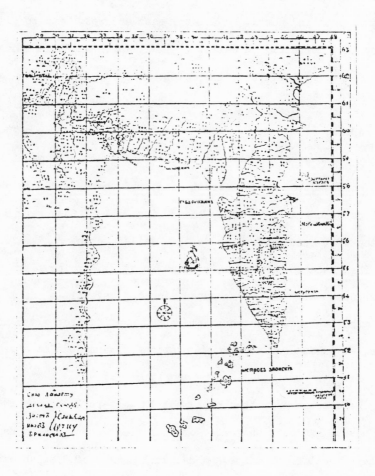

In 1719 Ivan M. Evreinov and Fedor F. Luzhin, two geodesists
(land surveyors) began their expedition with orders from Peter as
follows: "You are to go to Tobolsk, and taking guides you are to
go to Kamchatka and farther, whither it is indicated to you, and
you are to describe the local places [where or whether] America
is joined with Asia, which must be done very carefully, not only
in the south and north, but in the east and west, and to place
everything correctly on a map..."[39] If there was a land connection between Asia and America, it would be found on the east
or south part of Kamchatka, which had not been thoroughly explored
and mapped.

Evreinov and Luzhin reached the west coast of Kamchatka in
1720, crossed to the east coast, wintered there, and surveyed the
east coast of Kamchatka. In the spring of 1721 they were back
on the west coast. From there they sailed to the Kurile Islands
and then back to Okhotsk. At Kazan in 1722, Evreinov reported to
Peter personally about the expedition and gave him a map made from
it. The map shows southern Kamchatka, and together with earlier
maps, gives an accurate representation of Kamchatka as a peninsula
of Asia.[40]

Were there any other maps made in western Europe on the basis
of Russian explorations? One other cartographer, Johann Baptist
Homann, received accounts and manuscript maps of Russian explorations
which he used in making maps of northeastern Asia. Homann was
a German mapmaker who lived in Nuremberg. He prepared a map

Homann map from Johann David Köhler, Schul- und reisen Atlas,
  Nuremberg, 1719.

Homann map from Johann David Köhler, <u>Schul-</u> <u>und</u> <u>reisen</u> <u>Atlas</u>, Nuremberg, 1719.

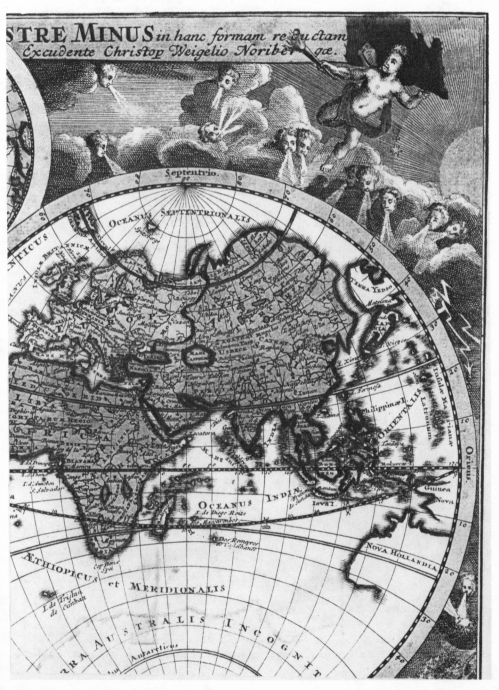

to accompany the German edition of Ides, published in 1707, but
the map did not appear with the book.[41]

On maps made prior to 1719, Homann depicts Novaia Zemlia as
an island, without any Cape Tabin or Ice Cape that could possibly
join to America. (See reproductions).[42] These maps may well reflect information Homann received from Russia.[43]

Homann published, sometime before 1722, a map showing Kamchatka
as a peninsula of Asia. He received this information from Russia,
at the order of Peter the Great. For his services as a mapmaker,
Homann was rewarded and given a position in Russian service.[44]

Philip Johann von Strahlenberg claimed his maps were used
by Homann in making maps.[45] Strahlenberg, a Swede who was captured at the battle of Poltava in 1709, made maps showing Kamchatka
as a peninsula of Asia. Strahlenberg was sent to Tobolsk in 1711;
he stayed in Siberia for eleven years. Strahlenberg made his
first map of Siberia in 1715, but it was lost in a fire. His
second map was confiscated in 1718 by Prince Matvei P. Gagarin,
the governor of Siberia. Strahlenberg claimed this map was confiscated because it indicated the location of mines of precious
metals in Siberia. Strahlenberg hated Gagarin, and expressed his
pleasure when Gagarin was executed in March, 1721, at Peter's
order, for abusing his position as governor. By 1721 Strahlenberg
had made a third map, which he sold before leaving Russia in 1723.
These maps, like the Russian manuscript maps, show Kamchatka as a
peninsula of Asia and do not indicate any unclosed peninsulas of

land in the northeast.[46]

Peter planned another expedition to the eastern seas in 1724. He selected Vitus Bering, a Dane who had been in the Russian navy since 1704, to head it. Bering's was the first Russian voyage to become widely known in western Europe. The belief arose that Bering was sent to determine the relationship between Asia and America--whether or not they were joined in the north. If they were joined, all hope of polar passages would vanish. If they were not, Russia would have taken a major step toward discovering a northeast passage. That this belief should have arisen in the eighteenth century is understandable, in view of western Europe's long preoccupation with trade in the east, and with finding some northern sea route to it. Peter had close ties with two maritime nations--the Dutch and the English--who were active in eastern trade through their East India companies. The English and Dutch had attempted to find a northeast passage, knowing how valuable it would have proven to be for eastern trade. Though Russians in Peter's time were exploring the northern coasts of Asia, the results of these explorations were not well known in western Europe. Geographers theorized that voyages could be made without difficulty in northern seas. Russia in Peter's time had acquired ships and a navy, and could utilize a northern sea route. If Russia gained access to a northeast passage, other European nations would be at an obvious disadvantage in eastern trade.

Later writers accepted the thesis that Bering's purpose was

to determine whether or not a land connection existed between Asia and America. Captain James Burney, in 1819, recorded his opinion that Bering sailed up the Kamchatka coast in search of a northeast passage, and turned back when "he had ascertained its separation from America."[47] Burney had sailed with Captain James Cook in the voyage for Great Britain to the North Pacific in 1778-79, and his account was given added importance because of this experience.[48] This same thesis was supported in 1823 by Vasilii N. Berkh, who wrote a monograph titled, Pervoe morskoe puteshestvie rossiian, predpriniatve dlia resheniia geograficheskoi zadachi: Soediniaetsia li Aziia s Amerikoiu? (The first Russian maritime voyage, undertaken to decide the geographical question: Is Asia joined to America?). Other nineteenth century Russian writers on Bering supported the same thesis, including Aleksandr S. Polonskii, Vasilii V. Vakhtin, Karl E. von Baer, A. S. Sgibnev, and Sergei M. Solov'ev.[49] The geographer and Arctic explorer, Adolf E. Nordenskiöld, and a Danish biographer of Bering, Peter Lauridsen, also supported the thesis.[50]

An American, Frank A. Golder, expressed the same idea in his Russian expansion on the Pacific, 1641-1850, published in 1914, and even more explicitly in his extensive study published in 1922 and 1925, in two volumes, with the title Bering's voyages: An account of the efforts of the Russians to learn the relation of Asia to America. Twentieth century Soviet historians held the same theme, with some variations on it. Lev S. Berg, in a book

written in 1946, stressed the importance of Gottfried W. Leibnitz
in persuading Peter to undertake the explorations, in order to
discover a northeast passage.[51] A decade later, Mikhail I. Belov
emphasized the importance of Peter's visit to the French Académie
des Sciences in 1717 and Peter's conversations with Guillaume
Delisle, in initiating his decision to send Bering on the voyage.[52]
Aleksandr I. Andreev, in a number of publications beginning in
1943, held that the settling of the geographic question was the
major purpose of the voyages.[53]

A new interpretation was put forward in 1941 by Aleksei A.
Pokrovskii, who published a collection of documents relating to
Bering's voyages. Pokrovskii questioned the traditional view
in his introduction to the collection, by noting that Peter's
instructions required Bering to go to America.[54] In 1960 Vadim
I. Grekov followed up on this interpretation and added to it
commentary on Peter's knowledge of the geography of the North
Pacific.[55] Boris P. Polevoi, in articles published in 1964 and
1967, developed the thesis further.[56] The thesis that Bering
was to go to America rather than to search for a northeast passage
was emerging. This interpretation was not the only one, for other
Soviet scholars (Aleksei V. Efimov, Dmitrii M. Lebedev, and Vasilii
A. Divin) recorded other views of the purposes for the voyages:
the search for trade in the east, protection of trade and of Russian
eastern empire, and extension of Russian holding in the east.[57]
In 1976 Evgenii G. Kushnarev published a monograph that again set

the Bering first voyage in the context of a search for a passage between Asia and America.[58]

In his book published in 1977, Bering's voyages: Whither and Why, the American historian Raymond H. Fisher examined the evidence presented by Soviet historians, Peter's instructions for the first voyage of Bering and the evidence relating to the second and concludes: "The purpose of Bering's first voyage, as we have seen, was not the commonly accepted one of settling the geographical question of the existence of a land connection between Asia and America--but rather, it was to go from Kamchatka to America and reconnoiter the coast."[59] The Soviet/Fisher thesis is compelling in many respects.[60] The examination of contemporary books and maps discussed in this chapter has revealed clear evidence in support of this thesis. These contemporary sources testify to Peter the Great's belief that there was no land connection between Asia and America.

Yet English-language texts published since the Fisher book continue to assert the earlier idea of the purpose of Bering's expedition, no doubt because the writers of them did not have Fisher's book available to them at the time of their writing. For example, J. Arthur Lower (1978) writes: "His [Peter's] last act before he died in 1725 was to appoint a Dane, Vitus Bering, to be leader of an expedition to discover whether Siberia was joined to North America."[61] In his biography of Peter, M. S. Anderson (1978) asserts "From 1719 onwards Peter made efforts to solve one of the greatest remaining puzzles of geographers, the question of whether

or not eastern Siberia was joined to North America. . . . "[62]

Another biographer, Robert K. Massie (1980), says Bering was sent

"to determine whether Eurasia and North America were joined by

land."[63] In an encyclopedia published in 1980 about discoverers,

Richard A. Pierce, one of the foremost American scholars of Russian

voyages, writes that the main task of the first Bering voyage was

"to determine whether Asia was connected with North America."[64]

Glynn Barratt, in an invaluable study of Russian naval activities

in the North Pacific, published in 1981, places the first Bering

voyage in the context of Peter's hopes to discover the Strait of

Anian between Asia and America, for purposes of trade via a north-

east passage.[65]

How did this idea become so dominant in the literature on

the Bering voyage? To begin to answer this question, it is

necessary to turn to the voyage itself, which is the subject of

the following chapter.

Footnotes

Chapter III

1. Nicolaas Corneliszoon Witsen, Aeloude & hedendaegsche scheepsbouw en bestier (Amsterdam: Casparus Commelijn, 1671). On
Peter's experiences during his travels of 1697-98 see Reinhold
Wittram, "Peters des Grossen erste Reise in den Westen" in
Jahrbücher für Geschichte Osteuropas, neue Folge, III:4 (1955),
373-403; N. A. Baklanova, "Velikoe posol'stvo za granitsei v
1697-1698 gg." in Petr Velikii: Sbornik statei, A. I. Andreev,
ed. (Moscow and Leningrad: AN SSSR, 1947), pp. 3-62.

2. Vincenzo Coronelli (1650-1718), Cosmographer of the Venetian
Republic, prepared many maps. His most famous work was the
12 volume Atlante Veneto, published from 1697 to 1701. The
reproduction here is from his Epitome cosmografica, o Compendiosa
in traduttione all'astronomia, geografia, & idrografia (Cologne,
1693). Giovanni Domenico Cassini (1625-1712) was a professor
of astronomy at Bologna when he was called to Paris in 1669 as
director of the Paris Observatory. The reproduction of the
Cassini map here is from Lloyd A. Brown, Jean Domenique Cassini
and his World Map of 1696 (Ann Arbor: University of Michigan
Press, 1941).

3. This map is similar to the one published in the Philosophical
Transactions of 1674, which was reproduced in Chapter I. The
map is from Melchisédech Thévenot, Relations de divers voyages

<u>curieux</u>, 2 vols. (Paris: T. Moette, 1696), I, preceding page one of "Relation des Isles Philippines."

4. See Lawrence C. Wroth, "The Early Cartography of the Pacific," in <u>The Papers of the Bibliographical Society of America</u>, XXXVIII:2 (1944), 85-268.

5. <u>Ibid.</u>, pp. 201-15. Chapter IX, "Japan, the Shuttlecock of the Cartographers."

6. Boris P. Polevoi, "Vodnyi put' iz ledovitogo okeana v tikhii; zabytyi nakaz A. A. Vinius 1697 goda," in <u>Priroda</u>, V (1965), 94. Witsen, according to Polevoi, had been informed that there was no land connection between Asia and America by F. S. Saltyko from Tobolsk, sometime between 1690 and 1692. See Boris P. Polevoi, "O kartax severnoi Azii N. K. Vitsena," in <u>Izvestiia AN SSSR, seriia geograficheskaia</u>, II (1973), 130.

7. Polevoi, "Vodnyi put'," 94.

8. See the discussions of Bruce and Perry in Chapter II.

9. Evert Ysbrandszoon Ides, <u>Three Years Travels from Moscow Over-Land to China</u> (London: W. Freeman [etc.] 1706), p. 104.

10. The Dutch edition of this work was published in 1704. The same printing plate that was used for the map in the Dutch edition was used for the English translation of 1704. Thus the English edition appears with a map containing Dutch legends.

11. Ides, <u>Three Years Travels</u>, p. 105.

12. See the quotation about the difficulties in sailing along the northern coast of Asia because of ice, given in Chapter II.

13. Nicolaas Corneliszoon Witsen, Noord en Oost Tartaryen, 2 vols. (Amsterdam: M. Schalekamp, 1785), II:676. The 1705 edition has the same sheets as the 1785 edition; the title has been changed to "Tartaryen." The translation of this passage is by Tracy Norris.

14. Johannes Keuning, "Nicolaas Witsen as a Cartographer," in Imago Mundi, XI (1954), 110.

15. Ibid., p. 109. The letter was written to Gijsbert Cuper, Burgomaster of Deventer.

16. Ibid. After Witsen's death, his books and maps were sold at auction, but it is not known what became of the materials for his large map. See Polevoi, "O kartax severnoi Azii," pp.131-32.

17. This is still conjectural, but the fact that Witsen said his new map was going to cover the area "near to America" suggests that this was the representation he intended to incorporate into the new large map.

18. Witsen's first map was the one that had the strong influence on western European cartographers. See Leo Bagrow, "The First Russian Maps of Siberia and Their Influence on the West-European Cartography of N.E. Asia," in Imago Mundi, IX (1952), 89-90.

19. Witsen's two smaller maps, reproduced here, were included in the Noord en oost Tartaryen of 1785, but not in the 1705 edition. This was verified by the Department of Rare Books of the New York Public Library, which has the only copy of Witsen's 1705 edition in America.

20. To the present time, this work has not been translated from Dutc[h] into any other language. A French translation of Witsen's comme[nts] about the area beyond Ice Cape, with an Ides' map, is included i[n] Cornelis de Bruyn, Voyages de Corneille Le Brun par la Moscovie, en Perse, et aux Indes Orientales (Amsterdam: Freres Wetstein, 1718), on page 142.

21. The great part of the Ides' book concerns China, of course, and the insertion about the Russian northeast is only a small part of the text, about an area which Ides did not visit.

23. Aleksei V. Efimov, Iz istorii velikikh russkikh geograficheskikh otkrytii (Moscow: Nauka, 1971), pp. 124-25; George Alexander Lensen, The Russian Push toward Japan (Princeton: Princeton University Press, 1959), pp. 27-30.

24. Another book may have been used, but this is the most likely one and the map reproduced here is from it. See Christoph Arnold, Wahrhaftige Beschreibungen dreyer mächtigen Königreiche, Japan, Siam, und Corea (Nuremberg: M. und J. F. Endters, 1672).

25. Lensen, The Russian Push, p. 30.

26. Ibid., p. 26.

27. Ibid., pp. 31-32.

28. A contemporary report on this was given in Friedrich Christian Weber, The Present State of Russia, 2 vols. (London: W. Taylor [etc.] 1723), I, 178.

29. Peter met Delisle on 17 June 1717 and showed him some manuscript maps of Siberia. Peter and Delisle attended a formal meeting of

the academy the following day. See A. I. Andreev, "Osnovanie akademii nauk v Peterburge" in Petr Velikii; Sbornik statei, edited by A. I. Andreev (Moscow, Leningrad: AN SSSR, 1947), pp. 283-333. The meeting is described on pages 289-90.

30. The Delisle map reproduced here is a redrawing from Guillaume Delisle, Atlas nouveau, contenant toutes les parties du monde (Amsterdam: J. Covens & C. Mortier [1741]).

31. On Delisle, see George Kish, "Guillaume Delisle," in Dictionary of Scientific Biography, IV, 22. Delisle tutored King Louis XV in geography.

32. Guillaume Delisle, "Determination geographique de la situation & de l'étendue des differentes parties de la terre," in Académie des Sciences, Paris, Histoire de l'Académie royale des sciences. Année MDCCXX (Amsterdam: Pierre de Coup, 1724), 473-98. The statement about Japan appears on page 494. He also wrote an undated "Lettre. . . sur la question, si le Japon est une Ile." A copy of it appears in Jean Frédéric Bernard, Recueil de Voyages au Nord, nouvelle edition (Amsterdam: Jean Frederic Bernard, 1732), IV:17-31.

33. This map is redrawn from Frank A. Golder, Bering's Voyages: An Account of the Efforts of the Russians to Determine the Relation of Asia and America, 2 vols. (New York: American Geographical Society, 1922), I, opposite page 2.

34. In his representation of Novaia Zemlia, Delisle had, like Witsen, shown a strait on the western side, but had attached Novaia

Zemlia to the coast of Asia by "Terre de Jelmer" in the east. On the undated map Novaia Zemlia is separated from Asia, giving evidence that Delisle had received information from Russia about its relation to the Siberian coast.

35. Presumably, the undated map was the earlier one, although this cannot be stated unequivocally.

36. See, for example, Leo Bagrow, "The First Russian Maps," pp. 90-91, where the Delisle map of 1706 is noted, while the later ones are not.

37. On Bion, see Jacques Payen, "Nicolas Bion," in Dictionary of Scientific Biography, II, 132-33. The maps reproduced here are from Nicolas Bion, l'Usage des globes celeste et terrestre (Paris: Michel Brunet ₍etc.₎ 1728). The same maps appeared in earlier editions of this book. A microfilm of the 1710 edition is in the Map Room of the University of California, Berkeley, and a copy of the 1717 edition is in the History of Science Collections at Cornell University.

38. This map is commonly called the "Elchin map" though it was made by the cossack Ivan Eniseiskii. It is reproduced here from Aleksei V. Efimov, Iz istorii, p. 198.

39. Raymond H. Fisher, Bering's Voyages: Whither and Why (Seattle: University of Washington Press, 1977), p. 57. Fisher notes that Peter crossed out the word "where" but did not replace it; hence the bracketed "where or whether."

40. Ibid., pp. 58-59. The map is reproduced from Dmitrii M. Lebedev

Geografiia v Rossii petrovskogo vremeni (Moscow; Leningrad: AN SSSR, 1950), p. 241.

41. Leo Bagrow, *A History of Russian Cartography up to 1800*, edited by Henry W. Castner (Wolfe Island, Ontario: The Walker Press, 1975), p. 78. The German edition of the Ides book was published in 1707; the titlepage of the book indicates that a map was included. No copies of the book contain the map, however.

42. The maps are reproduced from Johann David Köhler, *Schul- und reisen Atlas*. . . (Nuremberg: J. E. Adelbulner, 1719). The titlepage of this atlas bears the date 1719, which is important in dating the Homann maps contained in the atlas, since the Homann maps themselves are not dated.

43. These maps differ from the map Homann made of the Ides map which appeared in his atlas of 1702-1710, which is reproduced by Leo Bagrow in "The First Russian Maps," following page 92, since they give a more rounded configuration of the northeastern part of Asia. Homann received cartographical information from Russia, though it is difficult to know how early. See the later commentary on Homann.

44. Brecher, "Johann Baptist Homann," in *Allgemeine deutsche Biographie*, XIII, 35-38. The dating of this map will be discussed in the following chapter.

45. For general biographical information about Strahlenberg, see Mariia G. Novlianskaia, *Filip Ioann Strahlenberg: ego raboty po issledovaniiu Sibiri* (Moscow: Nauka, 1966).

46. Strahlenberg and his maps will be discussed further in Chapter IV, where his map is reproduced.

47. James Burney, A Chronological History of North-Eastern Voyages of Discovery; And of the Early Eastern Navigations of the Russians (London: Payne and Foss, 1819), p. 123.

48. Burney was a scholar of earlier voyages as well as a participar of Cook's voyage. In his study of Bering's first voyage, he used the Strahlenberg printing of Bering's account, rather than the earlier English translations. He would perhaps have had a clearer idea of the purpose of Bering's voyage if the editor of the manuscript printed in Strahlenberg's book had not changed the text. See the commentary in Chapter VI.

49. These writings are cited in the bibliography. They are discuss by Raymond H. Fisher, in Bering's Voyages, pp. 16-18.

50. A. E. Nordenskiöld, The Voyage of the Vega round Asia and Euro (New York: Macmillan and Co., 1882), pp. 534-35; Peter Lauridse Vitus Bering: The Discoverer of Bering Strait, translated by Julius E. Olson (Freeport: Books for Libraries Press, 1969; re-printed from the original edition of 1889), p. 35.

51. Lev S. Berg, Otkrytie Kamchatki i ekspeditsii Beringa (Moscow; Leningrad: AN SSSR, 1946); Fisher, Bering's Voyages, p. 19.

52. Fisher, Bering's Voyages, p. 19.

53. Ibid.

54. Ibid., pp. 19-20.

55. Ibid., p. 20.

56. Ibid.

57. Ibid.

58. Ibid., pp. 20-21.

59. Ibid., p. 152.

60. The thesis that Bering was sent to explore North America is compelling because, as has been seen, Peter the Great knew that the mainland of northeastern Siberia was not connected to America. The problem with this thesis is that Bering did not go to America, even when he was so close to it in the north, and therefore it becomes necessary to speculate as to why Bering did not follow Peter's orders, or why he misunderstood them.

61. J. Arthur Lower, Ocean of Destiny: A Concise History of the North Pacific, 1500-1978 (Vancouver: University of British Columbia Press, 1978), p. 24.

62. M. S. Anderson, Peter the Great (London: Thames and Hudson, 1978), p. 115.

63. Robert K. Massie, Peter the Great: His Life and World (New York: Alfred A. Knopf, 1980), p. 819.

64. Richard A. Pierce, "Vitus Jonassen Bering," in The Discoverers: An Encyclopedia of Explorers and Exploration (New York: McGraw-Hill, 1980), p. 79.

65. Glynn Barratt, Russia in Pacific Waters: A Survey of the Origins of Russia's Naval Presence in the North and South Pacific (Vancouver: University of British Columbia Press, 1981).

Chapter IV

The First Kamchatka Expedition

Peter the Great named Vitus Bering to lead the First Kamchatka

Expedition and promoted him to captain of the first rank. He se-

lected another Dane, Lieutenant Morten Spanberg, and a Russian,

Lieutenant Aleksei I. Chirikov, as Bering's assistants. Peter

wrote Bering's official instructions late in December, 1724, or

early in January, 1725, but he did not discuss the instructions

with Bering at that time, for Peter was by then very ill.[1] Peter

died on 28 January 1725 and Bering's instructions were issued under

the authority of Peter's widow, Empress Catherine I.[2]

Bering's instructions were not delivered to him until 5 Februar

1725, the day he left St. Petersburg. An advance contingent of the

expedition, twenty-five men and as many wagonloads of goods, had

left earlier, on 24 January, under the leadership of Chirikov.

Rumors were circulating in St. Petersburg that Bering was going

to the North Pacific to determine whether or not a northeast passage

existed between Asia and America.[3] Admiral Fedor M. Apraksin, head

of the Russian navy, gave Bering the instructions and a map.

Peter's short instructions to Bering have been translated

many times. The English text given here is a contemporary trans-

lation from the first publication of the instructions in Russia.[4]

They were printed in a history of Russian discoveries written by

Gerhard Friedrich Müller. Müller knew Bering well and saw Bering's instructions himself.[5] Müller wrote his history in German and it was translated into Russian for simultaneous publications in German and Russian. It was printed in St. Petersburg by the Russian Academy of Sciences in 1758.[6] The text is as follows:

I. One or two Boats with decks to be built at Kamtschatka, or at any other convenient place, with which
II. Enquiry should be made in relation to the northerly coasts, to see whether they were not contiguous with America, since their end was not known. And this done, they should
III. See whether they could not somewhere find an harbour belonging to Europeans, or an European ship. They should likewise set apart some men, who were to enquire after the name and situation of the coasts discovered. Of all this an exact journal should be kept, with which they should return to Petersburg.[7]

Peter's first order, to go to Kamchatka and build ships there, proved to be a long and difficult assignment.[8] Bering and his companions caught up with Chirikov at Vologda, and the expedition then numbered thirty-three men. At posting stations along the route to Verkhoturie problems arose, since the officials in the towns had not been notified about the expedition and were unprepared to provide accommodations and horses for such a large number of people. The expedition went from Verkhoturie to Tobolsk, arriving there on 16 March. They had to stay in Tobolsk until mid-May because of bad weather. Thirty-four soldiers were added to the expedition at Tobolsk.

The expedition then traveled northward on the Irtysh River to Samarovsk. From Samarovsk, midshipman Peter A. Chaplin was sent ahead with some of the men to construct boats for the expedition at Eniseisk, where thirty blacksmiths and carpenters were added to the expedition's forces.

Route of the First Kamchatka Expedition given in

Frank A. Golder, Bering's Voyages, I:10.

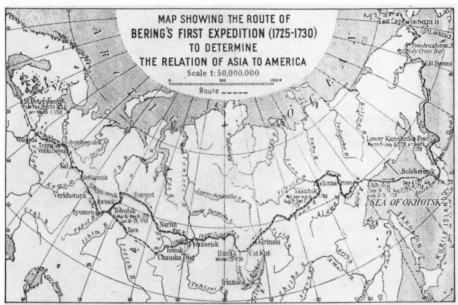

FIG. 3—Map showing the route of Bering's first expedition. Scale 1:50,000,000. Of the land journey, between St. Petersburg and Okhotsk, both the outward and the return routes are shown; of the sea voyage, between Okhotsk and Bering Strait (overland across Kamchatka), only the outward route is shown. (Based, for the land journey, on the text herewith and the tables (see bibliography) of Bering's report, and, for the sea voyage, on the map, reproduced in Fig. 6, accompanying Berkh's work of 1823 (see bibliography), which is based on the log book kept by midshipman Peter Chaplin.)

At Eniseisk the expedition divided. Bering with thirty of the men went on boats on the Enisei and Tunguska rivers to Ilimsk, arriving there 29 September. The other group, because shoals and rapids made it impossible to go by river to Ilimsk with the heavier materials, went overland to Ust-Kut, where they spent the winter making fifteen boats for the expedition's use.

During the winter (1725-26) Bering traveled to Irkutsk to learn what he could about the route to the eastern seaboard and Kamchatka.[9] He had managed to move his men and equipment across 75 degrees of longitude in a year, over a route unknown to him and in spite of difficulties in transport and with Siberian officials. But what he learned at Irkutsk was not encouraging: "The Accounts that he received, were such as gave him to understand that a more difficult Task could scarce be imposed on any Man, than that which had been lain upon his Shoulders."[10] At this time twenty carpenters and blacksmiths from Irkutsk and two coopers from Ilimsk were added to the expedition.

In the spring of 1726 the whole expedition embarked from Ust-Kut in the boats and went down the Lena River. By mid-June they reached Iakutsk. Here the expedition separated into three parts. Lieutenant Chirikov's group remained at Iakutsk for the winter. Bering's group went overland by horseback, leading a train of pack horses. They reached Okhotsk at the end of October 1726. Spanberg and the boats continued down the Lena to the Aldan River and then went up the Aldan, the Maia, and the Iudoma River with the heavy supplies, in order to avoid transporting them overland.

Late in December, Bering learned that Spanberg's boats had been frozen in near the mouth of the Gorbeia River, and that sleds, to be pulled by the men, were being built to transport the supplies to Okhotsk. Bering sent men and supplies, with dogsleds, to Spanberg's aid. Spanberg arrived in Okhotsk in January, 1727, without any of the supplies, which had been left at four places along the trail. Spanberg reported the hardships of the journey after he and his men left the Gorbeia River on 4 November. They had not been able to carry enough provisions with them, and were soon compelled to eat the flesh of dead horses and to use horsehides to make clothing and shoes. They had survived only because they found the flour Bering had been forced to leave behind at Iudoma Cross when some of the pack horses died.

Early in February, Bering sent Spanberg and ninety men with dogsleds, to retrieve the supplies left behind on the trail. In the first part of April, Spanberg and his men returned with about half of the supplies. Bering then sent twenty-seven men to Iudoma Cross to bring the remainder, and they returned in May. But the material left on the boats at the Gorbeia River could not be transported to Bering at the time, and orders were given that it should be returned to Iakutsk and from there be sent to Bering in Kamchatka. Much of the needed material for the expedition--including iron and tar--was therefore lost to the Bering expedition, after being transported with so much effort nearly all the way across Siberia from St. Petersburg.[11]

Spanberg sailed for western Kamchatka on 30 June 1727 in a newly-built ship, the Fortune. He was ordered to unload supplies on the western coast at Bol'sheretsk, to send men overland to eastern Kamchatka to prepare ship timbers, and to return to Okhotsk. Chirikov arrived at Okhotsk from Iakutsk on 3 July, with a supply of flour, which was loaded on Spanberg's ship, by then returned from Kamchatka, and on another ship. Bering and the expedition sailed from Okhotsk on 21 August.

At the Bol'shaia River the cargo was unloaded and put onto small boats for transport up the river to Bol'sheretsk, which was reached on 4 September. The journey from there across the mountains of Kamchatka was made under terrible conditions, by dogsled, with the aid of local inhabitants. Kamchatka in winter offered little to supplement the expedition's food supply, which was soon exhausted. Bering has been criticized for electing to make the overland journey across Kamchatka. For example, one recent writer notes "Thus far, the expedition's problems had been less of navigation than of transport and supply. But now, by choosing not to risk a voyage round Kamchatka to its eastern shore, Bering himself worsened those problems."[12] This criticism ignores the fact that southern Kamchatka had not been as yet circumnavigated and the mapmakers of the time placed the southern extremity of it too far south. (See the reproductions of the Homann and Strahlenberg maps later in this chapter.)

When Bering reached Nizhne-Kamchatsk on 11 March 1728, preparations were underway to build a ship for the voyage. Enough
trees had been cut before Bering's arrival to build one ship, and
these were transported to the building site by dog teams. On 4
April the ship was put in the stocks. Bering did not have tar for
the ship, but by burning large quantities of spruce, he was able
to obtain enough resin from the trees to use in its place. As
part of the ship's supplies, Bering had "a vast quantity" of plants
and herbs collected, from which he distilled a liquid "upon which
he was pleased to bestow the Name of Brandy, and of this he laid
in a plentiful Stock."[13] Seawater was boiled to obtain salt.
Fish oil was prepared as a substitute for butter, and fish were
salted to serve in place of beef or pork. "These Provisions,
such as they were, he embarked in such Quantities as would serve
his Crew, consisting of forty Men, for a whole Year."[14] The ship,
christened the St. Gabriel, was ready to sail in July 1728. Three
and one-half years had passed since Bering left St. Petersburg.
He had at last accomplished point one of Peter's instructions. He
wrote: "On July 14 we sailed from the mouth of the Kamchatka River
out to sea and followed the course laid down by the instructions
of His Imperial Majesty."[15]

After the long and difficult journey to Kamchatka, Bering's
voyage seems short and anticlimactic.[16] He sailed along the Kamchatka coast until 19 July when he directed his course to the
northeast. He encountered land again just above 60° north, on 20

July. Bering coasted along this land, continuing to the northeast.
On 1 August the St. Gabriel sailed into a bay and Bering explored
this bay, finding that it led to a river. After leaving the bay,
Bering again sailed eastward along the coast. Eight men from shore
approached the St. Gabriel by boat on 8 August. They told the
Russians they were Chukchi and that not far away from where the
Russians were, the land turned to the left (north). They told
the Russians that no promontory of any kind extended from their
land into the sea; in response to the question whether there were
islands or a land in the sea, the Chukchi replied that there was
no land, but an island not far away.[17]

The Russians reached this island on 10 August and named it
St. Lawrence Island. A boat was sent from the ship to the island,
where houses were found, but no people were seen. The Russians
sailed back to the Asian mainland. By 13 August the ship rounded
the southern point of the Chukchi Peninsula. Bering followed
the coast to the northeast and north, passing through the strait
between Asia and America. Because of fog, America was not sighted.
Soon the coast of Siberia was no longer in view either. Bering
sailed on to the north.

On 15 August the ship was at the latitude of 67°18'. Bering
"conceiving that he had now fully executed the Emperor's Orders,
as he saw no Land, either to the North or to the East, he resolved
to return, as thinking it to no Purpose to continue his Voyage
toward the West, or to run the Hazard of being driven by a contrary

Route of the First Kamchatka Expedition given in Frank A.
Golder, Bering's Voyages, I, facing p. 20.   It is based on
a map of Vasili N. Berkh, made in 1823.

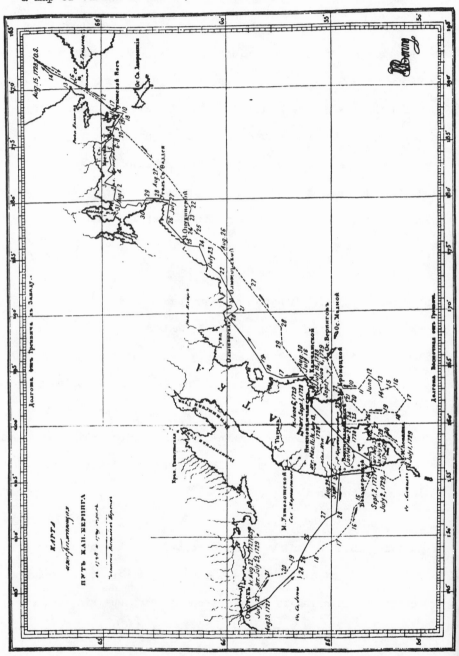

Wind beyond the Possibility of getting back during the Summer to Kamchatska. . ."[18] Or, as another translation records: "On the 15th of August we arrived in the latitude of 67°18' and I judged that we had clearly and fully carried out the instructions given by his Imperial Majesty of glorious and ever deserving memory, because the land no longer extended to the north."[19] Because of this decision to turn back, Bering has been criticized roundly. The kindest words used about him are "prudent" and "cautious" while the unstated criticisms have bordered on branding him a coward.

On their way south again the crew of the St. Gabriel did not sight the American coast, which was hidden by fog. On 16 August they discovered one of the Diomede Islands. On 20 August they were near land and forty Chukchi came in boats, offering fresh water, meat, fish, fox skins, and walrus tusks for sale. From this point Bering directed the course to the southwest. The one dramatic event on the return voyage occurred on 29 August, when the St. Gabriel was nearly wrecked somewhere on the Kamchatka coast. On 2 September they reached the Kamchatka River and they discovered that welcome provisions had come by ship from Okhotsk.[20]

What was Peter's second order to Bering? In the nineteenth century Peter's instructions to Bering were published in an official collection of Russian laws, the Polnoe sobranie zakonov.[21] They are prefaced with "About discovering the junction of Asia with America." The second order, in an awkward literal translation, is: "On these boats near the land, which goes to the north, and according to expectation (since its end is unknown) appears, that that land is part of America."[22] Translators of this order have given various renditions of it, based on their own translations of the text in Polnoe sobranie zakonov or on each other. Examples of English translations, with the year they appeared in English, are as follows:

Lauridsen (1889, translated from Danish)

II. With these you are to sail northward along the coast, and as the end of the coast is not known this land is undoubtedly America.[23]

Dall (1890)

2. With these boats ⌜you are directed⌝ to sail along the coast which extends northwards and which is supposed (since no one knows the end of it) to be continuous with America.[24]

Golder (1914)

II. To sail on these boats along the shore which runs to the north and which (since its limits are unknown) seems to be a part of the American coast.[25]

Golder (1922)

2. Sail on these boats along the shore which bears northerly and which (since its limits are unknown) seems to be a part of America.[26]

Lengyel (1943, translated from German)

2. You are directed to sail on these boats along the coast extending northward, which is supposed to be contiguous with America.[27]

Tompkins (1945)

2. You are to proceed in these along the coast which extends to the north and which seems, in all probability (since we do not know where it ends) to be part of America.[28]

Bagrow (1948, translated from Russian)

I. Sail on those ships towards the north along the land which must be supposed to be part of America as its end is unknown.[29]

Semenov (1963, translated from German)

2. In these vessels, sail along the coast which runs towards
the north and, because its end is not known, seems to form a piece
of America.[30]

In all of these translations, Bering is to explore some land

which is believed to be a part of America. All of the writers who

translated the text assumed that the land which was to be explored

was Kamchatka northward to the northeastern corner of Siberia--the

Chukchi Peninsula. Here Bering was to find out whether or not

mainland Asia was connected by land to America. If it was, no

sea passage between the continents would be possible; if not,

there was a navigable strait between the continents and the Russians

would have taken a major step in solving the question of a north-

east passage.

This interpretation has persisted. In 1981, for example,

Glynn Barratt translated the second order to Bering as follows:

"2. Sail in these same vessels, north up the coast which, since

its end is unknown, appears to be a part of America."[31] Barratt

accepted the traditional thesis that Bering was searching for a

northeast passage.[32] Barratt is critical of Bering because Bering

did not, after sailing through the strait between Asia and America,

continue his voyage westward along the Siberian coast to the Kolyma

River, a river known to the Russians.[33] Barratt writes: "Bering at

least firmly believed that he carried out his orders and was certain

that he had discovered a strait. So he had; but he had failed to demonstrate the fact."[34] Barratt's otherwise excellent study of the Russian Navy in the North Pacific is slightly marred by this acceptance of the traditional view of the purpose of Bering's first voyage. Russian manuscript maps published in the collection by Aleksei V. Efimov indicate that the Russians knew northeastern Asia was not connected to America before Peter sent Bering on the First Kamchatka Expedition.[35] The work of Soviet scholars, particularly Boris P. Polevoi, and the American scholar, Raymond H. Fisher, support the thesis that Bering was not sent to answer the question of a land connection between northeastern Asia and America.[36] As demonstrated earlier in this study, maps and accounts published in western Europe, based on information received from Russia, support the thesis that Peter the Great did not believe northeastern Asia was connected by land to America. But the view that Bering was sent to explore the Chukchi Peninsula (which he did) and to look for a passage between Asia and America (which he discovered) has persisted. The question of the interpretation of Peter's second order to Bering remains.

Raymond H. Fisher has studied Peter's instructions to Bering carefully. His translation of the second order, from Polnoe sobranie zakonov, is as follows:

2. ⌐you are to sail¬ on these boats along the land which goes to the north, and according to expectations (since its end is not known) that land, it appears, is part of America.[37]

As Fisher points out, this order does not indicate the direction Bering is to sail, only that he is to sail "along the land which goes to the north." It is Fisher's view that Peter wanted Bering to go to America, to sail east, not north.[38] From the instructions printed in the Polnoe sobranie zakonov it is not clear which direction Peter wanted Bering to sail. In the older interpretation the land of which "the end is not known" is northeastern mainland Siberia; in the newer interpretation it is not, since the Russians knew the "end" of northeastern Siberia.

All of the translations cited above are similar to the text in the Polnoe sobranie zakonov. They are subject to various interpretations, as has been shown; they are not translations from the Müller text cited at the beginning of this chapter. In that text the order reads:

II. Enquiry should be made in relation to the northerly coasts, to see whether they were not contiguous with America, since their end was not known.[39]

It is clear that the English translations cited above were based on the version of them recorded in the nineteenth century in the Polnoe sobranie zakonov, rather than on the Müller text. In Müller's text the verb is given: explored or examined (untersuchen in the German original; osmotrit--examined--in the Russian translation). The German text indicates that the northerly coasts (Nordliche Küsten) are to be explored; the Russian text states the northern coast (Severnoi bereg) is to be examined.

It is not possible, on the basis of either version of the instructions alone, to be certain of Peter's intent in sending Bering on the First Kamchatka Expedition.[40] It is clear that

Bering was sent to explore a land, the end of which was unknown and which was believed to be connected to America. The traditional view that this land was northeastern Siberia is doubtful, at best. If that were the case, Peter would have been sending Bering to verify something Peter already knew. The "end" of northeastern Siberia was not unknown. But what picture did Peter have of the geography of the North Pacific? This question leads to another: is it possible to identify the map given to Bering with the instructions?

Johann Baptist Homann, a German mapmaker and copyist, was employed to make maps for Russia.[41] The date of Homann's first commission from Peter is unknown, but Homann prepared a map to accompany the German edition of Evert Ides' Travels, published in 1707.[42] The map did not appear with the book, apparently, but it was in print prior to 1719, when a copy of it appeared in Johann David Köhler's Schul- und reisen Atlas.[43] In this map no peninsula of land extends from the Asian coast toward America that could suggest a land connection between Asia and America.

On the basis of information he received from Russia, Homann published two special maps, which can be dated as early as 1722. The two maps appear on one sheet: the left hand map is the earliest accurate depiction of the Caspian Sea; the map on the right gives the first printed presentation of Kamchatka as a peninsula of Asia.[44] The Kamchatka map is reproduced here.

Boris P. Polevoi, using this Homann map, formulated a new interpretation of Peter's instructions to Bering. The Kamchatka

Homann's map of Kamchatka, reproduced from the <u>Grosser</u> <u>Atlas</u>,1725.

Reproduced through the courtesy of the Department of Rare Books and Special Collections, Princeton University Library.

map has few names on it, but the entire coast of Kamchatka and the Chukchi Peninsula are delineated. Two unnamed lands without an "end" are shown, one east of Kamchatka (going off the map) and the other a finger-shaped piece of land in the north, opposite the Chukchi Peninsula. Polevoi identified this latter land as part of the "Big Land" (Alaska) shown as an island. He considered and subsequently rejected it as a possibility for "the land, which goes to the north" Peter sent Bering to explore. Rather, Polevoi argues, Peter wanted Bering to explore the land east of Kamchatka, the land which was called "Terra Borealis," "Terra Esonis," "Da Gama Land" or "Compagnie Land" on contemporary maps.[45]

Raymond H. Fisher concurs with Polevoi that the Homann map of Kamchatka was the one Bering received with the instructions. He concludes that Peter wanted Bering to go to America, along the southern coast of the land shown east of Kamchatka.[46] Fisher also considered the land east of the Chukchi Peninsula as Bering's destination, but dismissed it. He writes:

". . . we have accepted Polevoi's thesis that Peter's phrase 'the land which goes to the north' referred to the unnamed land east of Kamchatka on the Homann map. But it must be admitted that the description can apply as well, if not better, to the finger of land north of the unnamed land and east of the Chukotsk Penin- sula in the upper right corner of the Homann map. It too goes to the north, and since its end is left open, its end is unknown. Could this be the northward-going land Peter had in mind? If it were, then he must have wanted Bering to sail north along the east coast of this land to its supposed union with America and thence south to a city of European possession."[47]

In this study it will be argued that Peter sent Bering to explore the land east of the Chukchi Peninsula, intending that

123

Bering should follow the route Fisher described above. The Polevoi
and Fisher publications are convincing demonstrations of the inade-
quacy of the traditional belief that Peter sent Bering to explore
northeastern Asia in search of a passage between Asia and America.
But problems remain in the thesis that Peter wanted Bering to explore the land east of Kamchatka, since in this interpretation
Bering had to misunderstand or revise his instructions from Peter.[48]
Bering sailed north along the Kamchatka coast and the Chukchi Peninsula. But the identity of "the land, which goes to the north"
that Bering was sent to explore cannot be solved on the basis of
the Homann map of Kamchatka because the map has two unnamed lands
on it; both can be said to go "to the north" and the ends of both
are unknown.

Was the Homann map of Kamchatka the one given to Bering with
Peter's instructions? There are good reasons to believe it was
not. The Homann map of Kamchatka was printed as early as 1722.
In February, 1723, Homann was named "Moscow Agent" (consul), and
Peter the Great rewarded Homann for his services as a mapmaker.[49]
Homann was a copyist, not an originator of maps, and the maps he
made of northeastern Siberia were based on information he received
from Russia. Like Nicolaas Witsen before him, Homann undoubtedly
obtained approval, by sending proofs and drafts of his maps to
Russia, before he printed them. Homann died in December, 1724;
maps ascribed to him appeared in an atlas dated 1725. In these maps
more detailed presentations of Siberia and the North Pacific are
given. It is one of these maps, I believe, that Bering received

124

with his instructions.

In addition to the matter of dating--which is admittedly uncertain as the Homann maps do not have dates on them--there is another issue, which is one of completeness. While it is possible that the Homann map of Kamchatka could have been given to Bering, this map surely does not reflect the state of Russian knowledge of northeastern Asia, as the map has no indications of longitude or latitude on it. Russian manuscript maps include a grid.[50] Philip Johann von Strahlenberg, a Swedish prisoner of war who was in Siberia from 1711 to 1721, made maps which had indications of latitude and longitude on them.[51] Strahlenberg did not publish his great map of Russia until 1730, but he described making earlier maps while he was in Tobolsk. In his Prodrome of 1726 Strahlenberg discussed the fate of his maps.[52] In another work, he states specifically that eastern Asia in the maps of "Homan". . .
"are for the most Part, Copies of those Maps which I made in 1715 and 1718 at Tobolsky, (the Fate of which, and what happen'd to me concerning them, I mentioned in my Prodrome.) Both Maps were drawn upon two Sheets of Royal Paper, but the Persons into whose Hands they fell, and by whome they were publish'd, made some few Alterations (as of the Caspian Sea, for instance) and drew them into a narrower Compass."[53] (See the reproduction of Strahlenberg's 1730 map). That Strahlenberg is referring to a map made after 1722 is clear in the reference to the changed picture of the Caspian Sea; that he would not be referring to the Kamchatka map seems

The northeastern portion of Strahlenberg's map, from the English edition of 1738.

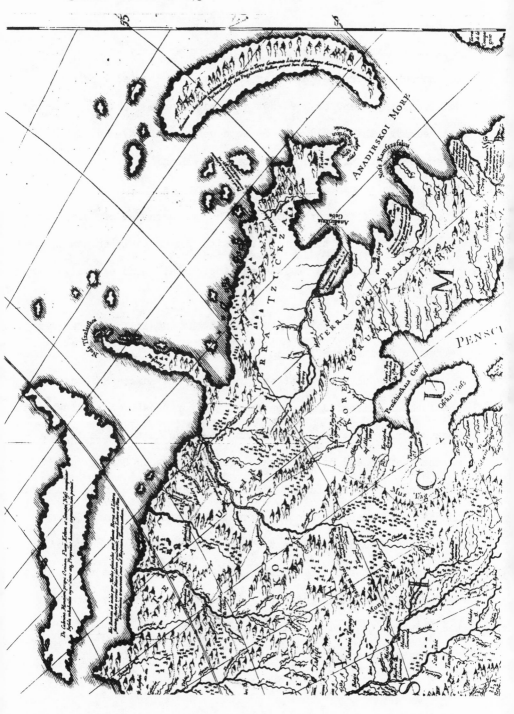

almost certain, since his own maps had indications of latitude and longitude on them.

Homann made a world map, dating from as early as 1722, according to the German scholar Christian Sandler, who studied Homann.[54] Unfortunately, Sandler does not give his source for dating the map this early. This world map--or some version of it--was, I believe, given to Bering with the instructions. On this map the land east of Kamchatka is named "Terra Esonis incognita." The eastern end of it is joined to North America. The northern end of Terra Esonis is not known.[55] In the north, opposite the Chukchi Peninsula, the finger-shaped land is labeled "incognita." The ends of it are unknown.

Evidence from the voyage supports the thesis that Peter sent Bering to explore the land in the north. Bering left the Kamchatka River in mid-July, at first sailing along the Kamchatka coast. On the 19th, he directed his course to the northeast. According to the Homann world map, the coast of Kamchatka was in the same longitude as the eastern end of the Chukchi Peninsula--thus Bering was directing his course toward the area of land with unknown boundaries on the Homann map.[56] According to the Homann world map, Bering should have reached land to the east. Instead, he encountered land again just above 60° north, directly ahead of him to the north. He followed his land, going to the east and north. By late July the ship had reached a position twenty degrees to the east of his starting meridian.[57]

Portion of the world map in Homann's <u>Grosser</u> <u>Atlas</u>, 1725.

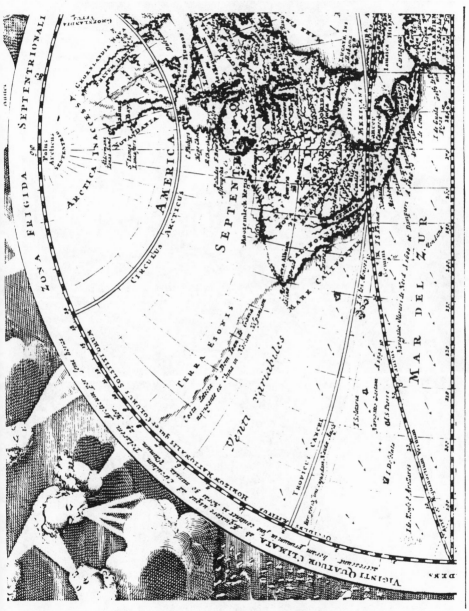

Reproduced through the courtesy of the Department of Rare Books and Special Collections, Princeton University Library.

128

Portion of the world map in Homann's <u>Grosser</u> <u>Atlas</u>, 1725.

Reproduced through the courtesy of the Department of Rare Books and Special Collections, Princeton University Library.

Homann's map of Asia, reproduced from Efimov, Iz istorii
russkikh ekspeditsii . . . 1948, facing p. 102.

An example of a Russian manuscript map, this one
by Ivan L'vov, dated about 1710. Homann's maps
were made on the basis of Russian maps. This map
is reproduced from the Atlas of 1964 edited by
Aleksei V. Efimov. [number 55].

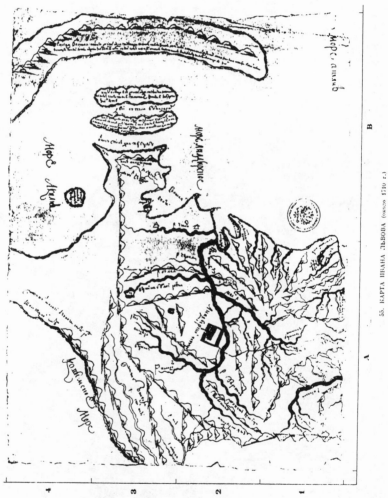

55. КАРТА ИВАНА ЛЬВОВА (около 1710 г.)

Bering sailed into a bay on 1 August and explored it. At this
point he could well have believed this was the sea shown on the
Homann map, separating the Chukchi Peninsula from the unknown land,
but far to the east of where it should have been according to the
Homann map.[58] When Bering discovered the bay led to a river, he
returned and continued eastward along the coast. The questions
asked of the eight Chukchi on August 8 correlate well with the
geographical depiction given on Homann's map. According to the
Homann map, the land should have turned north, as the Chukchi said
it did. The Russians asked if there was any promontory from their
land and the Chukchi answered no; the Russians asked if there were
islands or a land in the sea, and the Chukchi replied that there
was only one island. These questions correlate well with the information on the Homann map.[59] The Russians went to the island
but did not talk to people there and had no information about any
other land to the east. They returned to the mainland and followed
it around the southern point of the Chukchi Peninsula, passing
through the strait between Asia and America. Because of fog,
America was not sighted.[60] Soon the coast of Siberia was no longer
in view either. Bering sailed on to the north.

In his decision to terminate his voyage to the north, Bering
says he did so believing he had fulfilled Peter's orders. This
could not be the case if he were sent to search for a northeast passage,
or to go to America. It is the case if Bering were sent to explore
the "incognita" land of the Homann map. Either version of the

accounts quoted earlier support this thesis, since in one, Bering saw no land "either to the North or to the East" and in the other "the land no longer extended to the north."

What made Bering so sure he had fulfilled Peter's orders? Peter had directed Bering to find out whether the unknown land to the north was connected to America. Bering had followed the Homann map, as best he could. He found it completely erroneous in placing the Chukchi Peninsula directly north of eastern Kamchatka. Rather than finding himself on a course to the north, Bering had sailed northeast some thirty degrees east of his starting meridian at the mouth of the Kamchatka River. No matter how inaccurate the instruments for measurements might have been, it was clear that the northeast corner of Siberia was much further to the east than had been previously imagined.[61] In trying to make his experience fit with the Homann map, which was supposed to guide him in his voyage, Bering assumed he had sailed to the east of the land marked "incognita" on the map, and that it was not connected to America. Instead the land turned toward the west. Thus Peter's question was answered and his third order was invalid.

At the time when the ship passed through the strait and sailed beyond the sight of land, Bering asked Spanberg and Chirikov to express their opinions, in writing, about the future course that should be followed, a common practice in the Russian Navy. In his answer Spanberg wrote: "Because we have reached 67° 30' of the northern region and according to our opinion and the Chukchi's

The Homann world map, compared to a
modern map.

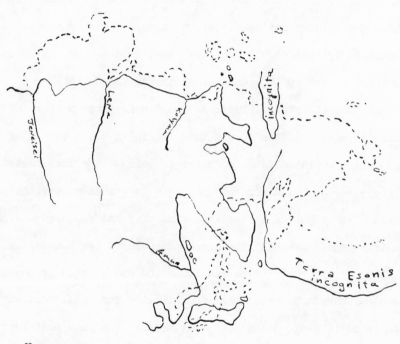

Homann ———
Actual - - - -

report have arrived opposite the extreme end and have passed east
of the land, what more needs to be done?"[62] Because the Chukchi
said there was no land in the sea, but only an island, Spanberg,
like Bering, assumed they had gone eastward of the unknown land
on the map. Chirikov, in his reply to Bering, recapitulated Bering's
statement to his lieutenant "That land of the aforesaid nos, about
which the opinion had been that it is joined with America, is
separated by the sea."[63] Chirikov wanted to follow the coast
further, to see if it again turned toward the north.[64]

During the winter, Peter A. Chaplin prepared a chart of the
first voyage.[65] After it was made, Bering's confidence that he
had fully completed Peter's orders to sail to the land marked
"incognita" on the Homann map may have been shaken, for the southern
coast of the Chukchi Peninsula, which they had explored during
their voyage, resembled the same peninsula on the Homann map. The
difference was that Bering had found the end of this peninsula
much farther to the east, and in following its coast northward,
had found it went to the northeast, rather than the northwest, as
Homann indicated. But had Bering gone far enough to the east to
have sailed the eastern coast of the land marked "Incognita" on
the map? Might the island they had discovered on the return voyage
have been one of the islands to the east of the Chukchi Peninsula
on the Homann map?

The St. Gabriel was repaired, and on 5 June 1729 Bering sailed
to the east of Kamchatka. He did this, he said, because of the

135

Bering's map of the expedition, compared to
a modern map.

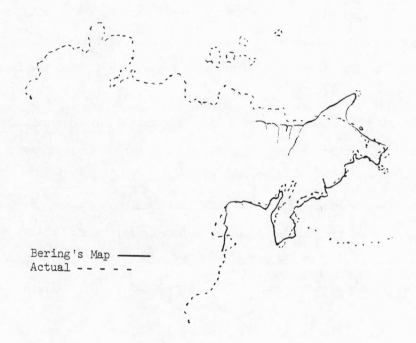

Bering's Map ———
Actual - - - - -

reports by the inhabitants of Kamchatka of land to the east. Bering made a short voyage to the east, but in foggy and stormy weather he did not sight the Commander Islands.[66]

This short voyage eastward had no apparent result.[67] It makes sense only in relation to a search for the land east of Kamchatka on the Homann map.[68] In this voyage Bering sailed over four degrees east of Kamchatka; the coast of the land to the east of Kamchatka ("Esonis Land") is shown at less than two degrees from Kamchatka. It is not surprising that Bering, when he neither sighted the land nor had indications of land nearby, gave up the search for the land east of Kamchatka on the Homann map. He directed his course to the southwest, around the Kamchatka Peninsula. Bering arrived at Bol'sheretsk on 2 July and then sailed from there on 14 July. He arrived at Okhotsk again on 23 July, and then Bering began the long journey home. He went overland to Iudoma Cross, then by boat and horseback to Tobolsk, reaching it on 10 January 1730. He returned to St. Petersburg on 1 March 1730, to make his report to the Admiral College.

Footnotes

Chapter IV

1. Peter had jumped into the waters of the Gulf of Finland in November 1724 to help save soldiers whose boat had been wrecked on a shoal near the shore. He later became ill, and by mid-January was nearing death. On the selection of Bering to lead the expedition, see Glynn Barratt, Russia in Pacific Waters, 1715-1825: A Survey of the Origins of Russia's Naval Presence in the North and South Pacific (Vancouver: University of British Columbia Press, 1981), pp. 16-17. Because of Peter's illness, Fisher believes Bering received little briefing on the expedition. See Raymond H. Fisher, Bering's Voyages: Whither and Why (Seattle: University of Washington Press, 1977), pp. 74-75.

2. According to the text translated by Golder, Bering's orders were given to him by Catherine I personally. Frank A. Golder, Bering's Voyages: An Account of the Efforts of the Russians to Determine the Relation of Asia and America, 2 vols. (New York: American Geographical Society, 1922), I, 9. In Golder's view, "Catherine was determined to carry out all the policies and ambitions of her husband." The continuance of the First Kamchatka Expedition in spite of Peter's death can be seen as more than the simple desire to see his wishes carried out, for it provides evidence that much care and planning had gone into the expedition.

3. According to a story attributed to Andrei K. Nartov, a close
associate of Peter's: "In the beginning of January 1725, in the
same month when the end of the life of Peter the Great was determined by the will of the Highest and when already His Majesty
felt the illness in his body, his still indefatigable spirit
labored for the benefit of glory of his fatherland, for he
drafted and wrote with his own hand the instructions of the
Kamchatka expedition, which was required to go and find out by
a voyage if northeast Asia is not joined to America," as quoted
in Fisher, Bering's Voyages, pp. 11-12. But, as Fisher says, th
story did not appear in print until the nineteenth century;
it reflects contemporary rumors that were spread that the purpos
of the voyage was to discover a passage between Asia and America
Ibid., pp. 17-18, 73-75.

4. Most scholars of the First Kamchatka Expedition have not used
this version of the instructions. As will be seen, the choice
of versions selected has an important bearing on the interpretat
The version given here was chosen, in addition to the reasons
stated in the text, because three contemporary texts were availe
for comparison: English, German, and Russian.

5. ₍Gerhard Friedrich Müller₎ A Letter from a Russian Sea-Officer,
to a Person of Distinction at the Court of St. Petersburgh (Lond
A. Linde and sold by J. Robinson, 1754), p. 7. This publication
will be discussed later in this study.

6. The German text is found in Gerhard Friedrich Müller, Sammlung
russischer Geschichte, 9 vols. (St. Petersburg: Kayserl. Academ

der Wissenschaften, 1732-64), III (1758) 111-2. The Russian
text appears in <u>Sochineniia</u> <u>i</u> <u>perevody</u>, <u>k</u> <u>pol'zie</u> <u>i</u>
<u>uveseleniiu</u> <u>sluzhashchiia</u>, edited by Gerhard Friedrich
Müller, (St. Petersburg: Imperatorskaia akademiia nauk,
1758), VII: 388.

7. Gerhard Friedrich Müller, <u>Voyages</u> <u>from</u> <u>Asia</u> <u>to</u> <u>America</u>, <u>for</u>
<u>Completing</u> <u>the</u> <u>Discoveries</u> <u>of</u> <u>the</u> <u>North</u> <u>West</u> <u>Coast</u> <u>of</u> <u>America</u>
(London: T. Jefferys, 1761), p. 1.

8. The account of the First Kamchatka Expedition which follows
records the difficulties Bering had in carrying out his first
instruction from Peter the Great. It is based on the various
editions of Bering's "Short Account" of the expedition. For
citations of these, see the bibliography.

9. Golder, <u>Bering's</u> <u>Voyages</u>, I, 12. The fact that Bering was
seeking information about the route can be seen as evidence
that Bering's map for the expedition was one of the Homann
maps discussed later, as they do not have details of the area
between Irkutsk and the eastern seaboard (Okhotsk is not shown,
for example). Bering's decision to go to Okhotsk was made on
the basis of what he learned in Irkutsk.

10. John Harris, <u>Navigantium</u> <u>atque</u> <u>Itinerarium</u> <u>Bibliotheca</u>, <u>Or</u>, <u>A</u>
<u>Complete</u> <u>Collection</u> <u>of</u> <u>Voyages</u> <u>and</u> <u>Travels</u>, edited by John
Campbell, 2 vols. (London: T. Woodward [etc.] 1744-48), II, 1018.
This quote may be an editorial insertion of John Campbell, but
it was certainly true, as Bering's later experience would reveal.

11. Barratt, who is critical of Bering for his actions on the

First Kamchatka Expedition, acknowledges the scope of this loss: "Men and material brought from St. Petersburg at huge expense had been lost within a few days' summer march of the Pacific littoral." Barratt, Russia in Pacific Waters, p. 19.

12. Ibid., p. 21

13. Harris, Navigantium, ed. Campbell, II, 1020.

14. Ibid.

15. Golder, Bering's Voyages, I, 18. In Dall's translation, this text reads: "On the 14th day of July we went out of the mouth of the Kamchatka river into the sea, in obedience to the autographic orders given me by his Imperial Majesty Peter the Great, as the map constructed for that purpose will show." William H. Dall, "A Critical Review of Bering's First Expedition, 1725-30, Together with a Translation of his Original Report on it," in The National Geographic Magazine, II (1890), 141.

16. The long account of the expedition's progress to Kamchatka given above is a reminder of the effort involved before the expedition sailed. This long journey and the events of it, perhaps, influenced Bering's actions during the voyage. Lieutenant Sven Waxell, a participant on the Second Kamchatka Expedition, writes: "It [the First Kamchatka Expedition] had consisted of only a small force and it had suffered from a shortage of provisions and other necessary things, for until then it had not been possible to know exactly what equipment

was needful; and, lastly, a series of accidents and mishaps had overtaken it." Sven Waxell, The American Expedition, translated by M. A. Michael (London: William Hodge and Company, 1952), p.49.

17. Fisher, Bering's Voyages, pp. 81-82.

18. Harris, Navigantium, ed. Campbell, II, 1020.

19. Dall, "A Critical Review," p. 141.

20. This ship was the first to round the southern tip of the Kamchatka Peninsula, an honor commonly ascribed to Bering's ship, the St. Gabriel.

21. The text appears in volume three of the Polnoe sobranie zakonov (St. Petersburg: Sobstvennoi ego imperatorskoi veli-chestva kantseliarii, 1830), III (no. 4649), p. 413. The instructions were published by Vasilii N. Berkh in 1823 in Pervoe morskoe puteshestvie rossiian, which was translated by William H. Dall in "Notes on an Original Manuscript Chart of Bering's Expedition of 1725-30, and on an Original Manuscript Chart of His Second Expedition; Together with a Summary of a Journal of the First Expedition, Kept by Peter Chaplin, and Now First Rendered into English from Bergh's Russian Version," Report of the Superintendent of the U.S. Coast and Geodetic Survey Showing the Progress of the Work during the Fiscal Year Ending with June, 1890 (Washington: Government Printing Office, 1891), Appendix no. 19, pp. 759-74. The text of the instructions appears on page 761. This text is identical to the version given by Dall in "A Critical Review."

22. My "translation." The problems of translating this text are evident.

23. Peter Lauridsen, Vitus Bering: The Discoverer of Bering Strait, translated by Julius E. Olson (Freeport: Books for Libraries Press, 1969), p. 13. The original of this work was published in 1889, translated from Danish.

24. Dall, "A Critical Review," p. 135.

25. Frank A. Golder, Russian Expansion on the Pacific, 1641-1850 (Cleveland: Arthur H. Clark Company, 1914), p. 134.

26. Golder, Bering's Voyages, I, 9, 11.

27. Emil Lengyel, Siberia (New York: Garden City Publishing Co., 1943), p. 68.

28. Stuart Ramsay Tompkins, Alaska: Promyshlennik and Sourdough (Norman: University of Oklahoma Press, 1945), p. 23.

29. L. Bagrow, "The Vitus Bering First Voyage Maps," Geografisk Tidsskrift, XLIX (1948-49), 34.

30. Iurii Semenov, Siberia: Its Conquest and Development, translated by J. R. Foster (Baltimore: Helicon Press, 1963), p. 143.

31. Barratt, Russia in Pacific Waters, p. 14.

32. Ibid., p. 1.

33. Ibid., p. 22. See also his description of Bering, pp. 16-17.

34. Ibid., p. 22.

35. Atlas geograficheskikh otkrytii v Sibiri i v severo-zapadnoi Amerike XVII-XVIII vv., edited by Aleksei V. Efimov (Moscow: Nauka, 1964). For example, see maps 47 (1701), 48 (ca. 1700),

49 (between 1699 and 1715), and 50 (1713).

36. See the bibliography for citations to these works.

37. Fisher, Bering's Voyages, p. 23.

38. Ibid., pp. 68-69.

39. Müller, Voyages, p. 1.

40. The problem, in whichever version of the instructions is used, is the identity of the "northern" coasts.

41. For biographical information see Brecher, "Johann Baptist Homann," in Allgemeine deutsche Biographie, XIII, 35-38.

42. Evert Ysbrandszoon Ides, Dreyjährige Reise nach China von Moscau ab zu lande durch gros Ustiga, Siriania, Permia Daour und die grosse Tartarey (Frankfurt: T. Fritsch, 1707). No copy of the book, apparently, contains a map.

43. Johann David Köhler, Schul- und reisen Atlas aller zu Erlernung der alten, mittlern und neuen Geographie (Nuremberg: J. E. Adelbulnern, 1719). The map is ascribed to Homann.

44. The map is reproduced here by courtesy of the Department of Rare Books and Special Collections, Princeton University Library. It is from Johann Baptist Homann, Grosser Atlas über die gantze Welt (Nuremberg: J. E. Adelbulner, 1725). This is the only copy of the atlas in the United States which has a dated titlepage and a table of contents indicating which maps were included in the atlas.

45. See the following articles by Boris P. Polevoi: "Iz istorii otkrytiia severo-zapadnoi chasti Ameriki" in Ot Aliaski do

ognennoi zemli, edited by I. R. Grigulevich (Moscow: Nauka,

1967), pp. 107-120; "O karte 'Kamchadalii' I. B. Gomana,"

Izvestiia, AN SSSR, seriia geograficheskaia (1970, no. 1),

99-105; "Petr pervye, Nikolai Vitsen i problema 'soshlasia

li Amerika s Aziei'" in Strany i narody vostoka, edited by

D. A. Olderogge; XVII, book 3, Strany i narody basseina tikhogo

okeana, edited by Y. V. Maretin (Moscow: Nauka, 1975), pp. 19-33.

46. Fisher, Bering's Voyages. The Homann map is discussed on pages
64 to 71.

47. Ibid., p. 106-107.

48. Ibid. Chapters three and four.

49. The date 1722 is ascribed to Homann's map on the basis of a
letter he wrote in 1723. See Endel Warep, "Über einige Karten
Russlands in J. B. Homanns Atlas vom Jahre 1725," Petermanns
geographische Mitteilungen, CVII:4 (1963), p. 310. On the
naming of Homann as Moscow Consul see Christian Sandler,
Johann Baptista Homann, Matthäus Seutter and ihre Landkarten:
Ein Beitrag zur Geschichte der Kartographie (Amsterdam: Meridian
Publishing Co., [196-?]), p. 49.

50. See, for example, map 61 in the Atlas edited by Efimov, dated
1722.

51. This statement may be somewhat conjectural, as Strahlenberg's
maps, which he made in Siberia, have apparently not survived.
See, however, footnote number 53.

52. Philip Johann Tabbert von Strahlenberg, Vorbericht eines zum

Druck verfertigten Werckes von der Grossen Tartarey und dem
Königreiche Siberien, mit einem Anhang von Gross-Russland
(Stockholm: B. G. Schneider, 1726), pp. 15-16.

53. Philip Johann Tabbert von Strahlenberg, An Historico-geographical
Description of the North and Eastern Parts of Europe and Asia
(London: J. Brotherton [etc.] 1738), p. 10.

54. Sandler, Johann Baptista Homann, legend on the map.

55. On this basis, it could be argued that Bering was sent to
explore the northern part of "Terra Esonis incognita" but all
the other evidence supports the thesis that the intended
destination was the land cited "incognita" on the map.

56. See the map reproductions. According to the Homann map, the
Chukchi Peninsula should have been straight north, not northeast.

57. The importance of having a map with a grid on it is clear, for
this would have convinced Bering he had sailed east of the
land marked "incognita" on the Homann map.

58. See the map reproductions. That Bering spent time exploring this
bay suggests he believed that it was the sea separating eastern
Siberia from the "incognita" land on the Homann map.

59. The statement that the land went north matched the position of
the "incognita" land; the statement that there was no promontory
or land near would have buttressed Bering's belief that he had
passed east of the land marked "incognita" on the map.

60. That Bering did not "discover" America when he was so close to
it has often been lamented. See his commentary on this matter

in a conversation with Delisle, which is discussed in the following chapter.

61. Again, the comparisons between the Homann map and a modern map are crucial in this argument.

62. Fisher, Bering's Voyages, p. 83.

63. Ibid.

64. This is the basis for criticism of Bering for those who believe he was searching for a northeast passage. Barratt, for example, writes: "Chirikov understood the nature of proof [of the existence of a strait] as he, apparently, had not." Barratt, Russia in Pacific Waters, p. 22.

65. See the reproduction of Chaplin's map in comparison with the Homann map and Dall, "Notes on an Original Manuscript Chart."

66. The Commander Islands are visible from the coast of Kamchatka on a clear day; a clear day, however, is a rarity in this part of the world.

67. For example, Lauridsen, in his biography titled Vitus Bering, struggles to find some meaning in this voyage. He writes: "If the wind had been favorable, he would very soon have reached Bering Island, where twelve years later he was buried." And Lauridsen holds that bad weather endangering the "frail vessel and the weather-worn rigging" prevented Bering from continuing his voyage. (p. 51).

68. Fisher, Bering's Voyages, p. 103. Fisher is using the Homann map of Kamchatka, without the grid, in his discussion.

Chapter V

The Earliest Printed Account of the

First Kamchatka Expedition

Rumors that Bering was being sent to the North Pacific to search for a sea passage between Asia and America had circulated before Bering left on his expedition.[1] There was at least one other conjecture about the purpose of the expedition current at the time, recorded by the French traveler Aubry de la Mottraye, who visited Russia three times, in 1707, 1714, and 1726. La Mottraye writes that Peter "was about discovering a North-East Passage to America, when Death put a Stop to the Course of his Undertakings."[2] According to La Mottraye, Peter had sent two ships for the purpose of discovering a northeast passage, without success, from Archangel in 1724. "But these Difficulties did not deter him; he ordered two other Ships to be built for the same Design, according to the Directions of Captain Barring, a British Subject; who set sail in the Year 1724 with a 100 Men for a second Attempt. The Account he had from them in 1726 was, that they had seen Land; and they gave him some Expectations of Success. I have heard nothing of it since that Time."[3] In spite of the obvious errors, there is some truth in La Mottraye's statement. Peter had sent ships from Archangel in 1724 to search for a northeast passage, and reports of land off the Siberian coast were received in St. Petersburg in 1725 from the cossack Afanasii

F. Shestakov.[4] Though La Mottraye assumed, apparently, that
Bering sailed from Archangel, his garbled report provides con-
temporary evidence of a belief that Bering's destination was
America.

During the time Bering was on his expedition, the idea that
he was seeking an answer to the question of the existence of a
strait between Asia and America was fostered by members of the
Russian Imperial Academy of Sciences, an institution founded by
Peter the Great. The foreign scholars who comprised its initial
membership did not arrive in St. Petersburg until after Peter's
death, however. The first meeting of the Academy, at which
sixteen members--all foreigners--were present, was held in November,
1726.[5] Two members of the Academy, Joseph Nicolas Delisle and
Gerhard Friedrich Müller, were particularly interested in geography.

Joseph Nicolas Delisle (1688-1768), the younger brother of
Guillaume Delisle, was a French astronomer and geographer.[6] Peter
invited Guillaume to Russia as a cartographer; Guillaume declined
the offer. In 1721 Peter invited Joseph Delisle to accept a
similar appointment in Russia to teach astronomy and to set up
an astronomical observatory. Peter wanted to have mapmakers who
were also trained in astronomy to prepare accurate maps of Russia.
The contract negotiations were prolonged, and Delisle finally
accepted an offer from Catherine I in 1725. He arrived in St.
Petersburg in 1726 to begin a four-year contract with the Academy,

and to work with Ivan Kirilov, director of cartographic studies for the Administrative Senate.[7] Delisle's twenty-one year service with the Academy was controversial, because of his practice of sending Russian maps and accounts of explorations to France, which held his first loyalty. For this practice he was criticized sharply.[8]

Delisle wanted to learn the results of Bering's expeditions, since he had a great interest in the cartography of the east, particularly in relation to the maps of his brother Guillaume.[9] Delisle was convinced Bering had been sent to settle the question of a sea passage in the north. In a letter of 25 May 1729 to Jean Frédéric Phélypeaux Maurepas, the leading proponent of French overseas explorations, Delisle states that Bering was sent by Peter "to search for the route by the north of Asia as far as the Eastern Sea."[10]

Gerhard Friedrich Müller had an equal interest in Bering's expedition. Müller (1705-1783) was a German, born in Westphalia.[11] While he was a student at Leipzig University, he came to the attention of Johann Burchard Menke, who was recommending scholars for the newly-formed Russian Academy of Sciences. Menke encouraged him to go to Russia. Müller arrived in St. Petersburg in November 1725 to take a position as adjunct (the rank below professor) in history, and like many other foreigners who joined the Academy, he sought rapid advancement. In 1726-27 Müller taught history and geography, and later began work in archives, a position suggested by the Academy's president, Lavrentii Blumentrost.

Müller did attain a prominent position in the Academy quickly. When Peter II moved the court to Moscow, Blumentrost went with it. The Academy remained in St. Petersburg, and Blumentrost entrusted the management of it to Johann D. Schumacher, the secretary of the Chancellery, the Academy's administrative body. This change was fortunate for Müller, who as a favorite of Schumacher's, became vice-secretary of the Chancellery. Schumacher thought so highly of Müller that when Schumacher went to Moscow in 1729 to be at court, he placed Müller in charge of the Academy.[12] It was due to Schumacher also, that Müller became editor of the Sanktpeterburgskiia Vedomosti and its German-language counterpart, the St. Peterburgische Zeitung, in January 1728.[13] This newspaper, published by the Academy of Sciences, served as a major vehicle of communication in St. Petersburg. Thus Müller reached a position of power and influence while still a very young man.

Delisle and Müller had studied a book and map which suggested that a passage by sea around the northeast corner of Siberia was possible. This two-volume work, titled Histoire généalogique des Tartars, was published in Leiden in 1726. Volume one of it was a translation of a manuscript on the history of the Tatars, with a genealogy of their rulers. The writer of this manuscript was Ebülgâzî Bahadir Han, Khan of Korezm (cited also as Abū al-Ghazi), who died in 1633. The manuscript, written in the Jagataic language, a branch of East Turkic, was finished in 1664 by the son of Abū al-Ghazi. The Swedish prisoner of war, Strahlenberg, obtained a copy of this manuscript in Tobolsk, and had it translated into German.[14]

Volume two of the Histoire généalogique was a separate work, a compilation made by Strahlenberg of material describing northern Asia. Strahlenberg shared his work with a friend, who translated both volumes into French and published them, together with Strahlenberg's map, without permission. The text which follows, found in volume two of the Histoire généalogique, could hardly have failed to excite proponents of a northeast passage:

> It has been believ'd till the present that Asia was joined on the N. E. to North America, and that for this Reason it was impossible to sail from the Icy Sea into the eastern Ocean; but since the Discovery of the Country of Kamtzchatka, 'tis known for certain that America is not contiguous to Asia, for the Russian Ships coasting the firm Land, pass at present Cape Suetoi Nos, or Holy Cape, and go traffick with the Kamtzchadals upon the Coast of the eastern Sea, about the 50th Deg. of Latit. but they must for this purpose pass between the Continent and a Great Island which lies to the N.E. of Cape Suetoi Nos. It is so lately discover'd, and it is so remote from the other Dominions of Russia, that we have not yet come to an exact Knowledge of it; what has been already related is all that I have been able to learn for certain of it, after a diligent Enquiry.[15]

A version of Strahlenberg's map with this text was also exciting. It was, in all probability, the first time Delisle and Müller had seen Kamchatka presented as a peninsula on a map.[16] In the map Kamchatka was separated from the rest of Asia by a great sea going northward to 50°, where the land was connected to the Asian

Strahlenberg's map from the Histoire généalogique
of Ebülgâzî Bahadir Han, in the English edition of
1729.

mainland by "a Space of Land not above 5 Deg. over, by means whereof
the Country of Kamtzchatka becomes contiguous with Siberia."[17]
In this map of Siberia a whole new land had appeared, one which
protruded out from Asia, from the point where the earlier maps of
Witsen and Guillaume Delisle had placed "Ice Cape." On the
Strahlenberg map, the area were "Ice Cape" had been was now
replaced by a land projection which connected Kamchatka to Siberia.

On Strahlenberg's map, the peninsula of Kamchatka extended
southward to a latitude of 40° north, almost to Japan. In this
map, the land of Jesso, therefore, about which Europeans had
speculated so much, appeared to be a part of Kamchatka. Müller
writes: "The notes to Albugazi and an accompanying map had made
common the opinion, that Kamchatka and Esso were one and the
same land."[18]

Müller turned to Nicolaas Witsen's Noord en Oost Tartarye
and extracted the portion of Witsen's book which described Jesso.
In 1728 he published this extract in the Kalendar ili
mesiatsoslov for the year 1729. The following year he wrote
a review of the Witsen book for the Kalendar for 1730.[19]
Müller did this, he says, because "Everyone spoke about
Kamchatka, as about an unknown world. The most detailed reports,
which Witsen communicated about the land of Esso, should,
according to my thought, give temporary knowledge of Kamchatka
until the return of Bering."[20] When Bering returned to St.
Petersburg, obviously, there were two members of the Academy

of Sciences who were eager to talk to him.

Was Bering prepared? Had he been briefed as to what he should reveal publicly about his voyage? Bering returned to St. Petersburg at a time of crisis in the government. Catherine I died in 1727; before her death she named a regency including her daughters Anne and Elizabeth, to guide Peter II during his minority. Peter II came under the influence of the old nobility, and symbolic of their orientation, the court moved back to Moscow. In January 1730 Peter II died of smallpox. He had not named a successor, and in the resulting uncertainty, the crown was offered to Anne of Courland (Anna Ivanovna), the daughter of Peter the Great's brother Ivan V. A group of aristocrats attempted to limit her authority by a set of conditions favorable to them, which she accepted. Once in Russia, however, on 25 February 1730, the new empress rejected the limitations in favor of autocratic rule.[21] Bering returned, then, at a time of confusion in the government.

Bering had been sent on a secret expedition by Peter the Great; he was an officer in the Russian Navy. It is questionable that Bering would have discussed his expedition without authorization. He may have sent a preliminary report about it to the court at Moscow before his arrival in St. Petersburg.[22] If he had done so, it is likely that there was little response. Surely Bering consulted with some superior officers in the Admiralty College immediately upon returning to St. Petersburg. But the

Admiralty College had problems of its own, for the Navy had fallen
into a state of neglect under the successors of Peter the Great.[23]
And the one person who clearly knew and understood Peter's
instructions for the voyage, Admiral Apraksin, was dead. Peter
the Great had shared the results of Russian explorations with
western Europeans. What would the policy of his successors be?

It is difficult to know, therefore, what guidelines, if any,
were given to Bering about what he should report. He undoubtedly
wanted to have recognition for his expedition, and in St. Petersburg there were people who wanted to hear about it. Bering would
clearly have emphasized what he had done: he had explored and
mapped the coasts of Kamchatka and northeastern Siberia; he had
learned that the "unknown" land was part of the Chukchi Peninsula.

The first public report about the Bering expedition appeared
in the 16 March 1730 issue of the Sanktpeterburgskiia Vedomosti,
and its counterpart, the St. Peterburgische Zeitung.[24] The
article also appeared outside Russia in 1730. It was translated
into Danish and printed in Copenhagen, in the Nye Tidende.[25]
The article was also translated into English and appeared in The
Historical Register of 1730. The text as it appears in The
Historical Register is as follows:

Petersburg, March 27. N.S.

Captain Berings, a Sea-Officer, return'd hither the
27th ult. from Kamtschatka, whither he was sent by the
Czarina Katharine, pursuant to the Orders of the Czar
Peter I. to examine the Frontiers of that Country extending
toward the North East, and to try to discover, whether,

as some think, it is join'd to the Northern Part of America;
or whether a Passage could be found that Way by Sea. The
Captain set out Feb. 5, 1725, with several Officers, Engin-
eers, Seamen, and Soldiers. Being arriv'd at Ochatskoy,
which is situate in the extreme Part of Siberia, he built
a Vessel there in the Spring 1727, and with it sailed over
the Sea of Pensinskoi and arriv'd at Kamtschatka. The
next Spring, which was in the Year 1728, he built another
vessel upon the River Kamtschatka, and steering to the
North-East, according to his Orders, he advanc'd as far as
67 Degrees 19 Minutes of Northern Latitude, and discover'd
that there was really a Passage to the North-East; and that
unless impeded by the Northern Ice, Men might go by Sea*
from Lena to Kamtschatka, and from thence to Japan, China,
and the East-Indies; and if the Inhabitants of the Country
may be believed, a Ship from Lena arriv'd at Kamtschatka
50 or 60 Years ago. The Captain brings a Confirmation,
that that Country joins to Siberia in the North. Besides,
the Chart which he sent hither in 1728, wherein his Journey
by Land from Tobolskoi to Ochotskoi was laid down, he has
made another of the Country of Kamtschatka, and of his
Voyage by Sea; whereby it appears, that it extends in Latitude from South to North from the 51st to the 67th Degree
of Northern Latitude. Its Longitude, from the Western
Coast, reckoning according to the Meridian of Tobolskoi,
is 85 Degrees, and from the utmost Confines to the North-
East, according to the said Meridian, is 126 Degrees; which
being calculated by the usual Meridian of the Canary Islands,
makes 173 Degrees on one Side, and 214 on the other. A more
circumstantial Account of this Discovery will be published
e'er long. Captain Bering set out from Ochotskoi the
Beginning of August last; so that he was above half a Year
upon the Road.

*There seems to be here an Error in the Print, and that
it should be to Lena from Kamtschatka.[26]

Who wrote the article? Peter Lauridsen, an early biographer

of Bering, assumed Bering wrote it himself, or that it was written

by close friends of his. Lauridsen knew only of the printing

of the article in the Nye Tidende, not of its original appearance

in St. Petersburg.[27] The content of the article does suggest

it was written by Bering or by someone who was close to him. The statement that Bering went "to examine the Frontiers of that Country extending toward the North East and to try to discover, whether, as some think, it is join'd to the Northern Part of America" is close to Peter's second order to Bering. The chronology of the expedition and the assertion that Bering sailed to the northeast "according to his Orders" further suggest Bering as the source of the information in the article.

But there are major differences between the newspaper account and Bering's report made to the Admiralty College on 10 March and his "Short Account" of his expedition, dated 30 April, which was sent to the Empress Anna.[28] The newspaper article states Bering had discovered "that there was really a Passage to the North East" which, unless ice prevented it, would have made sailing from the Lena River to Kamchatka, Japan, China, and the East Indies possible. In his "Short Account" Bering makes no mention of discovering a northeast passage--in fact the term is not even used! The newspaper article further emphasizes the northeast passage by noting that "if the Inhabitants of the Country may be believed" the voyage from the Lena River to Kamchatka has already been made. Bering does not report this information in his "Short Account," either. Finally, there is no notice given of Bering's second voyage, in 1729, to the east in the Sanktpeterburgskiia Vedomosti article, which is included in his "Short Account." Although there is evidence in the newspaper article that Bering supplied information for it, nevertheless it seems unlikely that he wrote it himself.

Who did write the article? Evidence in it suggests the
involvement of Joseph Nicolas Delisle. According to the article,
Bering sailed to 67° 19' north. The article gives the western
longitude of Kamchatka at 85° and the eastern extremity of Siberia
at 126° (from Tobolsk), figures which do not agree with Bering's
"Short Account" and the later maps based on the expedition.
Bering's figures for latitude and longitude were corrected after
his return to St. Petersburg, and before the official accounts
were submitted, indicating that the figures given in the
newspaper article were supplied by Bering soon after he reached
St. Petersburg.[29] These earlier figures--the ones in the article
in the Sanktpeterburgskiia Vedomosti--appear on a sketch map made
by Joseph Delisle, based on a conversation he had with Bering about
the expedition.[30] Delisle writes to Maurepas on 25 June 1730
that he had met Bering and had discussed the voyage with him, but
he does not give a date of that meeting.[31] Delisle's map, giving
the same figures of longitude and latitude as the newspaper
article, is good evidence that Delisle's conversation with Bering
took place shortly after Bering returned to St. Petersburg. The
indication at point "E" on the Delisle map, with its statement
that this is the point where ice often prevents passage around
the cape, corresponds with the statement in the newspaper article
that the northeast passage can be made "unless Ice prevents it."[32]

Delisle was not alone when he met with Bering, for Delisle

Delisle sketch map, reproduced from the
frontispiece of Frank A. Golder, Russian
Expansion, 1914.

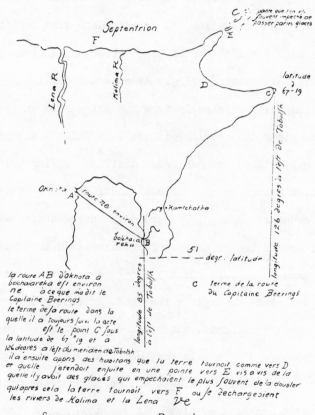

SKETCH ILLUSTRATING BERING'S FIRST VOYAGE

Made by J. N. Delisle and based on his conversation with Bering

[Delisle Manuscripts. xxv, 6]

needed an interpreter in conversations with Bering, a function
Gerhard Friedrich Müller often performed.[33] Müller's known
interest in Bering's expedition and his position as editor of
the Sanktpeterburgskiia Vedomosti suggest that Müller wrote the
article for the newspaper which he edited. It would be difficult
to identify anyone more likely to be the writer of the article.[34]

How much information did Bering share with Delisle and Müller?
Delisle made a sketch map of northeastern Siberia on the basis of
his conversation with Bering. Because the detail given in the
sketch map differs greatly from the later maps of the expedition,
it seems clear that Bering did not show Delisle any official maps
of the expedition, even in rough draft.[35] Bering told Delisle
and Müller enough of his official instructions so that Peter's
second order to Bering is recorded in the newspaper article.
The difference in the newspaper article is in the orientation
of the land to be explored. The newspaper article states that
Bering was sent to explore the land "extending toward the North
East" rather than north, which was what Bering had found.

What maps did Delisle and Müller discuss with Bering? In
his letter of May 1729 Delisle writes to Maurepas that the best
map of northern Asia available at the time was the one by
Strahlenberg published in the Histoire généalogique of 1726.[36]
Delisle attributes this map to Strahlenberg. He writes that
Strahlenberg had made four maps of northern Asia--the first was
burned in a fire at Tobolsk; the second was confiscated by

Prince Gagarin, the Governor of Siberia; the third Strahlenberg
had to sell before he left Russia. This latter map, dated 1717,
was given to the Academy of Sciences and is "now in my hands"
says Delisle.[37] The fourth was in Stockholm, with Strahlenberg.[38]

Strahlenberg, in his notes to the Histoire généalogique,
writes about "a Great Island" which lies to the northeast, which
"is so lately discover'd, and is so remote from the other Dominions
of Russia, that we have not yet come to an exact Knowledge of
it. . ."[39] Delisle, in 1729, tells Maurepas of the report of a
great land discovered in 1723, lying north of an island at the
mouth of the Lena River. Delisle writes "Ils disent que sur cette
grande terre il y a un grand nombre d'habitans, quantité de
zibelines, renards, castors, fouines et beaucoup de bois. Ils
ajoutent que la distance de cette grande terre à la côte
septentrionale de l'Asie est de 48 heures de navigation. . . .
Le tems et la suite des découvertes nous apprendront si cette
grande terre n'est pas contigue à l'Amérique. . ."[40] Bering
had set out to discover if an unknown land in the north was
connected to America. He found none. Thus the newspaper article
states "the Captain brings a Confirmation, that that Country
joins to Siberia in the North."[41] "That Country" does not refer
to the mainland of Siberia, but to the unknown land Bering was
sent to explore.

After his meeting with Bering, Delisle again writes to
Maurepas; in a letter dated 25 June 1730 Delisle states he

discussed Bering's voyage and Peter's instructions for it. In spite of signs of land to the east at the northern part of his voyage--winds coming, apparently, off land to the east, birds flying eastward, trees floating in the sea, larger than those growing on the Siberian coast--Bering did not go in search of land to the east. He did not, because he had strict orders to follow the coast of the land he was sent to explore. He would go to America only if the land joined to America. Delisle's text reads:

> Ainsi, le capitaine Beerings étant à ce terme de sa route, il y a eu plusieurs indices d'une terre voisine à son orient, comme d'un vent de terre qui venoit de l'est et des glaces amenées par ce vent, des oyseaux qui venoient aussy de l'est, et enfin de sapins déracinez, que la mer apportoit de l'est, quoyqu'il n'en croisse point d'aussy grands à la côte que le capitaine Beerings avoit à sa gauche. Malgré ces indices le capitaine Beerings n'a pas été plus loin, parce que l'ordre précis qu'il avoit étoit de suivre le nord-est pour s'assurer de l'extremité de la Tartarie de ce côté la; si cependant il avoit rencontré la côte de l'Amérique, il avoit ordre de la parcourir jusqu'à ce qu'il y eût trouvé quelque lieu connu et fréquenté par les vaisseaux d'Europe.[42]

Bering believed he had sailed east along the coast of the "incognita" land of the Homann map; it was not connected with America.

The importance of Bering's voyage, for Delisle and Müller, was its confirmation that there was a sea passage between Asia and America and the potential such a passage would hold for a northeast passage from Europe to Asia. Delisle and Müller were convinced, before they met Bering, that a search for the passage was the purpose of the voyage. Their orientation and education was western European and included a long emphasis on the search for northern sea routes to the east. Was there an easy passage from the Lena River to Kamchatka? On Strahlenberg's map such a voyage appears feasible, since there is no promontory extending northwards between the Lena River and Kamchatka. Bering "corrected" this view. This promontory is a portrayal of the one on the Homann map, though now shown reaching much farther to the east and north than it had on the Homann map.[43] Because of this promontory, Bering's critics were to accuse him of failing in the presumed purpose of his voyage, for he had not sailed around it in order to prove a passage from the Lena River to Kamchatka was possible.[44]

Bering, as noted above, never claimed he had verified the possibility of a northeast passage, nor even mentioned the term northeast passage, in his "Short Account" of his voyage. Bering had revealed the true nature of the geography of northeastern Siberia, and stated he had followed Peter's orders concerning the unknown land in the north. He had gathered extensive information on eastern Siberia and had formulated recommendations for improving Russian administration of it.[45] He presented his reports and maps to the Admiralty College and to the court.

If the newspaper article in the Sanktpeterburgskiia Vedomosti had had no further impact than appearances in four languages in newspapers of the time, it might have been only a historical oddity, a reflection of the view of Delisle and Müller (and the

common belief of their contemporaries) that Bering's First
Kamchatka Expedition was part of the search for a northeast
passage. But this was not the case. The newspaper article was
incorporated into what scholars have commonly believed to be the
earliest printed account of the First Kamchatka Expedition, a
fact that had an enduring effect on the writings about Bering's
voyage, as will be seen in the following chapter.

Footnotes

Chapter V

1. Raymond H. Fisher, Bering's Voyages: Whither and Why (Seattle: University of Washington Press, 1977), p. 73.

2. Aubry de la Mottraye, The Voyages and Travels of A. De La Motraye, 3 vols. (London: For the Author, 1723-32), III, 145.

3. Ibid.

4. Fisher, Bering's Voyages, pp. 164-65.

5. For histories of the Academy, see Alexander Vucinich, Science in Russian Culture: A History to 1860 (Stanford: Stanford University Press, 1963); Akademiia nauk SSSR, Institut istorii estestvoznaniia i tekhniki, Istoriia akademii nauk SSSR, 3 vols. (Moscow, Leningrad: AN SSSR, 1958-198-).

6. For general biographical information on Delisle, see Petr Petrovich Pekarskii, Istoriia imperatorskoi akademiia nauk v Peterburge, 2 vols. (St. Petersburg: Imperatorskaia akademiia nauk, 1870-73), I, 124-49 and Seymour L. Chapin, "Joseph Nicolas Delisle," in The Dictionary of Scientific Biography, IV, 22-25.

7. The relationship between Delisle and Kirilov worsened after an initial period of cooperation in mapmaking. Delisle did not want to print Kirilov's maps until complex astronomical observations could have been made to verify the positions given on them. See Mariia G. Novlianskaia, Ivan Kirilovich Kirilov: geograf XVIII veka (Leningrad: Nauka, 1964) and Leo Bagrow,

"Ivan Kirilov, Compiler of the First Russian Atlas, 1689-1737,"
in Imago Mundi (London, 1938) II, 78-82.

8. For example, one writer said Delisle "was essentially an
agent of the French government." O. M. Medushevskaya,
"Cartographic Sources for the History of Russian Geographical
Discoveries in the Pacific Ocean in the Second Half of the
18th Century," in The Canadian Cartographer, IX:2 (December,
1972), 100. See also Albert Isnard, "Joseph-Nicolas Delisle,
sa biographie et sa collection de cartes géographiques à la
Bibliothèque nationale," in Comité des travaux historique et
scientifique, Bulletin de la Section de Géographie, XXX (1915),
34-164.

9. M. H. Omont, "Lettres de J.-N. Delisle au Comte de Maurepas
et à l'Abbé Bignon sur les travaux géographiques en Russie
(1726-1730)," in Comité des travaux historique et scientifique,
Bulletin de la Section de Géographie, XXXII (1917), 144.

10. Ibid., p. 142.

11. For general biographical information on Müller see Pekarskii,
Istoriia, I, 308-430; L. Stieda, "Gerhard Friedrich Müller,"
in Allgemeine deutsche Biographie, XXII, 547-53.

12. Pekarskii, Istoriia, I, 312.

13. Carl Eichhorn, Die Geschichte der "St. Petersburger Zeitung"
1727-1902 (St. Petersburg: Buchdruckerei der St. Petersburger
Zeitung, 1902), p. 22.

14. The work was published as Ebülgâzî Bahadir Han, Histoire

généalogique des Tartars, 2 vols. (Leiden: A. Kalewier, 1726).
The English translation appeared as A General History of the
Turks, Moguls, and Tatars, vulgarly called Tartars, 2 vols.
(London: J. and J. Knapton, 1729-30). The University of
Minnesota Library copy is entered under Abu al-Ghāzi. Strahlen-
berg commented on his relationship to this publication in his
An Historico-geographical Description of the North and Eastern
Parts of Europe and Asia (London: J. Brotherton[etc.] 1738),
pp. vii, 127-28.

15. Ebülgâzî Bahadir Han, A General History, II, 663-64.

16. Müller knew this work. See Materialy dlia istorii imperatorskoi akademiia nauk, VI, 168-69. Delisle commented on
it in a letter written to Maurepas in 1729. Omont, "Lettres,"
p. 141.

17. Ebülgâzî Bahadir Han, A General History, II, 642.

18. Materialy dlia istorii, VI, 168-69.

19. Svodnyi katalog russkoi knigi grazdanskoi pechati vosemnadtsatogo veka 1725-1800, 5 vols. (Moscow: 1963-66), IV, 229.

20. Materialy dlia istorii, VI, 169.

21. Marc Raeff, editor, Plans for Political Reform in Imperial
Russia, 1730-1905 (Englewood Cliffs: Prentice-Hall, 1966).
The chapter "The Succession Crisis of 1730," on pages 41-52,
prints the "conditions" as well as giving a background to the
choice of Anna as empress.

22. During the course of the expedition Bering made reports on it;

the court may well have received a report on the maritime part
of the expedition before Bering went to St. Petersburg to repor
to the Admiralty College.

23. See Glynn Barratt, Russia in Pacific Waters, 1715-1825: A
    Survey of the Origins of Russia's Naval Presence in the North
    and South Pacific (Vancouver: University of British Columbia
    Press, 1981), especially page 23.

24. Vadim I. Grekov, "Naibolee rannee pechatnoe izvestie o pervoe
    kamchatskoi ekspeditsii (1725-30 gg.)" in Izvestiia AN SSSR,
    seriia geograficheskaia (Moscow) no. 6 (November-December, 1956
    108-12. The text of the article is given on pages 108-09, which
    Raymond H. Fisher translated in Bering's Voyages, pp. 12-13.
    Neither Grekov nor Fisher identified the author of the article,
    and both assumed the article had little impact beyond its first
    publication.

25. Peter Lauridsen, Vitus Bering: The Discoverer of Bering Strait,
    translated by Julius E. Olson (Chicago: S. C. Griggs, 1889),
    pp. 35-36.

26. The Historical Register for the Year 1730, XV:60 (London: R.
    Nutt, 1730), 291.

27. Lauridsen, Vitus Bering, pp. 35-36, 203 note 10. Not realizing
    that the notice in the Nye Tidende in 1730 was a translation
    from the article in the Sanktpeterburgskiia Vedomosti, Lauridse
    assumed that Bering, or one of his close friends, had written
    the account. Part of his reasoning for this belief was because

the article was included in Friedrich Christian Weber, <u>Das</u> <u>veränderte</u> <u>Russland</u>. Lauridsen writes: "That Bering himself was the author, would seem to be shown by the fact that Weber, who knew and associated with Bering, uses <u>verbatim</u> the same expressions concerning the first expedition." (p. 203) See the commentary on Weber in Chapter VII.

28. The texts that were used for comparison here are the English translation of the <u>Sanktpeterburgskiia</u> Vedomosti article that appeared in <u>The</u> <u>Historical</u> <u>Register</u> and the English translation by Brookes of Bering's "Short Account" which was published in Du Halde's work on China in 1736.

29. There were two manuscript versions of Bering's map. See William H. Dall, "A Critical Review of Bering's First Expedition, 1725-30, Together with a Translation of his Original Report on it," in <u>The</u> <u>National</u> <u>Geographic</u> <u>Magazine</u>, II (1890), 111-69 and A. W. Greely, "The Cartography and Observations of Bering's First Voyage," in <u>The</u> <u>National</u> <u>Geographic</u> <u>Magazine</u>, III (1892), 205-30.

30. This map is shown as a frontispiece to Frank A. Golder, <u>Russian</u> <u>Expansion</u> <u>on</u> <u>the</u> <u>Pacific,</u> <u>1641-1850</u> (Cleveland: The Arthur H. Clark Company, 1914) but is not discussed in the text.

31. Omont, "Lettres," p. 162.

32. <u>The</u> <u>Historical</u> <u>Register</u>, XV:60, p. 291.

33. [Gerhard Friedrich Müller] <u>A</u> <u>Letter</u> <u>from</u> <u>a</u> <u>Russian</u> <u>Sea-Officer,</u> <u>to</u> <u>a</u> <u>Person</u> <u>of</u> <u>Distinction</u> <u>at</u> <u>the</u> <u>Court</u> <u>of</u> St. <u>Petersburgh</u>

(London: A. Linde [etc.] 1754), p. 11

34. Raymond H. Fisher concurs in this conclusion, in correspondence on the subject.

35. Compare the sketch map made by Delisle with the later manuscript maps of the expedition.

36. Omont, "Lettres," p. 141.

37. Ibid., p. 142.

38. Ibid.

39. Ebülgâzî Bahadir Han, A General History, II, 664.

40. Omont, "Lettres," p. 146.

41. The Historical Register, XV:60, p. 291.

42. Omont, "Lettres," p. 161.

43. See the comparison between the Homann map and Bering's map.

44. This criticism was voiced early after Bering's return from the first expedition and has continued. Those who thought Bering was sent to search for a possible northeast passage at the northeastern point of Siberia have criticized him for his failure to sail further west, to the Kolyma River or the Lena River. And his reputation has suffered because of it. For example, Barratt writes: "So perished Bering, whom it is customary to regard as a great mariner and eminent explorer. Certainly, it was a large achievement to have turned a fabled strait into a charted one." He later adds, "On his first expedition he had shown great caution." Barratt, Russia in Pacific Waters, p. 40.

45. So much attention has been placed on Bering's sea voyages, in

this study as elsewhere, that the real importance of the two
Bering expeditions may be missed. In the eighteenth century,
whether or not there was a strait between Asia and America was
not of utmost importance, because the route to be sailed along
the northern coast of Siberia was simply not feasible for ships
of that time, as Peter well knew, and the efforts made to map
the arctic coasts during the Second Kamchatka Expedition would
verify. The most lasting result--and the most important one--of
the Bering expeditions was to establish official Russian presence
in northeastern Siberia.

Chapter VI

The Eighteenth Century Printings of Bering's

"Short Account"

The little article in the Sanktpeterburgskiia Vedomosti

caused some stir among readers in western Europe. In Copenhagen

it was of interest not only because Bering was born in Denmark,

but also because of the potential the Russian discovery might hold

for a northeast passage to the East Indies, a possibility of

much interest to the Danish East India Company.[1] Strahlenberg

was in Stockholm in 1730, and in his book published that year he

mentioned reading a report on the Bering expedition "in the common

News-papers."[2] Weber, the Hanoverian minister in Russia during

Peter the Great's reign, incorporated the newspaper article in his

book on Russia.[3] The Spanish minister to Russia, the Duke de

Berwick y de Liria, mentioned the Bering expedition in his correspon-

dence to Spain. Any notice of enterprises directed toward America

would be of concern to Spain, as the Spanish claimed all the lands

bordering on the Pacific Ocean on the basis of Balboa's "discovery"

of the Pacific Ocean in 1513.[4] It is noteworthy that the article

in the Sanktpeterburgskiia Vedomosti asserted Bering had dis-

covered there was a passage in the northeast, from the Lena River

to Kamchatka, and from there to "Japan, China, and the East-

Indies." Nothing was said about going to America. De Liria

registered no protest over the Bering voyage, nor could he, as there was no mention in it of sailing to America. Receipt in Spain of information about Russian explorations in the eastern seas was reduced after November, 1730, for diplomatic relations between Spain and Russia were severed then, and not renewed for many years.[5]

In London the article about Bering's expedition rekindled the desire to search for a northeast passage. The young Russian minister to Great Britain, Antiokh D. Kantemir, was approached by the merchant/adventurer John Elton, with his "Project for discovering a navigable passage from the town of Archangel around Novaia Zemlia to Japan, China, the Indies, and America."[6] Kantemir hired Elton for service in Russia. Elton arrived in St. Petersburg on 29 December 1732 but ended up going to Persia rather than Kamchatka.[7]

Russians could not have been pleased by this attention to their activities in eastern Siberia, for they were anxious to avoid arousing the jealousy of other European countries. One of the things Bering's expedition had revealed was how tenuous the Russian presence in northeastern Siberia really was.[8] Another discovery made by Bering was the extent of the fur trade in northeastern Siberia, and especially the lucrative trade between Siberia and China.[9] This was hinted at by Strahlenberg, who wrote the following under the entry for "Beaver" in his book: "In the Russian Language, called Bobri, and in the Tartarian, Condus; In the Province of Kamtschatki in Siberia, are very large ones; The Skins are about four Foot long, and two and a half Foot broad, the Hair is black,

short and soft; These Skins are sold in China for about sixty
Rixdolars a-piece, and in Russia, not for above twenty Rubels,
and therefore few are brought to Russia; But whether these are
the right Sort of Beaver, is yet uncertain."[10] This "beaver"
was the sea otter, the animal which was to play such an important
part in later Russian voyages to the Aleutian Islands and America.[11]

To dampen any ideas of an easy northeast passage, manuscript
maps were made based on Bering's expedition, and were presented
to heads of various European countries. At least twelve manuscript
maps have survived.[12] They are beautifully prepared maps, in a
large format, and are decorated with watercolor illustrations and
elaborate cartouches. They are confined to Siberia from Tobolsk
eastward and so do not include the area of Novaia Zemlia, thus
avoiding the old question of the possibility of sailing around it
on the north, or through the Strait of Vaygach.[13] Where the mouth
of the Lena River would be, cartouches or decorations are shown.
In the northeast, northward of the point reached by Bering in his
voyage, a great imaginary promontory stretches to above 73° north.
Any viewer of this map gets the clear understanding that Russia was
not claiming any easy water route from the Lena River to Kamchatka.

The maps of the Bering expedition fostered doubts that
Bering had discovered a passage from the Lena River to Kamchatka,
for Bering had not sailed westward along the coast that led to
the Lena, around the promontory. Bering was criticized for this
by members of the Academy of Sciences, and by those who believed

Manuscript map of the First Kamchatka Expedition in the
James Ford Bell Library. (right portion only).

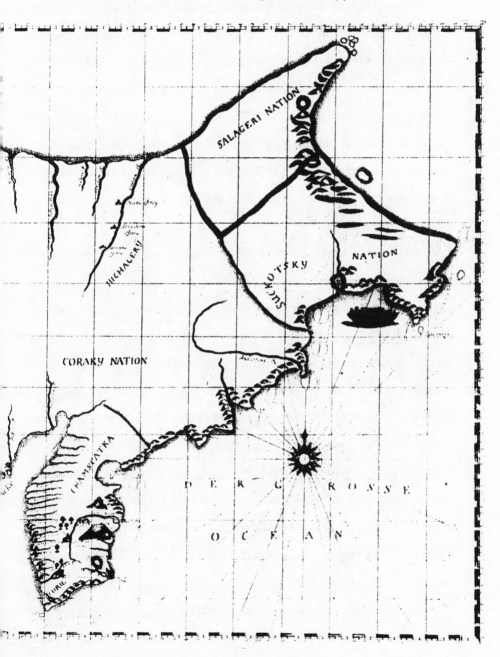

his purpose was to discover a northeast passage.[14] The Admiralty College criticized Bering, too, and pointed out that he had <u>not</u> fulfilled Peter's instructions completely.[15] He had not gone to America, to see how far it was from the northeast corner of Siberia. Bering admitted he had not done this, but defended himself, undoubtedly, by pointing out that he had no authorization to go to America, unless the coast of the land he was exploring had joined America, which it had not.[16] Bering was promoted to the rank of captain-commander, and was promised a reward of 1,000 silver rubles.[17]

The presentation of maps of the Bering expedition to selected western Europeans was one matter; the publication of Bering's account of the expedition was another. In spite of the statement in the <u>Sanktpeterburgskiia</u> <u>Vedomosti</u> that a more complete report on the Bering expedition would be published soon, none was published at the time.[18] On the strength of Bering's reports and recommendations, a second expedition was planned shortly after he returned from the first. Members of the Admiralty College, the Academy of Sciences, and the Senate worked jointly on the plans for the Second Kamchatka Expedition.[19] Joseph N. Delisle prepared a map for it.[20] In his recommendations for a second expedition, Bering proposed a voyage to America and another to search for a route to Japan, to open trade there; the Admiralty College added the assignment of mapping the arctic coast, a reflection of its hopes of finding a sea route to the northeast, if possible, which would be

of the most benefit to it.[21] But the purpose and results were
to be kept secret from western Europe and all participants in the
expedition had to sign an oath promising to keep the expedition
secret.[22] The Second Kamchatka Expedition, under Bering's leadership, set out from St. Petersburg in the spring of 1733.

A paraphrase of Bering's "Short Account" of the First Kamchatka
Expedition, with a map, was printed in 1735. It appeared in
volume four of Jean Baptiste du Halde's Description historique,
géographique, chronologique, politique, et physique de l'empire
de la Chine, published in Paris. The complete work was a monumental
set of four folio volumes, with many illustrations and maps, printed
with the approval of the King of France. The compiler of this
massive work, Du Halde, was the editor of Lettres édifiantes et
curieuses écrites des missions étrangères par quelques missionnaires
de la Compagnie de Jésus. His Description . . . de la Chine was
based on the reports of the Jesuit missionaries in China.[23]
The maps in the work were prepared by Jean Baptiste Bourguignon
d'Anville, geographer to the King of France.[24]

Where did Du Halde get his information on the Bering expedition? He stated he received the map from "the King of Poland"
who told him he could make whatever use he liked of it. The reader
of the account was left to infer that the "Short Account" came
from the same source.[25] The King of Poland at the time was either
Augustus II, who reigned to 1733, or his son Augustus III, who
succeeded him. The Russians supported both against the claim of

Printed version of the map of the First Kamchatka
Expedition, printed by Du Halde in 1735.

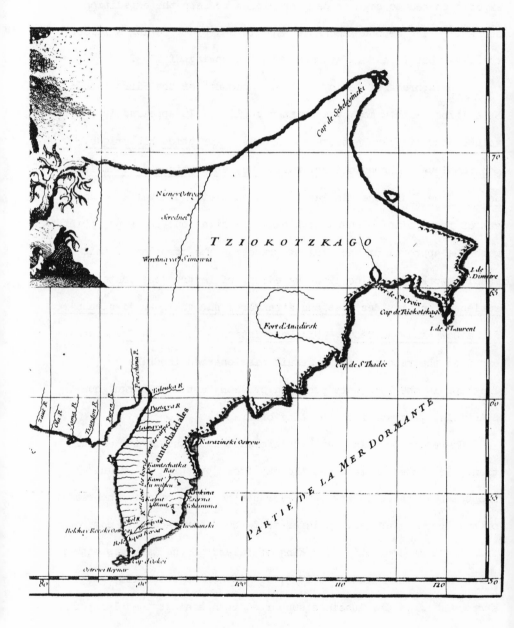

Stanislas Lesczynski to the Polish throne. It seems unlikely
then, that either King Augustus would have sent materials
on Bering's expedition to a Jesuit in Paris for publication.
There is no indication that Du Halde ever traveled to Poland.

Joseph Nicolas Delisle, in his letter of 25 June 1730 to
Maurepas, says he hoped to be able to send Bering's accounts of
his voyage to France soon.[26] That he was successful in obtaining
a copy of Bering's account, and a map, seems certain. The Russians
believed that Delisle was the source of Du Halde's publication
on the Bering expedition, and later Delisle was carefully watched
to prevent him from sending more information to France.[27] It
was for this practice that his contract with the Academy of
Sciences was ultimately terminated in 1747.[28]

In addition to this evidence, there is also internal evidence
in the text of the "Short Account" which Du Halde published, for
it incorporates information from the Sanktpeterburgskiia Vedomosti
article in it! The beginning of the Du Halde version of the
"Short Account" states that Bering "as public Accounts inform'd
us," was sent on an expedition to find out whether Asia was
connected to America, or if there was a sea passage between them.[29]
As noted before, Bering in his "Short Account" had not mentioned
any such purpose. Since the Du Halde printing of the "Short
Account" was widely circulated, translated, and known in western
Europe, this inclusion put the purpose of the First Kamchatka
Expedition squarely into the context of the discovery of a sea

passage between Asia and America. Ever since 1735, scholars who have studied the first Bering voyage have been confronted with this statement of its purpose in the first printed account of it.[30]

The map printed by Du Halde was not based on one of the manuscript maps sent to the heads of western European countries by the Russians, for the configuration of it does not conform to the one which emerges from a composite of the manuscript maps which have survived.[31] Rather, the map printed by Du Halde bears close resemblance to another manuscript map--an early one--by Peter Chaplin.[32] Close comparison of the map printed by Du Halde and the one made by Chaplin reveals other similarities.[33] It appears reasonable to predicate that the map in Du Halde's work was not based on the manuscripts distributed to western Europe by the Russians (France was not among them, because of the relationship between France and Russia at the time) but rather on a manuscript map made very soon after Bering returned from his expedition--one which Delisle sent to France.

Does all of this mean that Delisle was committing espionage, eighteenth century style, on behalf of France? Not necessarily. At the time the article was published in the Sanktpeterburgskiia Vedomosti, apparently Bering, Delisle, and Müller assumed that a more complete account of Bering's expedition would be published.[34] Delisle may have sent the "Short Account" and map to Maurepas before the decision to withhold further information about the

181

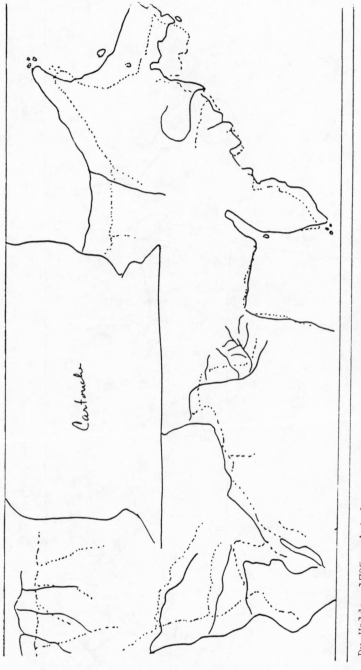

Cartouche

Du Halde, 1735 printed map ———   Manuscript maps, composite – – – –

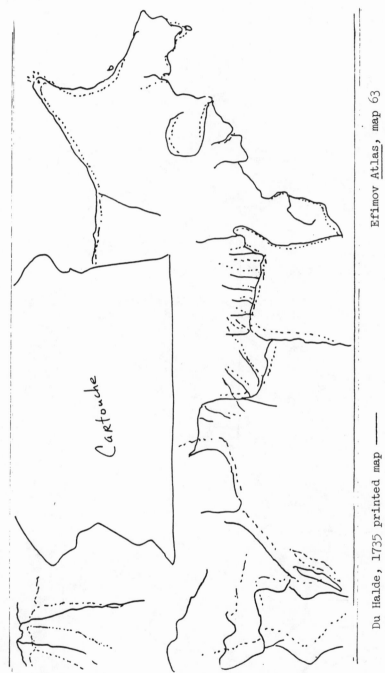

Cartouche

Du Halde, 1735 printed map ——

Efimov Atlas, map 63

First Kamchatka Expedition was made, a decision which could well have resulted in view of the interest raised in wester Europe by the publication of the newspaper article about it.[35] That Bering's accounts and maps were shared with Delisle was not surprising, as Delisle was the geographer working on Russian maps.[36]

Delisle would not have given Du Halde permission to publish the Bering material in 1735, for by that time all reports of Russian explorations were to be kept secret. But the French obtained a second copy of Bering's "Short Account," this one from Stockholm. The latter was translated from Swedish to French in 1733 at the order of the French minister to Sweden, Charles Louis de Biaudos, the Count de Casteja.[37] Instead of printing this translation from Swedish, Du Halde printed the Delisle text, with the map.[38] If questions were raised, the Swedes could have been identified as the source of the "Short Account" Du Halde printed. In identifying the "King of Poland" as the source of the map, Du Halde could not damage Russian/French relations. Presumably Du Halde had no reason to believe Delisle would get into trouble with Russian officials because of the publication of the Bering material.[39]

The Du Halde Description . . . de la Chine was an impressive work, and plans were soon made to translate it into English. One of Britain's most successful publishers, Edward Cave, announced his intention of publishing an English translation of Du Halde's opus in 1735.[40] Cave, the founder and publisher of the highly

successful Gentleman's Magazine, offered the public an opportunity
to subscribe to his translation of Du Halde, promising that the
English version would be every bit as good--and in some respects
even better--than the French original. He intended to publish
the work as a serial, with two sheets of it appearing each fort-
night.[41]

Cave must have been somewhat shaken in 1736, when the publisher
John Watts published a four-volume English abridgment of the Du
Halde Description . . . de la Chine. The translator of this
edition was a physician, Richard Brookes.[42] In this work, The
General History of China, the Bering "Short Account" appears in
volume four, accompanied by a reduced version of Du Halde's map.[43]
This is a straightforward translation of Du Halde's text, with
the preliminary statements from the Sanktpeterburgskiia Vedomosti
article incorporated into it. Dr. Brookes had some difficulties
with the transliteration into English of some Russian place names,
for example, he has "Seniseiski" for Jeneisei, "Tenissee River"
for the Jeneisei River, "Slim" for Ilim, "Himski" for Ilimsk,
"Jackutski" for Iakutsk, "Tudoma" for Iudoma, etc. He also
stated that Bering went to "Bolchayrecski Ostrog, or the Town of
small Barks upon the great River" where he found only "fourteen
small Russian Families."

The publication of the Watts edition of the Description . . .
de la Chine should have discouraged Edward Cave, for it went into
a second edition before the first pages of Cave's serial publication

of the text were printed, in 1738. But this did not deter Cave.

He used the Gentleman's Magazine to promote his own translation

of the Du Halde work, and to criticize the Watts edition of it.[44]

The Cave translation of Bering's "Short Account" was not

printed until 1741. A map was included, based on the Du Halde

printed map, but with Bering's route added on it. The "Short

Account" in Cave's translation is an abridgment of the text given

by Du Halde. The Cave translation states of Bering: "By his

Instructions, signed by the Czar he was obliged to inform himself

of the North-eastern Frontiers of that Country, in order to

discover whether they were contiguous to, or what might be their

Distance from the Continent of North America, and if any Passage

could be obtained that Way by Sea." The latter is, of course,

from the Sanktpeterburgskiia Vedomosti article. Other than this

accidental, though nearly true, presentation of the orders of

Peter the Great and improvement in the transliteration of Russian

place names, the Cave translation is no better than the one made

by Brookes, for it again places the voyage in the context of a

search for a northeast passage.[45]

In 1747 the first volume of Ausführliche Beschreibung des

chinesischen Reichs, the German translation of Du Halde's De-

scription . . . de la Chine, appeared in Rostock. Volume four,

containing the "Short Account," was published in 1749. The transla-

tor added notes to Du Halde's text.[46] The German translation of

the "Short Account" includes the information from the Sanktpeter-

burgskiia Vedomosti. At the end of the "Short Account" the translator adds new materials, which he says "were made known a short
time ago" about the Second Kamchatka Expedition.[47]

A new English account of the First Kamchatka Expedition
appeared in London in 1748, in the Navigantium atque Itinerarium
Bibliotheca, Or, A Complete Collection of Voyages and Travels.
This collection was first published by John Harris in 1705.[48]
After the death of Harris, John Campbell, a Scot, decided to publish
a second edition, with many additions from more recent explorations.
Campbell was a vigorous proponent of British overseas trade,
dedicating his work "To the Merchants of Great-Britain" in the
hope that it would stimulate trade, "the surest Means of making
us a great, wealthy, powerful and happy People."[49] Volume one of
Campbell's collection was printed in 1744; volume two in 1748.
Section VIII of the latter is titled "A distinct account of part
of the north-east frontier of the Russian empire, commonly called
the country of Kamschatka or Kamschatska, including the voyages
of Captain Behring for discovering towards the East. . . ."[50]

The Campbell text is not another translation from Du Halde.
It is a new text, though its source is not certain. On 21 November
1747, the British minister in St. Petersburg, the Earl of Hyndford,
wrote to the Earl of Chesterfield: "I have in consequence of my
first instructions been endeavouring to learn, what discoveries
this court has made to the north-east of Russia, and I have been
so lucky, as to procure a copy of the journal and map of the

famous Captain Bearing, who took a survey of the coast of Kamschatka
and of the islands towards Japan, which I hope to be able to send
your Lordship by the next courier, but this must be kept a secret,
for, if Czernishew [the Russian minister in London] comes to the
knowledge of it, some people here may be sent to finish their days
in that country. . . ."[51] Lord Hyndford arrived in Russia late
in 1744. He apparently had difficulty in performing this part
of his "first instructions" as he was not able to get this copy
of Bering's journal and map until three years after his arrival
and almost two decades after the voyage itself.

British officials hoped to get information on the Second
Kamchatka Expedition, not another account of the First Kamchatka
Expedition.[52] In spite of Lord Hyndford's cautions about secrecy,
someone gave the Bering material to John Campbell for publication
in his collection of voyages. Du Halde, after all, had published
the account and map years earlier. What was it but another copy
of the text already printed by Du Halde?[53]

The map Campbell had was not the one used by Du Halde. At
first examination the two maps appear to be the same, which is
not the case. Campbell's map fits the composite of the surviving
manuscript maps described earlier, which Du Halde's did not.[54]
Near the eastern border of Campbell's map, the "I. St. Demetrius"
has been added.[55]

A comparison of Campbell's text with the text of the "Short
Account" printed by Du Halde suggests that Campbell indeed had an

authentic copy of Bering's text. In the "Short Account" printed
by Du Halde there is a gap in the record from 20 August 1728,
when the Russians encountered the 40 Chukchi, to September 2,
when they returned to the mouth of the Kamchatka River. The
Campbell version records: "On the 29th of August they met with a
great Storm, attended with a thick Fog, by which they were driven
upon the Coast of some Country East of Kamchatka, and where they
were obliged to come to an Anchor. Upon their endeavouring to
weight it the next Day, their Cable broke; however, they were so
Lucky as to escape with no other Loss than that of their Anchor."[56]
This passage records the near-wreck of Bering's ship on the coast
of Kamchatka (not some country east of Kamchatka), an event not
recorded in the Du Halde text.

In 1729 Bering sailed in search of land to the east, a voyage
not mentioned in the Du Halde version of the "Short Account."
Campbell's version states: "On the 5th of June 1729, they repaired
their vessel and put to Sea, steering due East from the Mouth of
the River Kamschatska, in Hopes of discovering that Land, which
the Inhabitants affirm'd might be seen in a clear Day; which,
however, they were not so happy as to meet with, though they
continued that Route for 30 Leagues, and then meeting a Storm
at East-North-East, they were obliged to return to the Mouth of
the Bolschoy reeschi, after having passed round the South Point
of Kamschatska, which was a Voyage that was never performed
before."[57] Campbell also published Peter's instructions to

Bering for the voyage, as follows:

      I. You shall cause one or two convenient Vessels
to be built at Kamtschatska, or elsewhere.
      II. You shall endeavour to discover, by Coasting
with these Vessels, whether the Country towards the North,
of which at present we have no distinct Knowledge, is a
Part of America, or not.
      III. If it joins to the Continent of America, you
shall endeavour, if possible, to reach some Colony belonging to some European Power; or in case you meet with any
European Ship, you shall diligently enquire the Name of
the Coasts, and such other Circumstances as it is in your
Power to learn; and these you shall commit to Writing, so
that we may have some certain Memoirs by which a Chart may
be constructed.[58]

His statement that he had an original copy of Bering's journal

is further buttressed by his inclusion of a table of the

latitudes and longitudes of places, calculated from Tobolsk,

which he says would "serve as a Kind of Test, by which all

subsequent Accounts may be tried with respect to their

Veracity. . . ."[59]

     John Campbell had an authentic copy of a report on Bering's

expedition.[60] But he translated it into the third person, and

added his own editorial comments to it, thereby lessening the

value of his publication as an authentic document. The original

manuscript which he used has been lost, apparently.[61] Camp-

bell viewed Bering's first voyage with tunnel vision resulting

from his belief that Russians were searching for a northeast

passage. He ignored both the instruction for the voyage, which

he printed, and the fact that Bering sailed eastward in 1729

in search of land and included this comment: "Before I speak of

the second Expedition of Captain Behring, it may not be amiss to
observe, that if there be any truth in the Accounts of Vessels
sailing from the Mouth of the River Lena in the Manner before-
mentioned, it amounts to a direct Demonstration, that the Dutch
ships employed to discover a North-east Passage in 1670, advanced
far enough to have made that Passage. . . . I think at this Day
the North-east Passage seems, without any just Reason, to be
treated as a thing known to be impracticable. . . ."[62] John
Campbell believed in northern sea passages. Following his account
of the First Kamchatka Expedition, Campbell recorded what he
knew of the Second Kamchatka Expedition, which was not much.[63]
Campbell's concern was for the effect the Russian discoveries
would have had on Britain's search for a northwest passage,
and he was highly critical of the Russians for withholding information about their discoveries.[64]

Another French version of the "Short Account" appeared in a
two-volume work printed in Amsterdam and Paris in 1757. This
was the first French translation of Strahlenberg's book on Russia,
which in this translation was titled Description historique de
l'Empire russien. The translator and editor of the Strahlenberg
text was Jean Louis Barbeau-de-la-Bruyère. He was born in
Paris, but spent fifteen years in Holland. When he returned to
France in 1731, he brought with him a number of maps which were
little-known there and were of interest to French geographers.[65]
In his translation of Strahlenberg's book, Barbeau-de-la-Bruyère

edited and abridged the original greatly, so that it could well

be considered a new work, rather than a translation. The trans-

lator also added material about Russian explorations, including

Bering's "Short Account."[66]

The text that Barbeau-de-la-Bruyère published was not the

Du Halde version of the "Short Account," but the French transla-

tion obtained by Casteja in 1733 from Stockholm. The text is in

the first person, and it is the earliest printing of the "Short

Account" in that form. A comparison of the text printed by

Barbeau-de-la-Bruyère with the manuscript, which is in the Bib-

liothèque Nationale, reveals that the editor has made almost no

alterations in printing the manuscript, and therefore it is

closer to the original of Bering's "Short Account" than any other

printing in the eighteenth century. The statement of Bering's

instructions is therefore of great interest. The text published

by Barbeau-de-la-Bruyère begins: "Le 5 Février 1725 je fus dépêché

par l'Amiral Général de ce tems-là, le Comte Apraksin, pour entre-

prendre une Commission en Sibérie, & alors on m'ordonna par une

Instruction dressée à cette fin, de m'informer entre autres

choses des limites de ce pays, & particulierement si le coin

Oriental de Sibérie se trouvoit séparé de l'Amérique."[67] The

manuscript version of this part of the text states that Bering

was to find out "de combien le coin Oriental de Sibérie se

trouvoit éloigné de l'Amerique." Only two words have been

changed in the printed version of the text. The "de combien"

of the manuscript is changed to "si" and the manuscript's
"éloigné" is printed as "séparé." The change has altered the
stated purpose of the voyage from "to find out how far America
was from the northeast corner of Siberia" to voyage "to find out
if the northeast corner of Siberia was separated from America."
Thus in the only eighteenth century printing of the "Short
Account" which did not incorporate the Sanktpeterburgskiia
Vedomosti interpretation of its purpose, or was influenced by
the bias of an editor, the purpose of the First Kamchatka Expedition can again be read in the context of a search for a northeast passage.

But is the "coin Oriental" of Siberia necessarily a part
of the mainland? And who made the change in the text and why?
In 1757 Joseph N. Delisle was living in Paris; when Barbeau-
de-la-Bruyère was going to print the text of Bering's "Short
Account," he might well have consulted with Delisle about it.
Indeed, the notes to the text are good indications that
Delisle was involved, as they provide information which would
have been familiar to Delisle, not Barbeau-de-la-Bruyère.[68]

I believe Delisle changed the manuscript wording of the
second instruction to Bering. Delisle knew that Bering was
sent to explore an unknown land in the north; he knew that
Bering was to go to America only if the land connected with
America. This land was the wedge ("coin" in French) shown on
the Homann map, east of the Chukchi Peninsula. Bering was to

go to America only if this land connected with America. Thus
Delisle changed the wording of the instruction, to indicate
Bering was to find out _if_ the northeast corner of Siberia (the
unknown land) was separated from America.

At the point where Bering turns southward again in his
first voyage, the text records: "Le 15 Août nous arrivâmes
sous 67 degrés 18 minutes de latitude; mais nous ne passâmes
pas outre, parce qu'il me sembloit avois satisfait à l'instruction
qu'on m'avoit donnée, sur-tout ne pouvant découvrir aucune terre
du côté de l'Orient des Tchuktschi."[69]

Bering turned back, he says, because he had been unable
to discover any land to the north or to the east of the
Chukchi Peninsula. He had not found, in other words, the
unknown land shown on the Homann map.

Footnotes

Chapter VI

1. The Danish East India Company was founded in 1728, and many
Danes would have been interested in Russian explorations that
might affect trade in the East. The hope of discovering a
northeast passage persisted, and Danes later considered sending
an expedition to the north in search of one. Sometime between
1742 and 1756, Waxell writes: "At the present time it can be
seen from the newspapers that the Danish Crown will perhaps
soon fit out a similar expedition, which will probably have
the same outcome as the earlier expeditions undertaken by
England and Holland. To put the matter in a nutshell, I can
say in advance what is likely to happen and be accomplished:
they will not achieve their object; they will lose many men,
and if they are just a bit unlucky, they will lose their ship
as well." Sven Waxell, The American Expedition, translated by
M. A. Michael (London: William Hodge and Company, 1952), p. 53.

2. Philip Johann Tabbert von Strahlenberg, Das Nord- und ostliche
Theil von Europa und Asia (Stockholm: In Verlegung des Autoris,
1730), p. 10; Strahlenberg, An Historico-geographical Description of the North and Eastern Parts of Europe and Asia (London:
J. Brotherton [etc.] 1738), p. 309.

3. See the section on Haven in the following chapter.

4. Glynn Barratt, Russia in Pacific Waters, 1715-1825: A Survey of the Origins of Russia's Naval Presence in the North and South Pacific (Vancouver: University of British Columbia Press, 1981), pp. 31-32. For further information on Spain in the Pacific see Warren L. Cook, Flood Tide of Empire: Spain and the Pacific Northwest, 1543-1819 (New Haven: Yale University Press, 1973), and O. H. K. Spate, The Spanish Lake (Minneapolis: University of Minnesota Press, 1979).

5. Barratt, Russia in Pacific Waters, p. 31.

6. The text of it is given in Aleksei V. Efimov, Iz istorii russkikh ekspeditsii na tikhom okeane (Moscow: 1948), pp. 251-52.

7. On Elton's activities in Russia and Persia see Jonas Hanway, An Historical Account of the British Trade over the Caspian Sea, 3 vols. (London: Mr. Dodsley [etc.] 1753), I, viii, 13-70.

8. Strahlenberg notes that Prince Matvei P. Gagarin, the governor of Siberia, plotted to make Siberia a separate kingdom. Gagarin was executed for his actions in Siberia. Strahlenberg, An Historico-geographical Description, pp. 261-65. Bering's account of Kamchatka indicated how few Russians were settled there; after his departure from Kamchatka, in 1731, the Kamchadals revolted against the Russians.

9. It is usual to cite Bering's Second Kamchatka Expedition as the one that "opened up" the fur trade in the North Pacific, but it is clear from the accounts of Bering's voyage to America (see the section on Steller in the following chapter) that the

Russians were aware of the value of sea otter pelts in the Chinese market.

10. Strahlenberg, An Historico-geographical Description, p. 335.

11. It was the discovery of the sea otters on Bering's Island that set off the Russian "fur rush" eastward along the Aleutian Islands to America. See Raisa Vsevolodovna Makarovna, Russkie na tikhom okeane vo vtoroi polovine XVIII v. (Moscow: Nauka, 1968), translated by Richard A. Pierce and Alton S. Donnelly as Russians on the Pacific, 1743-1799 (Kingston: The Limestone Press, 1975).

12. One of these manuscripts is in the James Ford Bell Library at the University of Minnesota. For details about it, see John Parker, The Strait of Anian: An Exhibit of Three Maps in the James Ford Bell Collection at the University of Minnesota, Portraying Sixteenth and Eighteenth Century Concepts of the Waterway between Asia and America, which is now known as the Bering Strait (Minneapolis: The James F. Bell Book Trust, 1956).

13. Although the area represented on the map includes the area in which it is found, Novaia Zemlia is not shown. See the reproduction of the manuscript map.

14. It has been suggested that because sceptics in the Academy refused to accept his findings, Bering went on a second expedition to "complete" his earlier work. Barratt, Russia in Pacific Waters, pp. 23-24; Frank A. Golder, Bering's Voyages:

An Account of the Efforts of the Russians to Determine the
Relation of Asia and America, 2 vols. (New York: American
Geographical Society, 1922), I, 25. The view that Bering
failed in his first expedition is common and widespread.
"St. Petersburg, however, decided that the results of the
expedition were unsatisfactory, and Bering was given new
instructions defining the scale and the mission of the second
Kamchatka expedition (1733-1743) and the Great Northern Ex-
pedition." Anatoli Sadyrev, "The Russian Columbus," in Soviet
Life, VIII:299 (August, 1981), p. 34.

15. Raymond H. Fisher, Bering's Voyages: Whither and Why (Seattle:
University of Washington Press, 1977), p. 74; Golder, Bering's
Voyages, I, 25.

16. This was the same answer Bering gave in response to Delisle's
question of why he did not go to the east when there were
signs of land there.

17. Barratt, Russia in Pacific Waters, p. 25.

18. As noted in the earlier discussion of the article, at the time
of writing, presumably, it was believed that a more complete
report on the expedition would be published.

19. Barratt, Russia in Pacific Waters, pp. 29-31.

20. Fisher, Bering's Voyages, pp. 136-38. At this time, Delisle
was apparently in good standing with the Admiralty College.
See the discussion of Delisle in the following chapter.

21. Bering had proposed voyages to America and to Japan; he had

added, in his fifth proposal, a statement "If it is considered desirable, it is possible to explore unhindered the northern lands or the coast of Siberia from the mouth of the Ob River to the Enisei and from there to the Lena River. . . . " Fisher, Bering's Voyages, p. 113. He had not suggested mapping the arctic coasts of Siberia, which is what the Admiralty College directed him to do. The Admiralty College wanted to send the Second Kamchatka Expedition to the Pacific Ocean, by sea around Africa, to the East Indies, and then northward. See Barratt, Russia in Pacific Waters, pp. 26-28.

22. The earliest ukaz regarding secrecy for the Second Kamchatka Expedition was dated 2 May 1732; a more complete statement was made on 28 December 1732. Fisher, Bering's Voyages, pp. 144-46.

23. For a short biography of Du Halde, see Eyriès, "Jean-Baptiste Duhalde," in Biographie universelle ancienne et moderne, XII, 182-83.

24. On Anville, see Rossel, "Jean Baptiste Bourguignon d'Anville," in Biographie universelle ancienne et moderne, II, 296-98. Anville (1697-1782) was appointed royal geographer in 1718. The Bering map also appeared in Anville's Nouvel atlas de la Chine (La Haye: H. Scheurleer, 1737), and this is sometimes cited, erroneously, as the first printing of the map.

25. It is easy to make this assumption. For example, Raymond H. Fisher writes: "Du Halde states that he received a copy of

Bering's account and map from the King of Poland; but Albert
Isnard . . . tells us that the Russian Academy suspected
Joseph N. Delisle of having provided the map and document
for the "Relation succincte" and expressed its displeasure
by removing him from the office he then held in the academy."
Fisher, Bering's Voyages, p. 181.

26. M. H. Omont, "Lettres de J.-N. Delisle au Comte de Maurepas
et à l'Abbé Bignon sur les travaux géographiques en Russie
(1726-1730)," in Comité des travaux historique et scientifique,
Bulletin de la Section de Géographie, XXXII (1917), 162.

27. V. G. Churkin, "Atlas Cartography in Prerevolutionary Russia,"
translated by James R. Gibson, in The Canadian Cartographer,
XII:1 (June, 1975), 6-7.

28. Albert Isnard, "Joseph-Nicolas Delisle, sa biographie et sa
collection de cartes géographiques à la Bibliothèque nationale,"
in Comité des travaux historique et scientifique, Bulletin de
la Section de Géographie, XXX (1915), 48. See also the section
on Delisle in the following chapter.

29. Jean Baptiste Du Halde, The General History of China, translated by Richard Brookes, 4 vols. (London: J. Watts, 1736),
IV, 429.

30. See the bibliography for editions of the Du Halde work.

31. I made this composite outline on the basis of maps reproduced
in Leo Bagrow, "The Vitus Bering First Voyage Maps," in
Geografisk Tidsskrift, XLIX (1948-49), 32-40.

32. This map is from _Atlas geograficheskikh otkrytii v Sibiri
    i v severo-zapadnoi Amerike XVII-XVIII vv._, edited by Aleksei V.
    Efimov (Moscow: Nauka, 1964).

33. Bagrow in "The Vitus Bering First Voyage Maps" states that
    the Du Halde printing of the map was closest to a Russian
    manuscript map in Stockholm. (p. 35). This map, however,
    fits the composite map presented here, and the representation
    of the Anadyr River, for example, is much different on this
    map from the one in Du Halde. The similarities between the
    Du Halde map and the early Chaplin map (Efimov no. 63) are
    not only in the general outline, but also in such details as
    the course of the Anadyr River and the contour of the nor-
    thern coast of eastern Siberia.

34. Bering's "Short Account" may have been intended for publica-
    tion, and Bering could well have assumed it would be published.
    At the time, no policy about publication of the results of the
    First Kamchatka Expedition had been formulated, presumably.

35. Delisle was obviously wrong in sending the account and map
    to France, though it seems unlikely that he would have stated
    openly to Maurepas that he hoped to do so, if he had thought
    he was sending a secret journal and map. The idea that Bering
    was sent in search of a northeast passage can be seen as a
    disguise for the real purpose--to go to America--but the
    Russians did not want to raise all the old hopes of an easy
    northeast passage either. The interest that was shown in

western Europe in the northeast passage may well have prompted the decision to keep the results of the First Kamchatka Expedition secret.

36. Ivan Kirilov, the Russian who prepared the first Russian atlas, was by this time much engrossed in administrative duties, and Delisle was the one who prepared a map based on Bering's maps. See the section on Delisle in the following chapter.

37. The manuscript in the Bibliothèque Nationale has written on it, "Traduit du Suedois a Stockholm le 5 febrier 1733 Pour S. E. M^r le Comte de Casteja ambassad. de france." The reference is to Charles Louis de Biaudos, the Count of Casteja.

38. A comparison with the text of the Du Halde printed account indicates that Du Halde did not use the copy translated from the Swedish. These differences are evident in statements about dates, numbers, and places, not just differences in phrasing.

39. Delisle had been in Russia for a decade at the time Du Halde published the Bering account and map. Assuming that the map and account had been sent soon after Bering's return in 1730, they had already been in France for five years.

40. For a biography, see The Rev. Canon Overton, "Edward Cave," in Dictionary of National Biography, IX, 338-40, and C. Lennart Carlson, The First Magazine: A History of the Gentleman's Magazine (Providence: Brown University, 1938).

41. The prospectus for this work was issued in 6,000 copies, as

"Proposals for printing Du Halde's History of China." See
John Nichols, Literary Anecdotes of the Eighteenth Century,
6 vols. (London: 1812-16), V, 44-45. I am grateful for
permission to use material on Cave and his publication of the
Du Halde History of China from a paper presented by Michael
Welch for the University of Minnesota Library School (Library
Science, 8-402, spring quarter, 1981). A copy of this paper
is on file in the James Ford Bell Library.

42. Very little is known about Brookes, aside from his translations of medical, scientific, and geographic works. See G. T.
Bettany, "Richard Brookes," in Dictionary of National Biography, VI, 436.

43. Du Halde, The General History, IV, 429-40.

44. See The Gentleman's Magazine, VII (March, 1737), 150; Ibid.,
VII (June, 1737), 366-67.

45. Jean Baptiste Du Halde, A Description of the Empire of China
and Chinese-Tartary, 2 vols. (London: Edward Cave, 1738-41),
II, 362-64. Cave presumably translated this text himself.
The instructions to Bering appear on page 382.

46. Jean Baptiste Du Halde, Ausführliche Beschreibung des chinesischen Reichs und der grossen Tartarey, 4 vols. (Rostock:
Johann Christian Koppe, 1747-49), IV, 86-93. The translator
of this text was Professor Johann Lorenz Mosheim, of Göttingen
University, who published the Historia tartarum ecclesiastica
in 1741.

47. <u>Ibid</u>., IV, 93. What the translator provides is a sprightly potpourri of speculation, misinformation, and fact about Bering's voyage to America and Steller's part in it.

48. John Harris, <u>Navigantium</u> atque <u>Itinerarium</u> Bibliotheca, Or, <u>A</u> <u>Complete</u> <u>Collection</u> <u>of</u> Voyages <u>and</u> Travels, edited by John Campbell, 2 vols. (London: T. Woodward ₍etc.₎ 1744-48).

49. <u>Ibid</u>., II, a2^{v}. For a biography of Campbell see "John Campbell," in <u>Biographia</u> <u>Britannica</u>, 2nd ed., 5 vols. (London: 1778-93), III, 209-15.

50. Harris, <u>Navigantium</u>, ed. Campbell, II, 1016-41.

51. Russkoe istoricheskoe obshchestvo, <u>Sbornik</u>, CIII (St. Petersburg: 1897), 452.

52. By this time the interest in western Europe was on Bering's and Chirikov's voyages to America, about which little had been published other than the notices that had appeared in newspapers. Bering's First Kamchatka Expedition was well-known through the editions and translations of Du Halde. It is not surprising, therefore, that the account of the first expedition was given to Campbell for publication in his collection of voyages.

53. As will be seen, the text and map printed by Campbell were quite different from the earlier printings in Du Halde. Hyndford states he had obtained a copy of the"original journal" of Bering. The "Short Account" of Bering's voyages has been published many times; Bering's journal has not been

published. See Fisher, Bering's Voyages, pp. 180-83. If Campbell did have a copy of Bering's journal, it must have been close in content to Bering's "Short Account," and it was not surprising that the printed version in Campbell was considered only another copy of the "Short Account."

54. See the maps. The Campbell printing of the Bering map, according to Dall, was "the most perfect yet published." William H. Dall, "A Critical Review of Bering's First Expedition, 1725-1730, Together with a Translation of his Original Report upon it," in The National Geographic Magazine, II (1890), 121-23. Dall believed that Cave's printing of the map "introduced numerous improvements and corrections into the charts of D'Anville, which accompanied the original edition of Du Halde."

55. Ibid., 122. This is further evidence that Campbell was not using the Du Halde map in preparing his map of the expedition.

56. Harris, Navigantium, ed. Campbell, II, 1021.

57. Ibid.

58. Ibid., II, 1020. The text as presented by Campbell is given here in the appendix and in Chapter VII.

59. Ibid., II, 1021.

60. "Lord Hindford, the English Ambassador Extraordinary and Plenipotentiary to Russia, managed to steal the journal and the map of Bering's and Chirikov's expedition." O. M. Medushevskaya, "Cartographic Sources for the History of

Russian Geographical Discoveries in the Pacific Ocean in the
Second Half of the 18th Century," translated by James R.
Gibson, in The Canadian Cartographer, IX:2 (December, 1972),
100.

61. Raymond H. Fisher attempted to locate this manuscript, without
success. See Fisher, Bering's Voyages, pp. 181-82.

62. Harris, Navigantium, ed. Campbell, II, 1022-23.

63. Ibid., II, 1023. Campbell reports on the Bering voyage of
1741, "of which all we know is this, that he sailed Southward to the Isles of Japan, and from thence Eastward about
eighty Leagues. At that Distance from Japan he discovered
Land, which he coasted Northwest, still approaching towards
the North-east Cape, without going ashore until he came to
the Entrance of a great River, where sending his Boats and
Men ashore, they never returned, being either lost, killed,
or detained by the Natives, which made his Discovery incom-
pleat, his Ship being stranded, and he afterwards died in
an uninhabited Island." Ibid., II, 1022-23. This report
is a confused and incomplete mixture of fragments from the
Spanberg, Chirikov, and Bering voyages, and indicates how
little was known in western Europe about them.

64. Campbell maintains that the Russians were concealing the
results of their explorations for their own benefit and concludes "The Russians look upon themselves as in full Possession of that great Secret, so long and so ineffectually

sought by the Northern Maritime Powers, of a short Passage
to the East-Indies and the South-Seas, and that too exclu-
sively of other Nations, from a Persuasion, that by discovering
this Passage, they have discovered also that the North-West
Passage, by which only we could interfere with them, is impracticable." Ibid., II, 1025. Russians had discovered a
great continent in the North Pacific, close to Kamchatka,
and this meant that the northwest passage would be less likely
than ever. Müller's map published in 1754 shows this great
land mass bulging from North America. (See Chapter VII).

65. See A. J. Q. Beuchot, "Jean Louis Barbeau-de-la-Bruyère,"
in Biographie universelle, ancienne, et moderne, III, 335-36.

66. Philip Johann Tabbert von Strahlenberg, Description historique
de l'empire russien, 2 vols. (Amsterdam; Paris: Chez Desaint
& Saillant, 1757), II, 264-310. This text is reproduced in
the appendix.

Chapter VII

Contemporary Reports on the First Kamchatka Expedition

In addition to the printings of Bering's "Short Account" there were other reports about the First Kamchatka Expedition published in various parts of Europe in the eighteenth century. The most important of these came from six individuals who had experience in Russia. Five of them knew Bering personally. Background information about these individuals is given here, to place their comments on the First Kamchatka Expedition in the context of their experience in Russia.

Friedrich Christian Weber

Friedrich Christian Weber, the minister from Hanover who was in Russia from 1714 to 1721, wrote a book on Russia which was extremely popular.[1] Weber showed himself to be flexible and good-humored from the beginning; shortly after his arrival in Russia he was invited to a "magnificent entertainment" at the home of Admiral Fedor Apraksin. Weber dressed in the plain, dark clothing he considered appropriate to his position but found that in order to get in to the party, he had to change to an outfit trimmed in silver and gold and have two footmen go ahead of him shouting "clear the way." At dinner, Weber drank "Hungary wine" and shortly afterwards was given a full quart of brandy. Weber reports "being forced to empty it in two Draughts,

I soon lost my Sense, though I had the Comfort to observe that the rest of the Guests lying already asleep on the Floor, were in no Condition to make Reflexions on my little Skill in drinking."[2] Weber thoroughly enjoyed his seven-year stay in Russia, and he was close to Peter and his associates during that time.

The 1721 edition of Weber's Das veränderte Russland was translated into French and English. In this edition, as noted previously, Weber states his belief that a northeast passage was impossible because Asia and America were connected by land in the north. Revised and enlarged editions of Weber's book were published in Germany in the late 1730s, including commentary on events which occurred after Weber left Russia. These were not translated into other languages.[3]

An account of Bering's First Kamchatka Expedition appeared in the later editions of Weber's book. Weber writes that Bering was sent on his expedition in order to find out if Asia was connected to America, or if there was a sea passage between them. The account of the Bering expedition is almost a verbatim printing of the article in the 16 March 1730 issue of Sanktpeterburgskiia Vedomosti.[4] At the end of the article, where the statement appears that Bering's return journey from Okhotsk to St. Petersburg took almost six months, Weber writes: "This Captain Bering, whom I knew personally, was six months on his return journey. . . ."[5] By adding this parenthetical phrase, Weber gave his account an added touch of authenticity, as it could be interpreted to mean that

Weber talked to Bering after the First Kamchatka Expedition.[6]

Weber probably did meet Bering at some time while Weber was in Russia--
perhaps even at that first memorable dinner at Apraksin's house--
but Weber did not talk to Bering after the First Kamchatka Expedition. Weber was not in Russia after 1721. Thus Weber's
account, which placed the purpose of the First Kamchatka Expedition as a search for a northern sea passage, was given the
status of a firsthand report, when all Weber had said was that he
had known Bering.

After giving the text from the Sanktpeterburgskiia Vedomosti,
Weber provided a historical background for the First Kamchatka
Expedition. According to Weber, the impetus for the expedition
dated back to the time when Tsar Alexis exiled a Polish officer,
Fedor Kozyrevskii, to Siberia. Fedor's son Peter and grandson
Ivan were with the military forces that brought Kamchatka under
Russian rule, and in the years 1711 and 1714 Peter the Great
ordered Ivan Kozyrevskii to gather information about the northeastern part of Kamchatka, particularly about the "nos" or cape
in the northeast. For years Ivan Kozyrevskii sent reports to
Peter, even after 1718 when Ivan became a monk, Ignatius. The
reports were the basis for Peter's great interest in the northeastern part of Siberia and were the reason Peter sent Bering
to explore there. These reports had convinced Peter the Great
and his successors to search for a sea passage to Japan, China,
and the East Indies. If the attempt to discover the sea passage

would be successful, Weber concludes, Russia would gain far more by discovery than could be won by conquest.[7]

Peder von Haven

A Dane, Peder von Haven (1715-1757), was the author of two books in which notices about Bering's expeditions appear.[8] Haven went to Russia for the first time in 1736, when he was twenty-one. Trained as a theologian, Haven took an appointment in Russia to serve as secretary and pastor to his countryman, Peter Bredal, who had served in the Russian Navy since 1703.[9] During part of the three years Haven was first in Russia, Bredal commanded the Azov fleet in actions against Turkey, and thus Haven traveled to the south of Russia. Haven left Russia in 1739, and in 1743 he published a book based on his travels there, the Reise udi Rusland. This book was translated from Danish for a German edition in 1744. Since Bredal knew Bering well, the notice Haven gives (which may have come from Bredal) is intriguing. Haven writes about two caravan routes, one to Kamchatka and the other to China. Kamchatka, he notes, was almost unknown until Bering was sent there to learn about it. Bering spent the first years in Kamchatka studying the language, and then came back with a full report. Bering went to Kamchatka again as governor and built a colony there and a seaport. He built ships, with which he explored the Kamchatka coasts, searching for a route to China and Japan.[10] This account obviously has several errors, but it does identify one important aspect of the

Bering expeditions: the importance the Bering expedition had for establishing Russian control over eastern Siberia.[11]

Haven was agin in Russia from 1743 to 1746, this time to St. Petersburg as chaplain to a Danish diplomatic mission. In 1747, Haven published the Nye og forbedrede efterraetningar om det Russiske rige. Inserted in volume two of this work is a summary of Bering's first expedition, a short statement about Spanberg's voyage to Japan, and a report on Bering's voyage to America. The last was taken from an official document submitted to the Admiralty Office by Sven Waxell, a Swede who sailed with Bering in the Second Kamchatka Expedition. Waxell, as first officer of Bering's ship, the St. Peter, took command of the ship when Bering was ill, and after Bering's death was the officer in charge. He sent his report to the Admiralty College in November, 1742.[12] The publication of this document was illegal. Haven writes: "Both Bering's and Spanberg's daily journals are inserted in my Efterraetningar. I got these rare writings from Captain Spanberg himself."[13]

Morton Spanberg (1698-1761) headed the part of the Second Kamchatka Expedition charged with discovering a route to Japan. He sailed from Okhotsk in June, 1738, and explored the Kurile Islands. In 1739 Spanberg sailed again, and this time reached Japan, and traded with the Japanese.[14] News of Spanberg's voyage reached St. Petersburg on 6 January 1740. Reports of Spanberg's voyage appeared in Amsterdam, on a map by "Guillaume Delisle" (dead since 1725) and "Jean Kyrilow" (Ivan Kirilov, who died in 1737).[15] The information recorded on the map was credited to Mr. Swartz, a representative of Holland who was in St. Petersburg. It reports that Spanberg had discovered thirty-four islands. Though the Russians could not understand the language of the people on the islands, the islanders were friendly and had "plenty of gold money."[16]

Similar reports were published in France and Great Britain in 1740.[17] An account in The London Magazine ties Spanberg's discovery to trade, stating that from the islands "it is thought they may sail to Japan, China, and so round to the East Indies, Persia, &c. which will greatly increase the Trade and Commerce of Muscovy."[18] The first of two articles in The Gentleman's Magazine reports "The People, who are almost like the Japanese, shew'd him Gold and Copper Coins, which it seems they have great Plenty of."[19] In the next article about the voyage, a letter from Spanberg is quoted, ending "The Curious will be pleased with the Journal I shall give of my Discoveries, which at the same time will shew the Advantages which the Russians will reap by Trade to China and Japan."[20] The promise of the publication of this journal was not fulfilled, and the Russians could not have been pleased by these unauthorized reports on the activities of the "secret" Second Kamchatka Expedition.[21]

Spanberg was on his way to St. Petersburg to report in person on his discoveries, when he received an order from the Admiralty

College to repeat his voyage. The stated reason was that the Admiralty College, and the Academy, did not believe Spanberg had reached Japan, but only Korea. Spanberg returned to Okhotsk to discover that all supplies there had been appropriated by Bering for the voyage to America. It was 1742 before Spanberg could sail again, on a voyage made in unfit ships. Spanberg did not reach Japan on this voyage.[22]

Spanberg was annoyed and frustrated, when he had to repeat his voyage and in 1745 he left Siberia without permission, to go to St. Petersburg. For this Spanberg was court-martialled, and sentenced to death, a sentence later commuted to a reduction in rank for three months. Spanberg was assisted with his case by the Danish ambassador in St. Petersburg, and it was during this time, presumably, that Haven met Spanberg.[23]

Spanberg gave Haven an official account of Bering's voyage to America (a voyage he had not participated in), a short account of the voyage to Japan (no more, really, than what had appeared in the newspapers), plus some information on the First Kamchatka Expedition. He did not give his own journal to Haven. Haven's book was little-known in Denmark, and less so outside Denmark, probably fortunately for Spanberg.[24]

The First Kamchatka Expedition, as reported by Haven, was put in the context of a search for a northeast passage. When Bering sailed beyond the latitude of 67° north, according to the report, he "would have to sail through the highest icebergs of the sea

before he could come around the northeast cape of Siberia, where
the northeastern Siberians sometimes hunt and fish during the
summer. However, all these people assured him unanimously that
such a voyage from the Samoyed land at Archangel around the cape
and down to Kamchatka had really been undertaken by wayfaring
people, among whom most had lost their lives during the course
of the voyage, and the rest of them lost their health."[25] Concerned for the safety of his men and ship, Bering turned south
again. In this account, the assertion is not that a voyage
had been made from the Lena River or the Kolyma River to Kamchatka,
but from Archangel to Kamchatka.

Haven's statement about Bering's instructions, since it came
from Spanberg, is of interest. Haven reports that Bering's purpose
was "to explore the situation of Kamchatka in relation to other
lands."[26] In the context of Haven's statements about the northeast passage, this statement can be seen as an order to search
for such a passage, but this statement is very close to the purpose
of the First Kamchatka Expedition identified in this study.

Johann Georg Gmelin

In 1751-52 the four volumes of Johann Georg Gmelin's Reise
durch Sibirien were published in Göttingen. Gmelin (1709-1755)
was born in Germany and educated as a medical doctor.[27] He joined
the Russian Academy of Sciences, becoming a professor of chemistry
and natural history in 1731. Gmelin was a participant in the
Second Kamchatka Expedition; he was to survey the natural

history of the areas to be explored. Two other members of the Academy also participated: Louis Delisle de la Croyère, the half-brother of Joseph Nicolas Delisle, as astronomer, and Gerhard Friedrich Müller, as historian.

The academic contingent of the Second Kamchatka Expedition reached Tobolsk in January, 1734, where Bering was waiting for them, since De la Croyère and the other surveyors were to begin mapping the arctic coasts. Gmelin and Müller traveled to Tomsk, Eniseisk, and Krasnoyarsk and arrived in Irkutsk on 8 March 1735. They investigated the region around Lake Baikal and spent part of the winter of 1735-36 in Irkutsk. They next went to Ilimsk and in the spring traveled down the Lena River, rejoining Bering at Iakutsk. During the winter of 1736-37 their relations with Bering worsened, for Bering's chief concern was for the naval contingent of the expedition, and the complaints of the academicians about housing, supplies, and transportation were not well received.[28] The two academicians decided not to travel on to Okhotsk with Bering. Instead, they sent the student Stepan Krasheninnikov on an overland journey to Kamchatka to begin studies and preparations pending their own arrival later. Krasheninnikov wrote the first detailed description of Kamchatka, which was published in Russia in 1755.[29]

Gmelin and Müller spent the winter of 1737-38 in Irkutsk and tried to arrange for transportation to Iakutsk to continue the expedition to Kamchatka, without success. With no apparent

possibility of making the journey the following summer, they peti-
tioned to be relieved of further responsibilities with the Second
Kamchatka Expedition. After further explorations in Siberia,
they returned to St. Petersburg in February, 1743.[30]

Gmelin resumed his duties with the Academy, but he was soon
embroiled in quarrels within it. He was not happy at the Academy
and wanted to obtain a position in Germany instead. His relations
with Schumacher were impossible. At last Gmelin obtained a
leave from the Academy to visit Germany. He never returned.[31]

The publication of Gmelin's book about his travels was not
authorized by the Russian government. Concerns were expressed
in Russia when it became known that Gmelin was going to publish
the work. On 22 October/2 November 1751, Johann D. Schumacher
wrote to Leonhard Euler in Berlin, stating he feared Gmelin would
bring misfortune upon himself by the publication. "It would
be better," writes Schumacher, "to suppress this work. Nothing
can be published about the Kamchatka Expedition without first
consulting the Academy."[32] Gmelin had signed an oath to that
effect.

Gmelin acknowledged his oath about the expedition in the
introduction to his book, stating "The least of that is known
to me, and I would commit a punishable offense, if I would make
known to the world the little that is known to me about the sea
voyages, without the highest permission."[33] Gmelin apparently
believed that secrecy should be preserved only about the sea

voyages. His book, a very detailed diary of his travels, includes strong condemnations of the Russian administration in Siberia, particularly for its treatment of the inhabitants.[34] Gmelin denounced Russian officials in Siberia for drunkenness, laziness, greed, incompetence, and wickedness. Readers of it in the Russian Academy of Sciences found much in Gmelin's book that was "excessive, indecent, and suspicious," and not surprisingly, the work was banned in Russia.[35]

In spite of his statement that he could not reveal anything about the sea voyages, in the introduction to his book Gmelin discusses the reasons for Russian maritime explorations.[36] He traces this interest to the visit Peter the Great made to France in 1717, when members of the French Académie des Sciences questioned him about the extent of Siberia and whether or not it was connected to America. There were three ways of finding out, Gmelin writes. The first was to sail eastward along the arctic coast, as the English and Dutch had attempted to do. The Russians tried this under orders of Peter the Great in 1724. For information on this voyage Gmelin refers his readers to the eulogy of Peter published by the Académie des Sciences.[37] The second way was to sail the usual route to the East Indies from Europe, then along California to the north, and on to the north and west to reach the Arctic Ocean. The Russians had not attempted this. The third way was to start from Kamchatka and sail north as far as the land went, to see whether or not Siberia joined America in

the north. This third option was the route Bering followed on
his first expedition.[38]

That was all Gmelin said. In his voluminous book on Siberia,
Gmelin says nothing more about the Russian voyages. He had known
Bering; he had traveled for almost a decade with the Second Kamchatka Expedition. This experience suggests he would have better
knowledge of the sea voyages of the expeditions, and their purposes.
Perhaps he did not, and had confined himself to his studies of
natural history.[39] But on the other hand, he may have been
cautious about further disputes with his former employers in
Russia.[40]

Joseph Nicolas Delisle

Under the terms of his 1725 contract with the Academy,
Delisle was granted permission to send all his astronomical
observations to the Académie des Sciences. But in sending
information to France, Delisle did not limit himself to astronomical observations. During his twenty-two years in Russia,
Delisle sent an immense collection of maps (over four thousand
of them) and manuscripts to France.[41] Since Delisle was preparing maps for an atlas to be published by the Academy of Sciences,
he claimed he needed copies and translations of Russian geographic
materials for his work.[42] Delisle sent many maps to Maurepas,
the Secretary of the Navy, who, in granting Delisle permission
to go to Russia, had done so on the express condition that Delisle
would occupy himself with geographic work from which France could

benefit.[43]

Delisle's practice of sending maps and manuscripts to France did not go unnoticed, but the Russian officials wanted to avoid a public confrontation with him about it. A commission was established to watch him, but its effectiveness was uncertain.[44] In 1739 a Geography Department was established in the Academy of Sciences and Delisle was selected to head it, with the mathematicians Leonhard Euler and I. G. Hensius named to assist him and to try to prevent the sending of more maps to France.[45] The following year Delisle was removed from this position in the Geography Department. His contract with the Academy was renewed in 1745, after extended negotiations, but in May 1747 the contract was broken, and Delisle went back to Paris. Members of the Academy of Sciences were forbidden to correspond with him.[46]

On 8 April 1750, Delisle presented a lecture, "Nouvelles decouvertes au nord de la Mer du Sud," to the Académie des Sciences. Two manuscript maps were used to illustrate the lecture--the map Delisle had prepared for the use of the Second Kamchatka Expedition, and a new map, "Carte des nouvelles découvertes au nord de la Mer du Sud." In 1752 Delisle published his lecture in the form of a pamphlet titled Explication de la carte des nouvelles découvertes au nord de la Mer du Sud, with an accompanying map.[47]

The publication of Delisle's map and pamphlet caused great consternation in Russia, particularly within the Academy of Sciences.[48] Delisle had broken his pledge to maintain secrecy

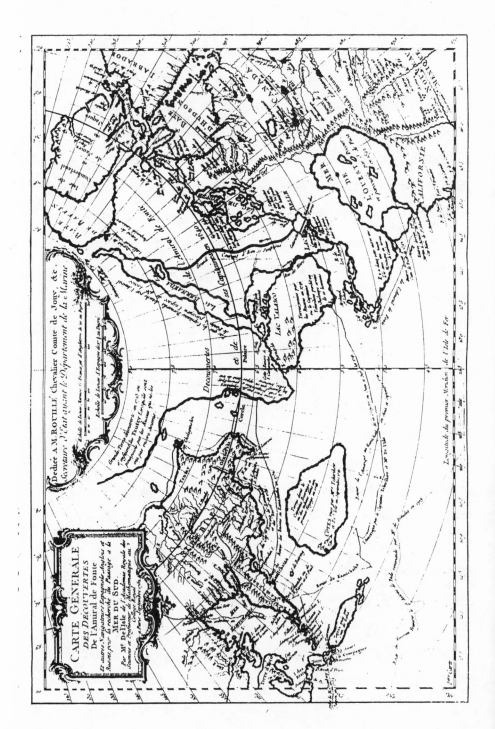

about the Second Kamchatka Expedition.[49] He begins his lecture by
referring to the two-and-a-half centuries of searching for a
northeast or northwest passage by sea to the East. Delisle speaks
of the North Pacific and asserts: "I am now to lay before the
company the discovery of all the countries and seas contained in
it, the knowledge of which I acquired during my long stay in
Russia, and since my return to France."[50] What Delisle presents
may indicate how successful the Admiralty Office had been in
keeping information from Delisle. For example, Delisle does not
state that Bering had reached America; he says Bering was shipwrecked on an island near Kamchatka shortly after he began his
voyage. Delisle's map and pamphlet feature the voyage of Chirikov
to America--or rather, in Delisle's view, the voyage Chirikov
was able to make to America because of the accomplishments of
Delisle's half-brother, Delisle de la Croyère, who sailed with
Chirikov and died just as the ship returned to Kamchatka.[51]
Delisle annoyed readers in Russia by stating that his map of
1731 had been the impetus for the Second Kamchatka Expedition
and that the expedition was formed according to his plans for
it.[52] Delisle further confuses his account of the Russian explorations by incorporating into his pamphlet a comparison of
the explorations with the "voyage" of Bartolome de Fonte, which was
fictitious. Delisle supports the De Fonte voyage on the basis
of the comparison. This resulted in many later publications
on the northwest passage.[53]

In his comments on the First Kamchatka Expedition, Delisle provides some information of importance to this study. He says he had received his earliest information about the longitudes of Kamchatka "near twenty years ago [1730]. . . by means of Captain Beering's map and journal."[54] He had used them in preparing his map of 1731. Thus he had, not only the map of the First Kamchatka Expedition, but Bering's journal as well. Bering, Delisle reports, "told me with his own mouth what he omitted in his accounts, viz. that, in his voyage along the eastern coast of Asia, betwixt the latitude of 50 and 60 degrees, he had all possible indications of a coast, or country, eastward."[55] Here Delisle's obsession with a land near Kamchatka--as presented on his map--is obvious, for in his letter of 25 June 1730 to Maurepas, Delisle states Bering told him of signs of land near the northern termination of his voyage, i.e., near the Chukchi Peninsula.[56]

Delisle says Bering believed he had accomplished his mission on the first voyage when he sailed beyond 67° north latitude, and "perceived the sea free towards the north, and east, and that the coast winded away north-westwards, and had further learned from the inhabitants, that between fifty and sixty years ago, a vessel had arrived at Kamtschatka, from the river Lena."[57] The latter part of this statement echoed the article in the Sankt-peterburgskiia Vedomosti.

Did Delisle know anything more about the Russian explorations? In his lecture he states he was going to begin publication of "all my geographical, astronomical, and physical collections;

and shall successively give new maps of Russia, both general and

particular. . . ."[58] He published no more maps of Russia, either

because he was slow in getting maps done (a charge made against

him in Russia), or because he had no further information (which

seems unlikely because of the immense collection of maps he had

amassed).[59]

Gerhard Friedrich Müller

The response to Delisle's Explication was not long in forth-

coming. The Academy of Sciences felt obliged to respond to it,

and Müller did so in the form of an anonymous work, Lettre d'un

Officier de la Marine russienne, which appeared in French and

German editions in 1753.[60] It was translated into English and

published in 1754, together with Delisle's Explication.[61]

Years had passed since Delisle and Müller were young colleagues

at the Academy, awaiting Bering's return from the First Kamchatka

Expedition. For Müller those years had been filled with experi-

ences which made him uniquely qualified to write about the Bering

expeditions.

Müller left Russia in August, 1730, to settle family business

matters in Germany following the death of his father. He also

traveled to Holland and England on behalf of the Academy. When

he returned to St. Petersburg in August, 1731, he found that

Schumacher's attitude toward him had changed completely, from

warm friendship to deep hatred. Müller later writes: "I deemed

it necessary to enter upon another learned field--that was
Russian history, which I intended not only to study industri-
ously myself but to make known in compositions from the best
sources."[62]

Plans for the Second Kamchatka Expedition were in progress.
Ivan Kirilov, Senior Secretary of the Administrative Senate, had
drawn up a memorandum on the expedition and had had it translated
into German for presentation to Ernst-Johann Biron, the favorite
of Empress Anna.[63] He had chosen a bad translator, however.
Bering suggested that Kirilov should have the translation redone
by Müller. "In this way," Müller states, "I got to know Kirilov,
whose acquaintance was not to remain without consequences."[64]

In the winter of 1732-33, Gmelin became ill "in the region
of the liver" and withdrew as a participant in the expedition.
In Müller's words, "Captain-commander Bering, with whom I had
close relations, had aroused in me the desire for this journey
even before there was any hope for me to go."[65] Bering told
this to Kirilov, who advised Müller to apply for Gmelin's place.
Müller was accepted. He writes: "I was glad, because in this way
I was removed from the confused condition of the Academy for a
long time, and was far from the hatred and hostility. . . ."[66]
Gmelin recovered from his illness, a recovery Müller ascribed
to Rhine wine, and Gmelin and Müller both participated in the
Second Kamchatka Expedition.

When Müller returned to St. Petersburg in February, 1743,

he found Schumacher hated him as much as ever.[67] Like Gmelin, Müller was soon embroiled in quarrels within the Academy. Müller got into difficulties over maps, too. In 1744, when he saw some of the maps for the Russian _Atlas_ to be published in 1745, he offered a number of suggestions for corrections of them. These suggestions were not welcome, and Müller began working on his own maps, a general map of Russia and a map of Siberia.[68]

Müller presented his maps to the Academy on 3 March 1746, but was told that he could not publish them without the permission of Empress Elizabeth, since they included information from the Second Kamchatka Expedition.[69] Instead of permission, on 7 April 1746 the following order was received: "Her Imperial Majesty has ordered that the charts relating to the Kamchatka Expedition in the possession of the Academy, rough drafts and clean copies, as well as those made on post-paper, all that exist, written or printed, nothing omitted, likewise the reports and descriptions from this same expedition recently sent to the Academy by Adjunct Steller, of whatever kind they may be, as well as lists of the things sent by him, be brought to Her Imperial Majesty's Cabinet the next day in the morning. . . ."[70] The government was particularly concerned about the materials from Steller (see the later commentary on Steller). Müller made a list of the maps and materials the Academy had and delivered it, with the materials, in person the next day.[71] The government's concern about maps of the Second Kamchatka Expedition was not unfounded, for a map based on the expedition was published in Nuremberg by the Homann publishing firm in 1746.[72] A similar one--though undated--appeared in Amsterdam at approximately the same time.[73] If the government had been aware of these maps, the departure of Delisle from the Academy in 1747 and subsequent actions toward Müller are not surprising, as they would have been suspected of supplying these maps to the foreign publishers.[74]

Müller's new contract of 1747 made him the "historiographer of the Russian Empire." He was told to confine his work to history of Siberia and a general history of Russia. He was forbidden to make any more maps or to have access to the Geography Department of the Academy. In January, 1748, Müller became a Russian citizen. In the fall of that year he was accused of corresponding with Delisle. His papers were confiscated, and he was subjected to house arrest and reduced to the rank of adjunct to the Academy.[75]

Müller's work in history was criticized. A lecture he prepared on the place of the Varangians in Russian history was the subject of controversy and resulted in a long investigation.[76] The first volume of his history of Siberia was received in the Academy without enthusiasm: "It has been noticed that in the first volume of the Siberian History which is already printed, the greater part of the book is nothing but a copy from official records, and otherwise the book would not have the proper size. . . ."[77] At a meeting of the Academy, Müller was accused

Redrawing of the Georg Moritz Lowitz map of 1746, courtesy of the University of Kansas Libraries.

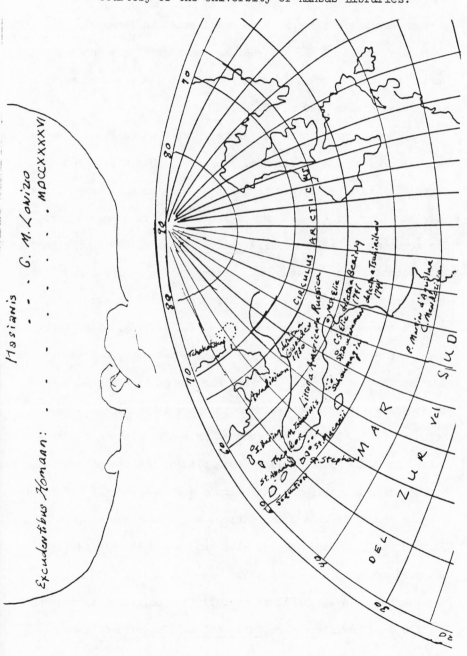

of feigning illness in order to be relieved of his duties with
the Second Kamchatka Expedition.[78] It should be noted that the
actions against Müller may have originated, in large measure,
as much a result of the anti-German feelings in the Academy
during the period following the reign of the Empress Anna, as
a personal attack against Müller.[79]

Müller's fortunes in the Academy improved in 1751, when he
was restored to the position of professor. His maps were returned to him in 1752, and he began to work on a history of the
Russian discoveries and a map of them.[80] He was named to write
the rebuttal to Delisle's Explication, which he did in one month.
This rebuttal was the anonymous Lettre, which Müller based largely
on the report made to the Admiralty Office by Sven Waxell.[81]

In the Lettre, Müller notes that Delisle's problems with
the Academy were well known, for Delisle had not produced on time
the maps he was expected to make, and the publication of the
Academy's Atlas of 1745 was made in spite of Delisle's work, not
because of it. He had been removed from his position as "mapmaker" in 1740. Ivan Kirilov, not Delisle, was the pioneer of
mapmaking in Russia. The map Delisle had made was not the impetus
for the Second Kamchatka Expedition, which had been planned before
Delisle made the map. Müller also had seen "with his own eyes" that
the work of Delisle de la Croyère was questionable, to say
the least.[82] In sum, Müller carefully and politely discredited
Delisle, and devastated the Explication. In spite of this

rebuttal, Delisle's pamphlet and map set off a new interest,
represented in a number of publications, in the old question of
northeast or northwest passages.

About the First Kamchatka Expedition, Müller writes: "What
I advance here, is no more than I have often heard from Mr.
Beering himself, nay, whose instructions I myself have seen,
which were as follows: Firstly, To make the best of his way to
Kamtschatka, and there to build two small vessels. Secondly,
With these to reconnoitre the furthest northern part of the
eastern coasts of Siberia, and to see whether in any part they
joined with America. Thirdly, Afterwards to enquire on the
American coasts after some European settlements and plantations,
or to try whether he could not meet with a ship, to learn the
names, and the bearings of the coasts. Fourthly, To draw up an
exact account of all his proceedings and observations, and then
to return to St. Petersburgh."[83] In this English translation,
at least, Müller's version of the instructions supports the
idea that Bering was sent to explore the coasts of Siberia and
therefore reflects the traditional interpretation of the purpose
of the voyage. However, Müller continues, Bering turned back
on the first voyage because "he perceived the coast to stretch
away to the west, in the manner as some of the inhabitants, who
came aboard his ship, had before informed him; from whence he
had concluded that there could be no continent, by which Asia
and America were joined. . . ."[84] Here the emphasis has

shifted. Bering, according to this latter statement was not looking for a sea passage, but a "continent" that connected Asia and America.[85]

Müller states that the coast did not go westward, as the inhabitants had reported, for there was a cape called "Serdtse Kamen" westward on the coast, and west of that, the great Chukchi Promontory, which went to the northwards to between 70 and 71 degrees north. Delisle's statement that Bering had been told about a voyage from the Lena River to Kamchatka was not true, Müller says, since news of this had only been discovered when one of the academicians of the Second Kamchatka Expedition (Müller) discovered the report--Bering certainly did not have any information about the voyage during the First Kamchatka Expedition! (Müller makes this assertion in spite of the statement in the Sanktpeter-burgskiia Vedomosti.)[86]

Müller, in the Lettre, denies any possibility of a northeast passage. The explorations undertaken during the Second Kamchatka Expedition proved it was impossible. "From so many unfortunate voyages, it may well be concluded what account is to be made of the passage through the Frozen-sea, which the English and Dutch formerly attempted with so much zeal and eagerness . . . after all, which of us are more likely to succeed in such an attempt, they, or we Russians, who are more inured to cold and fatigue than the former, and are able to bear the want of a thousand things, and who, though powerfully supported, yet failed in our enterprizes. To what purpose then are all these charges and labours of so many trials? Why, it is to find a shorter cut to the Indies, a considerable advantage I own, were one not obliged to go through a severe winter of three or four months by the way; after all, the nearest way to the East-Indies is to be found only on our maps and globes." [87]

Müller continued his work in Russian history and on the Russian voyages.[88] In 1754 a map of the North Pacific was prepared for the Academy of Sciences by Ivan Truscott, under Müller's supervision.[89] This same map, with slight modifications, was published in 1758, the same year that Müller's account of the Russian voyages was printed.[90] About the First Kamchatka Expedition, Müller concludes: "Capt. Bering went to sea, from the mouth of the river Kamtschatka, on the 20th of July . . . and steered North East, generally in sight of the coast of Kamtschatka; his chief endeavour was to describe this coast as exactly as possible upon a map, in which he succeeded pretty well, at least we have none better than his."[91] Müller states that Bering had not proved America and Asia were not joined in the north but only thought he had. The proof of that, Müller asserts, resulted from his own studies in the archives at Iakutsk in 1736-37! What Bering had been unable to do by sea, Müller had accomplished in the discovery of a manuscript describing a voyage from the Kolyma River to the Anadyr River in Kamchatka, made in 1648 by the cossack Semen Ivanovich Dezhnev.[92]

Georg Wilhelm Steller

Georg Wilhelm Steller (1709-1746) was born in Germany. He studied for the Lutheran ministry at Wittenberg University, then transferred, in 1731, to Halle University to study medicine. He joined Russian service as an army physician and then went to St. Petersburg, where he acted as an assistant to Johann Amman, a botanist with the Academy of Sciences. Steller became a member of the Academy in 1736. In 1738, when Gmelin asked to be released from participation in the Second Kamchatka Expedition, Steller took his place. Steller went to Okhotsk in 1740 and traveled with Bering to Kamchatka.[93]

Bering and the expedition went to Kamchatka and founded the port of Petropavlovsk.[94] On 4 May 1741, Bering called a council to determine the route to be followed on the voyage. Participants in the council included, besides Bering, his second-in-command, Aleksei Chirikov, Bering's other officers, and Louis Delisle de la Croyère. On the basis of the council and the confidence expressed in the accuracy of the map of Joseph N. Delisle, a route to Da Gama Land was selected.[95] The two ships, with Bering in the St. Peter and Chirikov in the St. Paul, sailed on 4 June 1741 to the southeast. They reached the latitude of 46° 5' on 13 June, which should have brought them to Da Gama Land. No signs of land were evident. The ships next went north for a week, and on 20 June they were separated.[96]

Bering directed his course eastward on 25 June, and Alaska

was sighted between 58° and 59° north latitude on 16 July.
Bering followed a northwesterly course along the land, searching
for a suitable anchorage. The ship anchored 20 July, at an
island the Russians named St. Elias. Steller went to shore, and
did all he could to survey the natural history of the island in
the short time he was allowed to remain there. Steller was out-
raged when he learned that Bering's main concern was to fill the
water casks for the homeward journey. The ship sailed by the
Kodiak Islands. When the officers of the St. Peter met on 10
August to discuss continuing the explorations, twenty-six of the
seventy-six crew members of the St. Peter were ill with scurvy.[97]

Because of shifting winds, the St. Peter sailed an erratic
course, so it was 29 August before the Shumagin Islands, named
for one of the crew who died there, were reached. By this time
Bering was too weak to command, and Lieutenant Waxell was in
charge of the St. Peter. The ship's boats were sent to shore
for water, and one of them was nearly lost in an encounter with
the islanders, who tried to detain the boat. The Russians fired
muskets to frighten them off. Much to Steller's disgust, the
barrels were filled with brackish water.

By early September the health of the crew was so precarious
that discussions began about seeking a place to winter, but the
officers set their hopes on reaching Kamchatka. Strong variable
winds prevented good progress, and a storm near the end of September nearly destroyed the ship. There was more discussion of

235

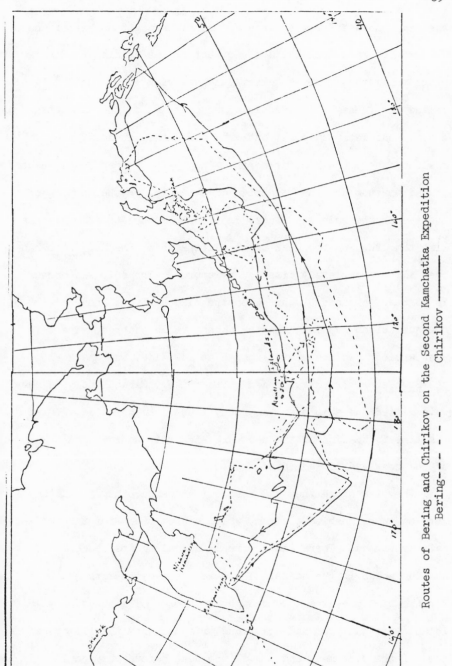

Routes of Bering and Chirikov on the Second Kamchatka Expedition

Chirikov ——————

Bering — - — - —

seeking a harbor for the winter. October brought no better weather
By 22 October, Waxell had decided that it was crucial to find a
place to winter. On 5 November land was sighted. The St. Peter
sailed into a bay. The Russians hoped it was on the Kamchatka
coast, near Petropavlovsk, but from a sighting at noon, they
realized they were too far north. They left the bay, but because
of bad weather and the condition of the ship, on the morning of
6 November the ship's officers decided to return to it. By this
time the crew was too weak to handle the ship; the St. Peter had
been almost completely disabled by storms. The ship was anchored
in sight of a sandy beach. When the tide went out, however,
the surf began running, and the anchor cable snapped. The ship
was carried toward a reef, exposed at low tide, and the keel of
the St. Peter struck submerged rocks twice. Miraculously, a huge
wave lifted the ship over the rocky reef, into quiet water. At
the time forty-nine of the men were sick with scurvy, and twelve
of the crew had already died.[98]

They had hoped they had reached Kamchatka; they found they
were on an uninhabited island, which had no trees for firewood--
only driftwood. There was a stream, and along its banks foxes
had dug holes in the banks. These were converted into quarters
for the sick men, who were brought to shore. The foxes on this
island were numerous and bold, and tried to gnaw the fingers and
toes of the sick men, and ate at the dead before they could be
buried. Steller says he killed over seventy foxes with an axe

in three hours one time, but that did not stop them from coming
to the camp, or make them less aggressive. He writes: "They crowded
into our dwellings and stole everything they could carry away,
including articles that were of no use to them, like knives,
sticks, bags, shoes, socks, caps. . . . While skinning sea ani-
mals it often happened that we stabbed two or three foxes with our
knives because they wanted to tear the meat from our hands."[99]
On 28 November, a week after the last of the sick men had been
taken off the St. Peter, the ship's cables broke in a storm, and
the ship was wrecked on the beach near the camp on shore. On 8
December 1741, Vitus Jonassen Bering died on this island, later
named for him. He was sixty years old.

The men spent the winter keeping warm, when they could, and
eating the food the island provided. Scurvy subsided among them,
to be replaced by what Steller considered to a worse plague--
gambling. In the card games, sea otter pelts served as money.
The following summer a vessel was constructed from the wreckage
of the St. Peter, and in it the survivors of the St. Peter,
forty-nine men, reached Kamchatka on 27 August 1742. They brought
with them a fortune in sea otter pelts.[100]

In 1743 several reports on Bering's voyage to America were
published in western Europe.[101] A notice in the Gazette de France
states: "Captain Bering, who went to make an attempt to find out
whether one could go to America by way of the Arctic Sea [Mer du
Nord] was wrecked on the coast of an island, and the captain

with the larger part of the crew died there. Steller, the botanist
of the Academy, and several sailors were fortunate enough to
resist the disease and from the wreck of the big boat built a
smaller one, on which they returned to Kamchatka. Steller says
that he met Captain Tscherikov who told him that he had been on
the coast of some unknown country whose inhabitants resemble
the Americans. But when he attempted to land he was repulsed
by the Americans, and after losing several soldiers and sailors,
he had to give it up."[102] An article in the Gentleman's Magazine
also cited Steller as its source.[103]

At the time these reports were written, Steller had not yet
even begun his homeward journey but was still exploring Kamchatka
and describing its natural history during his overland
journey to Bolcheretsk. In the summer of 1744 Steller sailed
from Kamchatka to Okhotsk and then continued his journey, arriving
in Iakutsk in October. A letter from Germany written by his
brother Augustin, which Steller received there in March 1745,
informed him that accounts in newspapers made him a hero for his
part in the Bering expedition.[104]

Steller was concerned, since the notices ascribed to him
could be viewed as a breach of his pledge of secrecy about the
Second Kamchatka Expedition. He felt the articles were the work
of his enemies.[105] Steller had made many enemies, including the na
officials in Kamchatka; he further complicated his situation when
he became intoxicated at a party at Irkutsk and accused Governor

Lorenz Lange of treason. Steller apologized the next day, and both seemed pleased to drop the matter.[106]

Steller reached Verkoturye in March, 1746, after a rapid journey, but then slowed his pace and enjoyed a spring visit at Solikamsk, with Grigorii Demidov, who was an amateur botanist. Once again Steller started toward St. Petersburg but changed his mind and went back to Solikamsk. On 16 August, Steller was arrested there and ordered to go back to Irkutsk to face charges. At the time, Professor Eberhard Fischer, the historian who was on his way to Siberia as Müller's replacement, was in Solikamsk. Steller entrusted his plants to Demidov, his writings to Fischer. He was already well on his journey to Irkutsk when word came that he was cleared of all charges. But Steller did not reach St. Petersburg again, for he died of a fever, at Tiumen, on 21 November 1746.[107]

No report of Steller's death was forwarded by the Academy or the government to his family. Augustin learned of his brother's death from a newspaper article. He wrote to correspondents in St. Petersburg and received no satisfactory answers to his questions. Then Augustin wrote a biography of his brother, in which he suggested that Steller's death was due to evil plottings of his enemies in Russia and that the secrecy of the government about the expedition proved it.[108] The Russian government felt obliged to reply. The response was in the form of an anonymous pamphlet of thirty-eight pages, titled Leben Herrn Georg Wilhelm Stellers,

published in Frankfurt in 1748. The author of it was almost
certainly Gerhard Friedrich Müller.[109]

Steller's "collected notes" were published, without authorization, in 1774, as Beschreibung von dem Lande Kamtschatka. The
editor, Jean-Benoit Scherer, added a biography of Steller to the
book. Scherer states he had learned, on good authority, that
Steller died while his sledge driver was drinking in a tavern,
leaving the sick Steller outside to freeze to death.[110] This
publication, based on a text obtained by Scherer from Fischer,
caused annoyance in Russia, of course.[111]

Steller's journal of the American voyage is a priceless
historical record of it. It also reveals that Steller was a
difficult person to deal with. At the beginning of the voyage,
Bering and Steller were close friends. Later, Steller quarreled
with Bering and with the other officers of the ship. His journal
indicates that Steller considered himself to be an authority
on almost everything--including navigation--and this trait
made him many enemies on board the St. Peter. In spite of his
quarrels with Bering, Steller provides this estimate of Bering:
"Vitus Bering was by birth a Dane, a righteous and devout Christian,
whose conduct was that of a man of good manners, kind, quiet,
and universally liked by the whole command, both high and low. . . .
As is well known, the late lamented was not born to quick decisions
and swift action; however, in view of his fidelity, dispassionate
temper, and circumspect deliberateness, the question remains

whether another with more fire and heat would have overcome equally
well the innumerable difficulties of and obstacles to his task . . .
The only blame which can be laid against this excellent man is
that by his too lenient command he did as much harm as his sub-
ordinates by their too impetuous and often thoughtless action.
He also had a somewhat too high esteem for his officers and too
good an opinion of their intelligence and experience, and as a
result they finally became too conceited, looked with contempt
on all those near them and finally on the commander himself, and
forgot their subordination, without thought of gratitude."[112]

What did Steller report about the First Kamchatka Expedition?
In the work published by Scherer, this report appears:"Bering's
instructions were to find out, 1. How far to the east is America
situated from the farthest northeastern border of Kamchatka? 2.
Whether such in the north, toward the Chukchi Promontory
(called by the ancients Promontorium Tabin) is not adjacent to,
or even, as many assume, connected by land to America. Bering,
according to the Scherer edition of Steller's journal, made his
first voyage "without having discovered anything at all."[113]

Steller's journal of the American voyage was published again
in 1793, edited by Peter Simon Pallas, a German naturalist in
Russia.[114] Pallas said he received a copy of Steller's manuscript
of his journal from Fischer.[115] This version, translated by
Frank A. Golder, includes the following: "The great monarch
Peter I, of glorious memory, was influenced by the discovery

of Kamchatka as well as by the representations of the Paris
Academy of Sciences to cause an investigation to be made, by
sending out the then Captain Bering in 1725, as to how far
America is distant from Kamchatka, the extreme northeastern
corner of the Empire, or whether it ₍America₎ might not in
the north be nearer to the extreme Chukchi headland, which
the old map makers called Promontorium Tabin, or even be
continuous with the latter."[116]

The problem with both these translations, of course, is
in Peter's second instruction. Both translations of the first
indicate that Peter did not send Bering to explore Kamchatka,
but to explore the sea between Kamchatka and America, which
agrees with the recent thesis that Peter knew Kamchatka
and America were separated, and therefore can be seen as
support for contenders that Bering was meant to go to America.

Golder, in his translation of the second instruction, added
after "it" the bracketed "America." In doing so, Golder makes his
version of the instructions closer to the meaning of them
proposed in this study, but destroys the similarity by the
phrase "or even be continuous with the latter," since "the
latter" refers to "the extreme Chukchi headland."[117] If the
insertion for "it" is "Kamchatka" we are back to the old thesis
that Bering was sent to explore northeastern Kamchatka.

If Peter had meant either Kamchatka or America in this
phrase, why didn't he say so? It would have been far less

awkward, and clear to Bering (and to historians). He did not,
I believe, because he was not referring to either Kamchatka or
to America, but to the land marked "Incognita" on the Homann
world map--the land without a name. Peter had a particular idea
of the geography of the North Pacific, one which was placed
on a map by Homann and was understood by Bering. In the
translations of Peter's instructions, the meaning is clear
if the insertion is "the unknown land." The instructions
were not clear, even to Bering's contemporaries, without the
Homann map on which they were based.

Steller stresses how easy it would have been for Bering
to have gone to America on his first voyage, and states that
it was not the fault of the expedition that they didn't see
America, since the fog prevented it. He concludes: "Upon
the return of Captain Bering the curious world received nothing
more, than a map and a defective account of the already-known
land of Kamchatka, besides some oral accounts of the Anadyr
cossacks, according to whom the Chukchi Promontory is really
separated from America by open sea. . . ."[118]

Unfortunately, this assessment of the First Kamchatka
Expedition is one that was widely accepted and has been per-
petuated by the misunderstanding of Peter the Great's orders
to Bering. It was Bering's misfortune that he tried to follow
Peter's orders about the unknown land on Homann's map exactly.
By sailing as far east as he had, Bering and his officers

were convinced that they had sailed around the unknown land
and had discovered that it was not joined to America. Bering
therefore was later criticized for not doing what he was not
instructed to do. He had not discovered a northeast passage.
Peter, by the time he sent Bering on the voyage, was clearly
convinced that a northeast passage, at least one from Archangel
to Kamchatka, was not feasible. From earlier Russian
explorations, Peter knew that Kamchatka was not connected
to America. Bering had not gone to America, and for that
he has been criticized. But Bering had no instructions to
go to America, unless the unknown land on the Homann map
joined to America. Bering believed he had fulfilled his orders
when he discovered it was not part of America.

Bering's achievements in the First Kamchatka Expedition
were real: he mapped and explored Kamchatka north to the
easternmost extremity of Siberia. He reported on Russian
administration of Siberia and made recommendations for improving
it. The First Kamchatka Expedition was an initial step in
Russian expansion to America, a beginning which Bering himself
built upon in the Second Kamchatka Expedition. How that
expedition was reported in western Europe is another fascinating
story, one which calls for further study--in another place.

Footnotes

Chapter VII

1. See the bibliography for editions and translations of Weber's book, which is an extremely valuable firsthand account of Peter's reign. In Massie's words, Weber "was a dignified, relatively open-minded man who admired Peter and was interested in everything he saw, although he saw some things of which he did not approve." Robert K. Massie, Peter the Great: His Life and World (New York: Alfred A. Knopf, 1980), p. 613.

2. Friedrich Christian Weber, The Present State of Russia, 2 vols. (London: W. Taylor, 1723), I, 5.

3. See the bibliography for the later German editions of Weber's book. Only the first German edition, printed in 1721, was translated into other languages.

4. Friedrich Christian Weber, Das veränderte Russland, 3 vols. in 1 (Frankfurt und Leipzig: Nicolai Försters und Sohnes seel. Erben, 1744), III, 157-58.

5. Ibid., III, 158. "Dieser Capitain Behring, den ich persönlich kennen lernen, hat auf seiner Rückrise bis nach Moscau sechs Monate. . . zugebracht."

6. Golder lists this work in "Near-Contemporary Accounts of Bering's Expeditions" and notes that Weber "knew and associated with Bering." Frank A. Golder, Bering's Voyages: An Account of the Efforts of the Russians to Determine the Relation of Asia and

America, 2 vols. (New York: American Geographical Society, 1922-25), I, 362.

7. Weber, _Das veränderte Russland_, III, 159-60. On Ivan Kozyrevskii, see George Alexander Lensen, _The Russian Push Toward Japan: Russo-Japanese Relations, 1697-1875_ (Princeton: Princeton University Press, 1959), pp. 31-35.

8. For a biography of Haven, see Bjørn Konerup (A. Jantzen), "Peder v. Haven," in _Dansk Biografisk Leksikon_, IX, 478.

9. Th. Topsøe-Jensen (C. F. Bricka), "Peter Christian Bredal," in _Dansk Biografisk Leksikon_, IV, 48-49.

10. Peder von Haven, _Reise in Russland_ (Copenhagen: Gabriel Christia Rothe, 1744), pp. 474-75.

11. "While the First Kamchatka Expedition (1725-29) of Bering revealed the underdeveloped state of the Okhotsk Seaboard and the Kamchatka Peninsula, the Second Kamchatka Expedition (1733-42) of Bering and Chirikov ameliorated this condition through the construction and peopling of new facilities and the discovery of new fur resources." James R. Gibson, _Feeding the Russian Fur Trade: Provisionment of the Okhotsk Seaboard and the Kamchatka Peninsula, 1639-1856_ (Madison: The University of Wisconsin Press, 1969), p. 13.

12. This report was translated by Golder, who was unaware of Haven's printing of it. Frank A. Golder, _Bering's Voyages_, I, 270-81. Haven's printing of the text was translated by Leonhard Stejneger, "An Early Account of Bering's Voyages"

in *The Geographical Review*, XXIV:4 (October, 1934), 638-42.
Stejneger had not consulted Haven's other writings, and was
not sure that Spanberg was the source of the text. Waxell's
own full account of the voyage, which was written prior to
1756, was not published until this century (see the bibliography).

13. Peder von Haven, *Reise udi Rusland* (Sorøe: Jonas Lindgren,
    1757), pp. 489-90. (This portion of the text translated by
    Mariann Tiblin). Haven says he got the accounts in 1746,
    when Spanberg was under arrest. He writes that "now" (in
    1757) Spanberg was dead, but Spanberg did not die until 1762.
    See Kaj Birket-Smit, "Morten Spangberg," in *Dansk Biografisk*
    Leksikon, XXII, 329-30. (Note that this name is often spelled
    "Spangberg" as well as "Spanberg.")

14. On the Spanberg voyages, see Lensen, *The Russian Push*, pp.
    46-60.

15. A copy of this map is included in Guillaume Delisle's *Atlas*
    nouveau, contenant toutes les parties du monde . . . (Amster-
    dam: Covens et Mortier ₍1741?₎). The source of it may have
    been Joseph Nicolas Delisle, who had worked with Ivan Kirilov
    on Russian maps. On Kirilov, see Mariia G. Novlianskaia,
    Ivan Kirilovich Kirilov: geograf XVIII veka (Leningrad: Nauka,
    1964).

16. The legend on this map is given in French and Dutch and was
    translated into English in John Harris, *Navigantium atque*

Itinerarium Bibliotheca, Or, A Complete Collection of Voyages
and Travels, edited by John Campbell, 2 vols. (London: T.
Woodward ₍etc.₎ 1744-48), II, 1023.

17. For example, an article about the Spanberg voyage appears in
the Gazette de France on 27 February 1740. See Frank A.
Golder, Russian Expansion on the Pacific, 1641-1850 (Cleveland:
Arthur H. Clark Company, 1914), pp. 330-33.

18. The London Magazine, IX (London: T. Astley, 1740), 155.

19. The Gentleman's Magazine: And Historical Chronicle, X (February, 1740), 95.

20. Ibid., X (April, 1740), 205.

21. Spanberg had signed an oath of secrecy about the Second Kamchatka Expedition, before it began. In accordance with that
oath, nothing could be revealed or published about the results
of the expedition without permission.

22. On this voyage, see Lensen, The Russian Push, pp. 57-60.

23. Haven states he met Spanberg in 1746, when Spanberg was under
arrest. (See footnote 13 above). Under a sentence of death,
Spanberg may well have sought to meet with Haven, who was the
chaplain to the Danish embassy in St. Petersburg.

24. The accounts of the voyages were published in a little-known
work in 1747; scholars of the Bering voyages were not aware
of this publication, apparently, until 1934, when it was
"discovered" by Stejneger. (See note 12 above).

25. Peder von Haven, Nye og forbedrede Efterraetninger om det Russiske Riga (Copenhagen: Paa Autors egen Bekostning, 1747), p. 22. This passage was translated by Mariann Tiblin, and compared to the translation by Stejneger.

26. This statement of the purpose of Bering's first voyage is in conflict with the old thesis that Bering was sent to find out if Kamchatka was joined to America, but the rest of Haven's account places the voyage in the context of a search for a northeast passage, as noted above.

27. For general biographies on Gmelin, see Petr Petrovich Pekarskii, Istoriia imperatorskoi akademiia nauk, 2 vols. (St. Petersburg: Imperatorskaia akademiia nauk, 1870-73), I, 431-57; Vladislav Kruta, "Johann Georg Gmelin," in Dictionary of Scientific Biography, V, 427-29; M. Gmelin, "Johann Georg Gmelin" in Allgemeine deutsche Biographie, IX, 269-70.

28. In Bering's proposals for the Second Kamchatka Expedition, he stated he would be ready to sail in four years, and the cost of the expedition would be 10,000 to 12,000 rubles. After four years, the cost was already 300,000 rubles, and Bering was still in Iakutsk. See Golder, Bering's Voyages, I, 33-34.

29. Stepan Petrovich Krasheninnikov, Opisanie zemli Kamchatki (St. Petersburg: Imp. Akademii Nauk, 1755). It was translated into French and English in the eighteenth century. A recent English translation, with an introduction and notes,

was done by E. A. P. Crownhart-Vaughan, as <u>Exploration</u> <u>of</u>
<u>Kamchatka</u>: <u>North</u> <u>Pacific</u> <u>Scimitar</u> (Portland: Oregon Historical
Society, 1972).

30. Leonhard J. Stejneger, <u>Georg</u> <u>Wilhelm</u> <u>Steller</u>: <u>The</u> <u>Pioneer</u> <u>of</u>
<u>Alaskan</u> <u>Natural</u> <u>History</u> (Cambridge: Harvard University Press,
1936), p. 121.

31. For a full account of Gmelin's troubles with the Academy, see
Lothar A. Maier, "Die Krise der St. Petersburger Akademie
der Wissenschaften nach der Thronbesteigung Elisabeth Petrovnas
und die 'Affäre Gmelin'" in <u>Jahrbücher</u> <u>für</u> <u>Geschichte</u> <u>Osteuro-</u>
<u>pas</u>, neue Folge, XXVII:3 (1979), 353-73.

32. Leonhard Euler, <u>Die</u> <u>Berliner</u> <u>und</u> <u>die</u> <u>Petersburger</u> <u>Akademie</u>
<u>der</u> <u>Wissenschaften</u> <u>im</u> <u>Briefwechsel</u> <u>Leonhard</u> <u>Eulers</u>, 3 vols.
(Berlin: Akademie-Verlag, 1959-76), II, 259.

33. Johann Georg Gmelin, <u>Reise</u> <u>durch</u> <u>Sibirien</u>, 4 vols. in 2,
(Göttingen: Abram Vandenhoecks seel., Wittwe, 1751-52), I,
sig.++2^V-++3^r.

34. Alexander Vucinich, <u>Science</u> <u>in</u> <u>Russian</u> <u>Culture:</u> <u>A</u> <u>History</u>
to 1800 (Stanford: Stanford University Press, 1963), pp. 100-01.

35. Pekarskii, <u>Istoriia</u>, I, 452.

36. Gmelin, Reise, I, ✝3 forward. The text here gives reasons
for Russian interest in explorations, a subject which is
prominent in the introduction, but is little-mentioned in the
text of the book.

37. "Eloge du Czar Pierre I" by Fontenelle in Académie des Sciences,

Paris, <u>Histoire</u> <u>de</u> l'Académie royale <u>des</u> sciences. <u>Année</u> MDCCXXV. (Amsterdam: Pierre Mortier, 1732), pp. 141-72.

38. Gmelin, <u>Reise</u>, I, sig. ↑5^r-↑7^r.

39. Gmelin's outstanding work was in botany, notably his <u>Flora</u> <u>Sibirica</u>, published from 1747 to 1769.

40. See Maier, "Die Krise." At one point it was suggested that Gmelin's activities might result in his being "headless."

41. Albert Isnard, "Joseph-Nicolas Delisle, sa biographie et sa collection de cartes géographiques à la Bibliothèque nationale," in Comité des travaux historique et scientifique, <u>Bulletin</u> <u>de</u> <u>la</u> <u>Section</u> <u>de</u> <u>Géographie</u>, XXX (1915), 34-164; Pekarskii, <u>Istoriia</u>, I, 149-55.

42. Delisle worked with Ivan Kirilov on maps. "At the same time Delisle familiarized himself with the materials of Russian surveys, ordered French copies of Russian maps for himself (on the pretext of not knowing Russian), and sent them to-gether with the originals and other material in great quantity to France." V. G. Churkin, "Atlas Cartography in Prerevolu-tionary Russia," translated by James R. Gibson in <u>The</u> <u>Canadian</u> <u>Cartographer</u>, XII:1 (June, 1975), 6.

43. Isnard, "Joseph-Nicolas Delisle," p. 44.

44. Churkin, "Atlas Cartography," p. 6.

45. <u>Ibid</u>., pp. 6-7. For information about the Geography Depart-ment, see Vera F. Gnucheva, <u>Geograficheski</u> <u>departament</u> <u>Akademii</u> <u>nauk</u> <u>XVIII</u> <u>veka</u> (Moscow-Leningrad: AN SSSR, 1946).

46. Isnard, "Joseph-Nicolas Delisle," p. 49.

47. Joseph Nicolas Delisle, Explication de la carte des nouvelles decouvertes au nord de la Mer du Sud (Paris: Desaint et Saillant, 1752); the accompanying map was titled "Carte de nouvelles decouvertes au nord de la mer du Sud . . . par Philippe Buache . . . "

48. Aleksandr I. Andreev, "Trudy G. F. Millera o vtoroi kamchatskoi ekspeditsii," Izvestiia, VGO, XCI:1 (January-February, 1959), 5-6.

49. The Academy's instructions to its members state "nobody, either among those sent on the expedition or among the professors residing here, must, on pain of severe punishment, say anything to foreigners in private, in public, in writing, or in speech about the discoveries made by this expedition until these discoveries have been published." O. M. Medushevskaya, "Cartographic Sources for the History of Russian Geographical Discoveries in the Pacific Ocean in the Second Half of the Eighteenth Century," translated by James R. Gibson, in The Canadian Cartographer, IX:2 (December, 1972), 100.

50. [Gerhard Friedrich Müller] A Letter from a Russian Sea-Officer, to a Person of Distinction at the Court of St. Petersburgh (London: A. Linde [etc.] 1754), p. 61. This portion of the work is a translation of Delisle's Explication.

51. For example, on the map Delisle indicates the route "par le Capitaine Tchirikow et M^r De l'Isle de la Croyere."

52. [Müller] Letter, p. 63.

53. On the impact Delisle had on British theorists for northern passages, see Glyndwr Williams, The British Search for the Northwest Passage in the Eighteenth Century (London: Longmans, 1962), pp. 142-53.

54. [Müller] Letter, p. 63.

55. Ibid., p. 62.

56. M. H. Omont, "Lettres de J.-N. Delisle au Comte de Maurepas et à l'Abbé Bignon sur les travaux géographiques en Russie (1726-1730)," in Comité des travaux historique et scientifique, Bulletin de la Section de Géographie, XXXII (1917), 130-64.

57. [Müller] Letter, pp. 61-62.

58. Ibid., p. 58.

59. Further study of Delisle might identify the reasons why he did not publish more Russian maps. Perhaps he did not have much information on the results of the Second Kamchatka Expedition, which was of most interest to the public of the time.

60. For the Academy's concern, see Andreev, "Trudy G. F. Millera"; Pekarskii, Istoriia, I, 143. For editions of the work, see the bibliography.

61. The English translation of the anonymous Letter by Müller

also included Observations upon the Russian Discoveries, &c.
by Arthur Dobbs, a great proponent of searching for northern
passages; a translation of Delisle's Explication and a translation of the De Fonte "voyage."

62. Samuel H. Cross, "The Contribution of Gerhard Friedrich
Mueller to Russian Historiography, with some consideration
of August Ludwig Schloezer." Ph.D. dissertation, Harvard
University, 1916, p. 78. For a biography of Müller, see
Pekarskii, Istoriia, I, 308-430.

63. For the text of Kirilov's Memorandum see Raymond H. Fisher,
Bering's Voyages: Whither and Why (Seattle: University of
Washington Press, 1977), pp. 184-87.

64. Materialy dlia istorii imperatorskoi Akademiia nauk, 10 vols.
(St. Petersburg: 1885-1900), VII, 253.

65. Ibid., VI, 270.

66. Ibid., VI, 270-71.

67. Cross, "Contribution," p. 118. "Who could have thought that
during so long a journey and so great an interval, his hostility toward me would not subside?" Müller wrote in 1748 in
a letter to a colleague.

68. Andreev, "Trudy G. F. Millera," p. 3.

69. Ibid.

70. Materialy dlia istorii, VIII, 78.

71. Ibid.

72. This map, ascribed to Georg Moritz Lowitz, is dated 1746 in

the cartouche. The University of Kansas Library has four
different states of this map. See Thomas R. Smith and
Bradford L. Thomas, Maps of the 16th to 19th Centuries in
the University of Kansas Libraries (Lawrence: University
of Kansas Libraries, 1963), pp. 16-17.

73. This map appears as plate 69 in R. V. Tooley, Maps and Map-
Makers (New York: Bonanza Books, 1962). It was from an Atlas
by Covens and Mortier, and the dating of the map is difficult. But if it was printed prior to 1754 it was an illegal
publication of Russian geographic materials. (See following
footnote).

74. The image of the North Pacific given in the maps cited in
footnotes 72 and 73 was not published in Russia until 1754,
and publication of that material outside of Russia before
that time had to have come out of Russia illegally. Delisle
or Müller would have been suspected of supplying the information for the foreign publication of these maps.

75. Pekarskii, Istoriia, 354-62.

76. For one view of this lecture, see Omeljan Pritsak, "The Origin
of Rus," in The Russian Review, XXXVI:3 (July, 1977), 249-73.

77. Pekarskii, Istoriia, I, 361.

78. Ibid., I, 363-65.

79. On the internal conflict in the Academy between the Russian
and German factions of it, see Vucinich, Science, pp. 84-89.

80. Andreev, "Trudy G. F. Millera," 4.

81. <u>Ibid.</u>, 5-7.

82. ₍Müller₎ <u>Letter</u>, pp. 3-6.

83. <u>Ibid.</u>, pp. 7-8.

84. <u>Ibid.</u>, p. 8.

85. The word "continent" in this passage is striking because it may refer to the unknown land in the north (as presented on the Homann maps) rather than a range of mountains or a peninsula connecting Asia to America, as other versions of the instructions do.   The point is, in this case Bering was not seeking a connection between Asia and America, but a <u>continent</u> at "the furthest northern part of the eastern coasts of Siberia."

86. The newspaper article in the <u>Sanktpeterburgskiia</u> <u>Vedomosti</u> (March, 1730) indicates "if the Inhabitants of the Country ₍Kamchatka₎ may be believed, a Ship from Lena arriv'd at Kamtschatka 50 or 60 Years ago." Müller was the editor of the newspaper.

87. ₍Müller₎ <u>Letter</u>, pp. 24-25.

88. It should be remembered that here we are considering only Müller's publications relating to the Russian explorations. Müller's work, both published and unpublished, gained him the title of "the father of Siberian history," and his collections of manuscripts relating to history, the so-called "Müller portfolios," are an invaluable source for historians.

89. Gerhard Friedrich Müller, <u>Nouvelle</u> <u>carte</u> <u>des</u> <u>decouvertes</u> . . . (St. Petersburg: l'Academie Imperiale des Sciences, 1754).

90. The German text was titled <u>Nachrichten von Seereisen</u>; the Russian, <u>Opisanie morskikh puteshestvii</u>. Both appeared in 1758. See the bibliography for the full citation.

91. Gerhard Friedrich Müller, <u>Voyages from Asia to America, for completing the Discoveries of the North West Coast of America</u> (London: T. Jefferys, 1761), p. 3.

92. Raymond H. Fisher, "Dezhnev's Voyage of 1648 in the light of Soviet Scholarship," in <u>Terrae Incognitae: The Annals of the Society for the History of Discoveries</u>, V (1973), 7-26.

93. For a biography of Steller, see Pekarskii, <u>Istoriia</u>, I, 587-616; Leonhard J. Stejneger, <u>Georg Wilhelm Steller: The Pioneer of Alaskan Natural History</u> (Cambridge: Harvard University Press, 1936).

94. The summary of Bering's expedition to American which follows is based largely on Frank A. Golder, <u>Bering's Voyages</u>, 2 vols., and particularly on Steller's account of the voyage which appears on pages 9-241 of volume two.

95. There is no evidence of disagreeement about the choice of the route. See Fisher, <u>Bering's Voyages</u>, pp. 138-42. Fisher concludes, "Thus the decision, which was at the root of much of the American expedition's failure to accomplish all it had been charged with doing, was in fact made in conformance with the official orders and in the expectation that this choice would best enable it to fulfill these orders." (p. 142).

96. The logbook of the <u>St. Peter</u> in Golder, <u>Bering's Voyages</u>, I,

65, indicates that the St. Paul simply fell behind the St. Peter, and was lost to sight during windy weather.

97. The logbook indicates that this was the reason for the decision to return. Golder, Bering's Voyages, I, 120.

98. Ibid., I, 281-82; II, 135-37.

99. Ibid., II, 209-10.

100. Ibid., II, 161-62; 216-17.

101. In addition to the reports discussed below, it is clear that notices were published in Germany, since Steller's brother was aware of them.

102. The French text, with an English translation, appears in Frank A. Golder, Russian Expansion on the Pacific, 1641-1850 (Cleveland : The Arthur H. Clark Company, 1914), pp. 326-27.

103. The first report in English of Bering's second voyage was published in October, 1743, as follows: "Extract of a Letter from Petersburg: Captain Behring, who was sent to discover a Passage to America by the North, was shipwrecked upon an Island hitherto unknown, where he, and most of his Company had perished, through Cold, Hunger, and Fatigue. This News was brought by M. Stöller, a Botanist, and Associate of the Academy of Sciences at Petersburg, who had accompanied Capt. Behring. Mr. Stöller, with the Assistance of some of his Companions, found Means to build, out of the Ruins of their great Ship, a little Shallop, in which himself, and 19 others,

after running through a Thousand perilous Adventures,
arrived at Kamschatka." The Gentleman's Magazine, XIII
(1743), 552.

104. Stejneger, Georg Wilhelm Steller, p. 442.

105. Ibid. Steller wrote the family that his reason for not
writing more often was for fear of breaking the rule
about secrecy, and said "I should like very much to
know who has been making me out a sailor and a windbag.
My desire is to fill gaps in the realm of science, not
vacant space in the newspapers."

106. Ibid., pp. 447-48.

107. Ibid., pp. 472-73; 484-87.

108. The title of it was "Zuverlässige Nachricht von dem
merkwürdigen Leben und Reisen Herrn George Wilhelm
Stöller," and it first appeared in Johann Heinrich
Gottlob von Justi, editor, Ergetzungen der Vernünftigen
Seele, V (Leipzig: 1747), 362-84.

109. Stejneger, Georg Wilhelm Steller, pp. 492-93.

110. Georg Wilhelm Steller, Beschreibung von dem Lande
Kamtschatka, edited by J.B.S. [cherer] (Frankfurt und
Leipzig: J.G. Fleischer, 1774), p. 16.

111. Scherer obtained the Steller manuscript from Fischer,
with or without his permission. He published it without
permission, and in his introduction to the book raised

the old questions about the circumstances surrounding Steller's death.

112. Golder, Bering's Voyages, II, 155-56.

113. Steller, Beschreibung, p. 5.

114. On Pallas, see Peter Simon Pallas, A Naturalist in Russia: Letters from Peter Simon Pallas to Thomas Pennant, edited by Carol Urness (Minneapolis: University of Minnesota Press, 1967). In a letter of 1780 to Pennant, Pallas mentioned ". . . Bering's expedition to the northward, to ascertain the separation between the two Continents." (p. 135)

115. Georg Wilhelm Steller, Reise von Kamtschatka nach Amerika mit dem Commandeur-Capitän Bering, edited by Peter Simon Pallas (St. Petersburg: J.Z. Logan, 1793), p. 3.

116. Golder, Bering's Voyages, II, 10.

117. Ibid.

118. Steller, Reise von Kamtschatka, pp. 6-7.

APPENDIX

The text of Bering's "Short Account" from Jean Baptiste
Du Halde, Description. . . de la Chine. Paris, 1735.

Relation Succinte du Voyage du Capitaine Beerings dans la Sibérie.

Quoique dans le Projet que j'ai donné de cet Ouvrage, je me
sois borné à cette partie de la partie, qui est soûmise à la
Chine, & que je ne me sois nullement engagé à entrer dans cette
autre qui appartient aux Russes, j'ai cru néanmoins qu'une nouvelle
découverte faite par les ordres du feu Czar, ne pouvoit être que
très-agréable à ceux qui ont du goût pour la Géographie.

On sçait, & les nouvelles publiques nous l'annoncerent il y
a peu d'années, que ce grand Prince, qui étoit tout occupé de la
perfection des Arts & des Sciences, & qui a créé en quelque sorte
dans ses Etats une Nation toute nouvelle, fit partir le Capitaine
Beerings, avec ordre d'aller jusqu'à Kamtschacka, afin d'examiner
les frontiéres de ce Pays-là, qui s'etendent au Nord-Est, & tâcher
de découvrir, si, selon l'opinion de quelques-uns, elles tiennent
à la partie Septentrionale de l'Amérique, ou si l'on pourroit y
trouver quelque passage par eau.

Ce Capitaine après avoir exécuté ponctuellement ces ordres,
revint à Petersbourg le premier jour de Mars de l'année 1730, &
apporta une Relation succinte de son voyage, avec la Carte qu'il
en avoit dressée. Cette Carte fut envoyée au Sérénissime Roy de
Pologne, comme un présent digne de son attention & de sa curiosité,
& Sa Majesté a bien voulu qu'elle me fût communiquée, en me

permettant d'en faire tel usage qu'il me plairoit. J'ai cru que le
public me sçauroit quelque gré de l'avoir ajoûtée à toutes celles
que je lui avois promises.

Ce fut l'an 1725 le cinq de Février que le Capitaine Beerings
reçut ordre du Comte Apraxim, Amiral de Russie, de faire un voyage
en Sibérie. Il devoit, suivant l'instruction qui lui fut donnée,
prendre connoissance des bornes de ce Pays-là, afin qu'on pût
juger de ce qu'il restoit d'intervalle entre l'extrêmité de la
Sibérie la plus avancée vers l'Est ou le Nord-Est, & le continent
de l'Amérique Septentrionale.

Il lui fut permis en partant, de prendre chemin faisant dans
les Villes de Sibérie, le nombre & l'espéce de gens dont il
pourroit avois besoin. L'Amirauté avoir même fait partir d'avance
un Lieutenant, accompagné de vigt-cinq hommes, & avec autant de
bagage & d'outils nécessaires que vingt-cinq chevaux en pourroient
porter. La suite du Capitaine Beerings étoit de trente-trois
personnes, y comprenant les Domestiques.

Il atteignit le détachement de son Lieutenant à Vvologda,
& poursuivant son voyage vers Tobolsk, il passa par les Villes de
Totma, Vvtiug Vvelikoi, ou la grande Oustioug, Soli, Vvitziogda,
Kai gorod, Solikamski, Verchoturia, Turinski, ou Japantzin, & Tumen.

Le jour de son arrivée à Tobolsk fut le 16 de Mars. La
saison étant trop avancée pour pouvoir continuer de voyager de la
même maniere, il resta là jusqu'au 15 de May. Alors il en partit,
ayant fait passer son monde, & chargé son bagage sur quatre Barques,

avec lesquelles il descendit la riviere d'Irtisch jusqu'à Samarofko

yam. Il avoit pris à Tobolsk un Moine de l'Order de saint Jerôme,

un Commissaire, des Officiers subalternes, & trente-sept Soldats.

Un peu au-dessous de la poste ou du relais de Samarofk, il

entra dans le fleuve Obi pour le remonter, en passant devant les

Villes de Surgut & de Narim. Il prit un peu au-dessus de cette

derniere la riviere de Keta, qui le conduisit jusqu'à Makofsk,

qui est une Forteresse (d'autres disent un Monastere.)

Les Peuples qui habitent ce Pays depuis Tobolsk, sont les

Ostiakes; ils étoient autrefois Payens, mais depuis quelque tems

ils ont embrassé le Christianisme, par les soins du Métropolitain

de Tobolsk. De Makofsk on se rend par terre à la Ville ou Forteresse

de Jeniseïski.

Ce fut là qu'il prit avec lui trente personnes, tant Char-

pentiers que Marêchaux, & il s'embarque sur quatre Batteaux, comme

il avoit déja fait. De la riviere de Jenissée, il entra dans celle

de Tunguska.

Cette riviere a trois grandes cataractes, & plusieurs autres

rapides, qui en occupent toute la largeur d'un bord à l'autre.

De plus le lit de la riviere est parsemé assez fréquemment de

rochers ou écüeils cachez sous l'eau. Tous ces embarras rendent

cette navigation très-difficile, & l'interrompent en plusieurs

endroits. Ainsi, on ne se tire de là qu'après avoir couru de

grands risques, & essuyé bien de la fatigue.

On quitte la riviere de Tunguska pour entrer dans celle d'Ilim.

Mais les Barques Sibériennes qui sont arrivées jusques-là, ne peuvent remonter cette riviere d'Ilim, qui a des sauts & peu de profondeur. Ainsi, le Capitaine fit mettre son bagage le plus gros sur de petits Batteaux, qui étoient descendus de la Ville d'Ilimski tout exprès. Le reste fut mis sur des traineaux.

Lorsqu'il fut arrivé a Ilimski, il fit prendre les devans à son Lieutenant, afin qu'il se rendit sur la riviere d'Uskut ou Kuta & sur celle de Lena. Il lui donna quelques Officiers sub- alternes, & environ trente-neuf Charpentiers, au moyen desquels il devoit dans le cours de l'Hyver, construire quinze Barques, pour servir à descendre la Lena.

Quant à lui, il trouva des difficultez à aller plus loin, & il prit son quartier d'hyver à Ilimski avec le reste de son monde. Il falloit faire provision de vivres, & parce qu'aux environs de Jakutski, où il devoit se rendre par la Lena, il n'y a point de bled, il y avoit des Ordres de la Chancellerie de Tobolsk, aux Villes d'Irkutski & d'Ilimski d'en fournir.

Dans le courant de cet Hyver, le Capitaine fit un voyage à Irkutski, pour s'aboucher avec le Vvaivode, ou Gouverneur, qui l'avoit été précédemment à Jakutski, & duquel il pouvoit apprendre mieux que de toute autre personne, la nature du Pays qu'il avoit à traverser, la maniere d'y voyager, & de se transporter jusqu'à Ochotski, & Kamtschatka. La suite du Capitaine fut renforcée à Irkutski d'une vigtaine de personnes, Forgerons & Charpentiers, parmi lesquels il y avoit deux Tonneliers.

Le Pays traversé par les riviere Tunguska, Ilim, & Lena,
jusqu'à celle de Vvitim, est habité par des Peuples nommés Tunguses,
qui font grand cas des Rênes, parce qu'ils en tirent de grands
avantages. Mais ceux d'entr'eux qui n'ont point de Rênes, établisse
leur demeure plus prés des rivieres, dont le poisson les nourrit,
& sur lesquelles ils naviguent avec des canots faits d'écorce de
bouleau. Ces Tunguses sont Payens.

Vers la fin de l'Hyver le Capitaine reprit son voyage avec
des traîneaux, jusqu'à Uskut. Ainsi au Printems de 1726 il descendi
la riviere de Lena dans quinze Barques plattes jusqu'à Jakutski.

Les deux bords de la Lena au-dessous de la riviere de Vvitim,
sont habitez par les Jakutes, & par quelques Tunguses. Les Jakutes
ont beaucoup de bétail, chevaux, & bêtes à corne, dont ils tirent
leur nourriture, & leur vêtement. Ceux qui n'ont que peu ou point
de bétail, se nourrissent de poissons.

Ils sont Payens, & adorent le Soleil, la Lune, les Oyseaux,
tels que le Cygne, l'Aigle, & le Corbeau. Ils ont une haute idée
de leurs Sorciers, qu'ils appellent Schamans. Indépendamment de
cela ils tiennent chez eux des Bolvvaners ou petites Images, qu'ils
nomment en leur langage Scheitans. Au rest, ce peuple paroît
avoir une origine commune avec les autres Tartares.

A son arrivée à Jakutski, le Capitaine demanda du monde
pour faciliter sa marche, & ayant obtenu ce secours, il ordonna
à un Lieutenant de suivre avec la plus grande partie de son monde,
& le gros du bagage, le courant de la Lena, jusqu'au confluent de

la riviere d'Aldan, de remonter tout de suite les rivieres d'Aldan,
de Maya, & de Iudoma. Il se persuadoit qu'on pourroit remonter
ainsi jusqu'à Iudomska Kresta, & que par ce moyen le voyage
devenoit plus facile, & moins pénible que par terre.

Pour lui, avec le petit nombre de gens qu'il s'étoit réservé,
il monta à cheval à Jakutski, pour se rendre à travers pays à
Ochotski. Il fit charger ses provisions sur des chevaux, cinq
Puds pesant sur chacun. Le pud est un poids de Russie, qui
revient à 35 ou 40 livres. Il avoit environ seize cens puds
pésant en provisions & bagages. Il n'est pas question de les
faire voiturer par charoy dans un pays de montagnes & de marais.

Le Capitaine laissa un Lieutenant à Jakutski, pour y passer
l'hyver, avec ordre de prendre au Printems le même chemin par
terre vers Ochotski Ostrog, & cependant il se rendit lui-même en
ce lieu, où il ne trouva autour de la forteresse que dix familles
Russes.

Sur la fin de Décembre 1726 il reçut des nouvelles du Lieutenant qu'il avoit fait partir de Jakutski, par lesquelles il
apprenoit, qu'ayant été surpris par les glaces à l'entrée de la
riviere de Gorbéa, à environ 450 vverstes, (ou 108 lieuës Françoises)
avant que d'arriver à Indomska kresta, il avoit fait construire
des traîneaux longs & étroits, sur lesquels il avoit fait charger
le bagage le plus nécessaire, & qu'il s'acheminoit à pied avec
son détachement.

Le Capitaine crut devoir aller au-devant de son Lieutenant,

menant avec les gens qu'il avoit les habitans d'Ochotski. Les
provisions étoient tirées par de grands chiens. Enfin le Lieutenant & sa troupe arriverent en ce lieu d'Ochotski le premier
jour de Janvier 1727.

Ils étoient partis de la riviere de Gorbéa le 4 de Novembre
d'auparavant, & comme ils n'avoient pû porter de provisions en
quantité suffisante, ils furent constraints, dans la nécessité
de la plus cruelle faim, de manger la chair des chevaux morts.
Ils se servirent de toutes les peaux qu'ils purent trouver, après
les avoir frottées de chaux, à se couvrir le corps, & à se garantir
les pieds de la rigueur d'un froid extrême. Ils furent forcez
d'abandonner leur bagage en trois endroits différens, tout man-
quant dans une route entiérement déserte.

Ce qu'ils trouverent de ressource, ne fut que dans un peu
de farine, que le Capitaine, par le défaut de quelques chevaux
qui étoient morts de fatigue, avoit été obligé de laisser à Iudomska
kresta.

Le même peuple d'Yakutes qui habite aux environs de la Lena,
demeure aussi sur les rivieres d'Aldan, & de Maya; mais les bords
de la riviere de Iudoma, & les environs de la forteresse d'Ochota,
sont occupez par une Nation qu'on appelle les Tunguses de mer, ou
suivant le nom propre de leur langage, Lamutki. Ils ont des Rênes
apprivoisez en quantité qui les voiturent, & leur fournissent la
nourriture & le vêtement. On trouve aussi des Tunguses établis
près des Lacs & de la Mer, pour être a portée du poisson qui les

nourrit: leur Religion n'est pas différente de celle des Yakutes.

Le Capitaine envoya au commencement de Février un Lieutenant avec 90 hommes, & quelques chiens, pour rapporter sur des traîneaux le bagage qui avoit été abandonné sur la riviere de Iudoma. Ce Lieutenant fut de retour à Ochotski dans le mois d'Avril; mais sans avoir pû suffire à rapporter tout le bagage; c'est pourquoi le Capitaine dépêcha encore 27 hommes pour Iudomska kresta, qui en revinrent au mois de May.

La neige tombe dans ce pays-là en telle abondance, qu'elle couvre ordinairement la terre de la hauteur d'un bras Russe, (ou cinq pieds & demi de France) & quelquefois davantage. Ainsi l'on est obligé pendant trois à quatre mois de voyager à pied, & de traîner soi-même son bagage sur de petits traîneaux chargez jusqu'à quinze pieds tout au plus.

C'est de cette maniere que la troupe du Lieutenant qui partit de la riviere de Gorbéa, fit sa route jusquà Ochotski: & comme c'étoit en hyver, ces pauvres voyageurs ne pûrent mieux faire, pour se garantir la nuit du froid mortel de ce climat rigoureux, ou pour se mettre à l'abri du vent, que de s'enfoncer bien avant dans la neige.

Le 30 de Juin, le Capitaine fit monter sur une barque nouvellement construite, un Lieutenant, pour qu'il traversât du Port d'Ochotski ostrog à l'embouchûre de Bolchaya rerca, ou de la grande riviere, avec tout le bagage & les outils. Ce Lieutenant avoit ordre de faire passer à Kamtschatka le Sous-constructeur, & les

Charpentiers de l'Equipage, pour qu'on y taillât le bois nécessaire
à la construction d'un vaisseau. Après quoi il devoit prompte-
ment retourner vers la Capitaine.

Cependant le Lieutenant qui avoit été laissé à Jakutski,
arriva le troisieme de Juillet à Ochotski, apportant avec lui,
selon l'ordre qu'il en avoit reçu du Capitaine, 2300 puds de farine.

Quand la barque revenuë de la riviere de Bolchaya, & une
autre qui étoit aussi arrivée du même endroit, eurent été chargées
des provisions & bagages nécessaires, le Capitaine s'embarqua le
21 d'Août, pour se rendre aussi de Ochotski ostrog à la riviere
susdite. Il laissoit un Pilote avec quelques gens pour garder la
partie des provisions qui étoit restée dans les glaces à l'entrée
de la riviere de Gorbéa, jusqu'à ce que le Pilote pût faire re-
descendre ses provisions jusqu'à la riviere de Notora, qui tombe
dans Aldan, où il devoit les livrer à la Chancellerie de Jakutski,
en tirant une reconnoissance de cette livraison. Après quoi le
Pilote, & les gens de sa suite devoient venir rejoindre le Capitaine à Kamtschatka, munis de quelques provisions, & charges de
fer & de goudron. Ils n'arriverent qu'en 1728.

Le Capitaine parvenu à l'entrée de Bolchaya rerca, fit monter
son bagage jusqu'à Bolchay recski ostrog, ou à l'habitation de
la grande riviere sur de petites barques. Il n'y a autour de la
forteresse qui est en ce lieu-là que quatorze petits ménages
Russes.

Delà le plus gros du bagage fut encore porté sur la riviere

à cent vingt Vverstes, près du haut Kamtschatka. Pour arriver jusques-là, on prit des traîneaux, tirez, selon l'usage du pays, par des chiens, & on travers de cette maniere l'intervalle de la riviere Bolschaya à celle de Kamtschatka.

Dans le cours de ce voyage, on avoit grand soin, pour passer la nuit, de s'enfoncer dans la neige. On se couvroit principalement par le haut. Il regne dans ces quartiers-là des ouragans très-violens, qu'on appelle Purgi, & quand les Voyageurs en sont surpris avant que de trouver à se gîter, ou se mettre à l'abri, ils courent risque d'être enterrez sous la neige.

Kamtschatka dans l'habitation d'en haut, ne consiste qu'en dix-sept familles Russes; dans l'habitation d'en bas il y en a cinquante, & un peu plus lon, où l'Eglise est placée, il y en a quinze. C'est ce qu'on a pû inférer des termes de la Relation. La Carte marque distinctement trois habitations; sçavoir, Kamtschatka d'en haut, celui du milieu, & celui d'en bas.

Les Garnisons des trois Forteresses ne composoient alors que cent cinquante Soldats, & ces Soldats ne sont établis là que pour lever les impositions dont les Habitans sont chargez. On donna à ces Habitans, pour les voitures qu'ils avoient fournies depuis Bolschay recski ostrog, le poids de 300 puds de la graisse d'une baleine qui avoit été jettée sur le rivage l'Automne précédent; & un peu de tabac Chinois acheva de satisfaire ces gens-là, & mieux peut-être qu'on n'auroit fait avec de l'argent.

A Kamtschatka, du côté du Sud, il y a une Nation qu'on nomme

Kurile. Dans la partie du Nord, il y a peu d'humains parmi les
Kamtschakdales, ausquels on puisse attribuer quelque Religion &
quelques Loix. Ils different peu de langage entr'eux tous.

Les Russes établis à Kamtschatka, n'ont, de même que les
naturels du pays, ni bled, ni bétail. Ils ont pour tout des chiens,
qui leur servent à transporter ce qu'ils veulent d'un endroit à
un autre, & dont la peau leur fournit aussi le vêtement. Ils se
nourrissent de poisson. L'Eté leur permet d'avoir quelque gibier.
Ils ont encore des carotes & des féves.

Il vient pourtant quelque peu de bled aux environs du Couvent
de Pakutsiska, qui n'est éloigné de l'Eglise de Kamtschatka que
d'un Vverste. Il y vient aussi du chanvre & des raves; mais dans
les plantations des Habitans Russes, qui sont plus en deçà que
les Forteresses, il se trouve des navets extraordinaires, puisqu'il
n'en faut qu'une demie douzaine pour le poids d'un pud.

Le Capitaine apporta au Couvent nommé ci-dessus, du seigle
& de l'avoine, & ces grains furent semez pendant son séjour dans
le pays, mais il n'en put voir le progrès.

Au reste, il gele de très-bonne heure dans ce pays-là. On
n'y sçait ce que c'est que de fumer la terre, & c'est aux hommes
à la labourer, puisque les bêtes leur manquent. Le peuple qui
est sous l'obéissance de la Russie, paye son tribut en fourrures.

Les coûtumes de ce peuple sont bien barbares: si une mere
accouche de deux enfans, l'usage est d'en étouffer un dès qu'il
paroît. La conservation de cet enfant passeroit pour un crime.

Un autre coûtome, aussi barbare pour le moins, c'est que quand
un pere ou une mere tombent malades, quoique toute maladie ne
soit pas mortelle, la personne malade est transportée dans la
Forêt voisine, en tems d'Hyver comme en Eté: on lui laisse à la
vérité des provisions pour quelques jours; mais il paroît difficile
qu'aucun d'eux en réchappe.

Ils ne prennant pas soin d'enterrer leurs morts; ils les
traînent seulement jusques dans le bois, où ces corps sont dévorez
par les chiens. Il y en a parmi eux qui abandonnent leur demeure,
s'il arrive que quelqu'un y rende le dernier soûpir. Les Kuriles
brûlent leurs morts, ce qui leur a été défendu inutilement jusqu'à
présent.

Le Capitaine étant descendu jusqu'à Kamtschatka l'inférieur,
trouva ce qu'il falloit de bois pour la construction d'un Vaisseau
presque tout préparé. Le bâtiment fût mis en chantier le 4 d'Avril
1728 & achevé le 10 de Juillet. Les bois nécessaires furent
traîhez par des chiens, & comme le goudron manquoit, on trouva
moyen d'y suppléer, & d'en tirer d'un certain bois nommé Lisnischnik,
en le faisant brûler, ce qui avoit été inconnu jusqu'alors au
Habitans de ce pays-là.

On composa une espéce d'eau-de-vie pour le voyage de mer qu'on
alloit entreprendre. Avec de l'eau de la mer on fit du sel. Les
provisions consistoient en carotes & en racines faute de bled:
de la graisse cruë de poisson devoit tenir lieu de beurre, & du
poisson salé remplaçoit toute autre viande. Le Vaisseau fut

chargé d'une si grande quantité de vivres de cette espéce, qu'elle
pouvoit suffire pour nourrir quarante hommes pendant toute une
année.

Le 14 du mois de Juillet on sortit de la riviere de Kamtschatka,
pour achever de satisfaire aux ordres de la Cour de Russie, &
à l'instruction signée de la propre main du Czar, Pierre le Grand.

On se trouva le 8 d'Août par 64 dégrez 20 minutes de latitude,
& aussitôt huit hommes, qui montoient une barque de cuir, quitterent
le rivage pour approcher du Vaisseau. Ils s'informerent d'où il
venoit, & pourquoi il étoit venu. Après cela ils dirent d'euxmemes,
qu'ils étoient Tzuktschi, qui est le nom d'une Nation connue
depuis assez long-tems des Russes, & qui habite effectivement
dans ce quartier-là.

On appella ces Tzuktschi plusieurs fois, & à la fin il s'en
détacha un, qui vint au Vaisseau en nâgeant sur des peaux de chien
Marin; mais un moment après les autres arriverent aussi; ils dirent
que le rivage de la mer étoit rempli des habitations de leur Nation,
& ils firent entendre que l'étenduë de la terre ferme étoit vers
le couchant.

Ils indiquerent aussi une Isle, qui n'étoit pas fort éloignée,
& que l'on découvrit effectivement quand on fut parti delà; mais
on ne vit personne sur cette Isle, quoiqu'il y parût quelques
maisons. On lui donna le nom de S. Laurent, parce que ce jour-là
étoit celui de la fête de ce Saint, qui arrive le 10 d'Août.

La hauteur se trouva le 15 du même mois de 67 dégrez 18

minutes. Ce fut le non plus ultrà du Capitaine Beerings, qui
crût avoir suffisamment rempli sa commission, & satisfait aux
ordres qu'il avoit reçus, sur-tout, parce qu'il ne voyoit plus
que les terres continuassent de courir de même du côté du Nord.
Il appréhendoit qu'en allant plus loin, s'il étoit accüeilli de
quelque vent contraire à sa route, il ne lui fût plus possible
de retourner à Kamtschatka avant la fin de l'Eté. Eh! comment
se résoudre à passer l'Hyver dans un pareil climat, au hazard
de tomber chez des peuples qui n'ont point été soumis, & qui
n'ont de l'homme que la figure? Toute la côte depuis le lieu du
départ de Kamtschatka, avoit paru relevé comme une muraille, par
une suite continuelle de montagnes couvertes de neiges.

Dans la retour, & le 20 jour d'Août, il vint environ quarante
personnes vers le Vaisseau sur quatre canots; c'étoit des Tzuktschi,
comme ceux dont on a parlé. Ils apportoient quelque viande, du
poisson, & de l'eau fraîche. Ils avoient aussi quinze pieces de
pelleterie; il y en avoit de deux sortes, dont l'une étoit de
renard blanc. De plus, il y avoit quatre dents de chevaux marins.
Les gens du Capitaine eurent le tout pour des épingles, & des
fusils à faire du feu.

Ces sauvages assûrerent que leurs compatriotes alloient vers
la riviere de Kohlima, qui va tomber dans la mer glaciale à l'Est
de la Lena, avec des marchandises qui étoient tirées par des
Rênes, & qu'ils n'avoient jamais fait ce voyage que par terre,
& non par eau. Les Russes leur étoient connus depuis long-tems,

& l'un même d'entr'eux avoit été en traitte à la Forteresse d'Anadirski.

On fut de retour à l'embouchure de Kamtschatka le 7 de Septembre, & on prit son quartier d'Hyver à Kamtschatka l'inférieur.

Le 5 de Juin de l'année 1729 le Vaisseau ayant été mis en
état de reprendre la mer, le Capitaine sortit de l'embouchure de
Kamtschatka, faisant route au Levant, & cela sur ce que les Habitans de Kamtschatka avoient dit, que lorsque le tems étoit clair
& serein, on découvroit en mer une terre.

Mais quoi qu'on fit alors plus de deux cens Vverstes en s'avan-
çant en pleine mer, on ne vit point de terre. C'est pourquoi on
changea de route, & on prit vers le Sud du côté de Schatzik, (la
relation ne dit pas ce que c'est) pour doubler la pointe de
Bolschay recski, c'est-à-dire, celle du continent de Kamtschatka,
dont on n'a point eu de connoissance avant celle qu'on en donne
ici. Dans le cours de ce voyage on livra aux Gouverneurs de Kamtschatka, & de Bolschay recski, le poids de huit cens Puds en farine
ou gruau, & en viande seche & sallée.

De l'embouchure de la Boschaya, on se rendit en traversant
la mer à l'embouchure d'Ochota, où l'on arriva le 23 de Juillet.
Le navire & tout ce qui en dépendoit, fut livré au Gouverneur
de la forteresse qui est en cet endroit-là; ensuite dequoi le
Capitaine prit la route de Iudomska kresta, sur des chevaux qu'il
loüa pour ce voyage.

On prit après cela des bateaux plats, pour descendre les

rivieres de Maya & d'Aldan, jusqu'à l'entrée de celle de Belaya.
Là on prit des chevaux pour gagner Jakutski. Toute cette route
depuis Ochotski se fit du 29 Juillet au 3 de Septembre.

A Jakutski on monta sur deux barques plattes, pour remonter
la riviere de Lena, & on le fit jusqu'au premier d'Octobre. Il
fallut s'arrêter au Village de Peledun, où les glaces commencerent
à s'opposer à la navigation. Il tomba de la neige, & la riviere
de Lena se glaçant, on partit le deux d'Octobre pour se rendre à
Ilimski, & de là à Jeniseïski. On rencontre dans cette route
des Villages & des habitations de Russes.

En partant de Jeniseïski, on prit une route différente de
celle que l'on avoit tenuë en allant, & on se rendit à la Ville
de Tomski, par la riviere de Tschulim, en rencontrant des Villages
de Russes ou de Tartares nouvellement convertis. On en trouve de
même entre Tomski & Tscheuski, qui est plus haut dans l'Obi.

De Tscheuski on prit par les déserts de Barabut, au sortir
desquels on traversa la riviere d'Irtisch. On trouve ensuite
jusqu'à Tobolsk des Villages Russes, ou, pour mieux dire, presque
tous Tartares. Le jour d'arrivée dans la Métropole de Sibérie
fut le 10 de Janvier 1730.

On en partit le 25 du même mois, pour se rendre à Petersbourg
par le même chemin qu'on étoit venu, & on y rentra le premier
jour de Mars.

A succinct Narrative of Captain Beerings's Travels into Siberia.

Altho', according to the Scheme which I first laid down for this Work, I might have clos'd it with the Account of that Part of Siberia which is subject to China, and that I am by no means oblig'd to enter upon that other Part which belongs to the Russians, yet I thought that a new Discovery, by the Order of the late Czar, could not fail of being very agreeable to those who have a Taste for Geography.

Not long ago, as publick Accounts inform'd us, this great Prince, who hath been always employ'd in perfecting the Arts and Sciences, and who has in a manner created in his Dominions a quite new Nation, ordered Captain Beerings to go as far as Kamtsckatka in order to examine the Frontiers of those Countries which lay to the North-east, and to endeavour to discover whether, as some are of Opinion, they joined to North-America, or whether there could be found any Passage by Sea.

Captain Beerings having punctually executed his Orders return'd to Petersburgh on the first Day of March 1730, and brought a short Account of his Voyage, with a Map which he had made of it: This Map was sent to the most serene King of Poland, as a Present worthy of his Regard and Curiosity; and his Majesty having been pleased to communicate it to me, with a Permission to make what use of it I pleas'd, I thought that the Publick would be somewhat oblig'd to me if I added it to all the others which I had promis'd.

On the 5th of February 1725 Captain Beerings received orders

from Count Apraxim, Admiral of Russia, to travel into Siberia:
He was oblig'd, according to his Instructions, to inform himself
fully of the Bounds of this Country, in order to the forming a
Judgment what might be the Distance between the utmost East or
North-east Point of Siberia, and the Continent of North-America.
He was allow'd, as he pass'd through the Cities of Siberia, to
take with him what Number and Sort of People he might have occasion
for; the Admiralty had also ordered a Lieutenant and twenty-five
Men before, with twenty-five Horses loaded with Baggage and
necessary Instruments, and Captain Beerings's Retinue consisted of
thirty Persons including his Domesticks: He came up with the Detachment of his Lieutenant at Vuolagda, and travelling towards
Tobolsk pass'd thro' the Cities of Totma, Vvirug, Vvelikoi or
Great Oustioug, Soli, Vvitziogda, Kaigorod, Solikamski, Vercho
turia, Turinski or Japantzin, and Tumen: He arrived at Tobolsk
the 16th of March, but the advanced Season making it impossible
to pursue his Travels in the same way, he staid there till the
fifteenth of May; then he left Tobolsk, and putting his Retinue
and Baggage on board four large Barks, he fell down the River
Irtisch to Samarof ko yam: From Tobolsk he took along with him a
Monk of the Order of St. Jerom, a Commissary, some Subalterns, and
thirty-seven Soldiers.

A little below the Post or Relay of Samarofk he entred the
River Obi, and in going up it he passed by the Cities of Surgut
and Narim, and a little above the latter he came into the River of

Keta, which brought him to Makofsk, which is a Fortress (or as
some will have it a Monastery): The People which inhabit this
Country from Tobolsk are the Ostiakes; they were formerly Pagans,
but some time ago, by the care of the Metropolitan of Tobolsk,
they embraced Christianity. From Makofsk we went by Land to the
City or Fort of Seniseiski; there he took with him thirty Men, as
well Carpenters as Smiths, and as he had done before embark'd in
four Vessels: From the River Tenissee he entred Tunguska; this
River has three great Cataracts, and several other strong Currents,
which take up the whole breadth from one Bank to the other; besides the Channel of the River is pretty full of Rocks or Shelves,
which do not appear above the Water; all these Obstacles make the
Navigation of this River very difficult, and in several Places
interrupt it, so that they ran great Hazard, and endured great
Fatigue before they could get clear of it: From the River Tunguska they passed into the Slim, but the Siberian Barks, which had
got thus far, could not get up this River which has some Falls in
it, and is very shallow; the Captain therefore ordered the heaviest
of his Baggage to be put in little Boats, which were fallen down
for that purpose from the City of Himski, and the rest was put
upon Sledges: As soon as he came to Himski he ordered his Lieutenant to march before till he should come to the River Uskut,
or Kuta, and the Lena; he put under his Command some Subalterns,
and about thirty-nine Carpenters, who might in the Winter build
fifteen Barks to serve him to go down the Lena: As for himself,

finding it inconvenient to go further, he took up his Winter-
Quarters at Himski with the rest of his Retinue: It was necessary
to take in fresh Provisions, and because about Jakutski, whither
he was to go by the Lena, there was no Corn, he had Orders from
the Chancery of Tobolsk to the Cities of Irkutski and Himski to
furnish him with it.

In the Winter the Captain went to Irkutski to have a Con-
ference with the Vvaivode, or Governor, who had been formerly at
Jackutski, and who could better than any one else inform him of
the Nature of the Country he was to pass, the manner of travelling in
it, and the Road to Ochotski and Kamtschatka: The Captain's
Company were reinforc'd at Irkutski with twenty Persons, Smiths
and Carpenters, among which there were two Coopers: The Country
thro' which run the Rivers Tunguska, Slim, and Lena, to the Vvitim,
is inhabited by a People called Tunguses; they are very careful
of their Rain-Deer, because they receive great Advantage from
them; but those among them who have no Rain-Deer dwell nearer the
Rivers, and support themselves by Fish: Their Vessels are Canoes
made of the Bark of the Birch. These Tunguses are Heathens.

Towards the end of the Winter the Captain set out again with
Sledges to Uskut, and in the Spring 1726 went down the River Lena
in fifteen flat-bottom'd Barks to Jakutski: Both sides of the Lena
below the River Vvitim are inhabited by the Sakutes, and by some
Tunguses; the Sakutes have plenty of Cattle, Horses, and horned
Beasts, which supply them with both Food and Clothing; and they

who have little or no Cattle live upon Fish: They are Pagans and worship the Sun, Moon, and Birds, such as the Stork, the Eagle, and the Crow; and they have a great Opinion of their Sorcerers, whom they call Schanians: Besides this they have in their Houses Bolvvaners, or little Images, which are called in their Language Scheitans; in other respects this People seem to have the same Origin with the other Tartars.

At his Arrival at Sakutski the Captain demanded a Supply of Persons proper to facilitate his March, and having obtained it he ordered a Lieutenant to follow with the greatest Part of his Retinue, and the heavy Baggage, and to keep the Course of the River Lena to the Place where the Aldan flows into it, and to go up the whole Course of the Rivers Aldan, Maya and Tudoma, imagining that by this way they could go quite up to Tudoniske Kresta, and by that means the Voyage would become easy, and less troublesome than by Land: He himself, with a few Attendants whom he kept with him, got on horseback at Takutski in order to cross the Country to Ochotski; he put his Provisions upon Horses, five Puds weight upon each, (a Pud is a Weight in Russia of about thirty-five or forty Pounds) and in the whole had about sixteen hundred Puds weight in Provisions and Baggage; there was doubtless no possibility of conveying it upon Carriages in a mountainous and boggy Country: The Captain left a Lieutenant at Takutski to winter there, with Orders in the Spring to take the same way by Land towards Ochotski Ostrog, and in the mean time he went himself to that Place, where he found about the Fort no more than ten Russian Families.

About the end of December 1726 he received Letters from the Lieutenant that he had parted from Takutski, by which he understood that having been surprised by the Ice at the Entrance of the River Gorbea, at about 450 Vverstes, or 108 French Leagues, short of Tudomskakresta, he had built long and straight Sledges, upon which he had loaded the most necessary Baggage, and that he march'd on Foot with his Detachment: The Captain judg'd it proper to go meet his Lieutenant, taking with him, besides his Attendants, some of the Inhabitants of Ochotski; the Provisions were drawn by great Dogs, but at last the Lieutenant and his Troop arrived at Ochotski the 1st of January 1727; they had left the River of Gorbea the 4th of November before, and as they could not carry a sufficient quantity of Provisions, they were constrained by extremity of Hunger to eat the Flesh of the dead Horses; and made use of all the Skins they could find, after they had rubb'd them bare, to cover their Body and to defend their Feet from the extremity of the Cold; they were forced to leave their Baggage in three different Places, being destitute of every thing in a Road intirely desart: All the Supply they met with was only a few Meals which the Captain, by the Cropping of some Cattle who died of Fatigue, was obliged to leave at Tudomskakresta.

The Country about the Rivers Aldan and Maya are inhabited by the same Takutes who dwell upon the Lena; but another People, who are called Sea-Tunguses, or, according to their Name in their

own Language, Lamukti, possess both sides of the River Tudoma,
and the Country around the Fort of Ochota; they have abundance
of tame Rain-Deers, which carry them, and furnish them with both
Food and Clothing: Their Religion is the same with that of the
Takutes.

The Captain, at the beginning of February, sent a Lieutenant
with ninety Men and some Dogs to bring upon Sledges the Baggage
which had been left upon the Banks of the Tudoma: The Lieutenant
returned to Ocotski in April, but not having had Strength enough
to bring back all the Baggage, the Captain therefore ordered a
second Detachment of twenty-seven Men to Tudomska Kresta, who returned to him in May.

The Snow falls in this Country in such abundance that it covers
the Ground generally a Russian Fathom deep, or five and an half
French Feet, and sometimes more; so that for three or four Months
one must travel on foot, and draw ones Baggage ones self upon
little Sledges, with not more upon them than fifteen Pounds; it
was after this manner that the Troop of the Lieutenant, upon leaving
the River Gorbea, travelled to Ochotski, and as it was in Winter
those poor Travellers had no better way to defend themselves in
the Night from the killing Cold of that severe Climate, or to
shelter themselves from the Wind, than by burying themselves deep
in the Snow.

The 30th of June the Captain put on board a Bark newly built,
a Lieutenant with all the Baggage and Tools, in order to cross over

from the Harbour of Ochotski Ostrog to the Mouth of the Bochaya
or Great River: This Lieutenant had Orders to send over to
Kamtschatka the Under-builder, and the Carpenters of the Retinue,
to cut Wood necessary for the building of a Ship, after which he
was to return with all speed to the Captain: In the mean while
the Lieutenant, who had been left at Takutski, arrived the 3d of
July at Ochotski, bringing along with him, according to the Orders
he had received of the Captain, 2300 Puds of Meal. The Bark which
came back from the River of Bolchaya, and another likewise which
came in from the same Place, being loaded with the Provisions and
the necessary Baggage, the Captain embarked the 21st of August to
pass from Ochotski Ostrog to the abovementioned River: He left a
Pilot to take care of that Part of the Provisions which was left
in the Ice at the Entrance of the River Gorbea, till he could send
back his Provisions by the River Notora, which falls into the
Aldan, where he was to deliver them to the Chancery of Takutski,
taking a Receipt of this Delivery; after which the Pilot, and the
Men left with him, were to join the Captain at Kamtschatka, stored
with some Provisions, and loaded with Iron, Pitch, and Tar, but
they did not arrive till 1728.

    The Captain being come to the Entrance of the Bolchaya rerea,
ordered his Baggage to Bolchayrecski Ostrog, or the Town of small
Barks upon the great River: There are round the Fort which is in
that Place only fourteen small Russian Families. From thence the
heavy Baggage was carried up the River an hundred and twenty

Vverstes near to High Kamtschatka, to get quite thither they made use of Sledges drawn, according to the Custom of the Country, by Dogs; and after this manner they crossed the Country that lies between the River Bolschaya and the Kamtschatka. During this March great care was taken to bury themselves deep in the Snow in the Night, which by its Depth was their chief Defence: There are in these Parts very violent Hurricanes, which are called Purgi, and when Travellers are caught on a sudden by them before they have time to lodge themselves under Shelter, they are in great danger of being buried under the Snow.

High Kamtschatka consists but of seventeen Russian Families, but in the Low there are fifty, and a little further, where the Church stands, there are fifteen: This may be inferr'd from the manner of Expression; and the Map sets down distinctly three Towns, High, Middle, and Low Kamtschatka: The Garrisons of these Ports did not at that time consist of above a hundred and fifty Soldiers, and these are only placed there to raise the Taxes which are laid upon the Inhabitants: We paid these Inhabitants for the Carriages they had furnished us with from Bolschayrecski Ostrog three hundred Puds weight of the Fat of a Whale which had been cast on Shore the Autumn before, and a little Chinese Tobacco, which compleatly satisfy'd these People, and perhaps better than Mony would have done: On the South of Kamtschatka there is a Nation called Kurile; on the North side there are few among the Kamtschakdales to whom any Religion can be ascrib'd; there is but little difference among them all in their Language.

The Russians establish'd at Kamtschatka have not, any more than the Natives, either Corn or Cattle; they have every where Dogs, which they use in conveying any thing they please from one Place to another, and whose Skins also afford them Clothing; they live upon Fish, and in the Summer they have some Game, besides Carrots and Beans: However there is some Corn about the Convent of Pakutsiska, which is no more than one Uverste from the Church of Kamtschatka; there is likewise some Hemp, and Radishes, and in the Plantations of the Russians, which are more on this side the Fort, there are extraordinary Turneps, half a dozen of which weigh one Pud. The Captain brought to the above-mention'd Convent some Rye and Oats, which Corn was sown during his Stay in the Country, but he never saw the Produce of it; besides its freezing very early in this Country, dunging the Ground is a thing unknown there, and the whole Tillage of it must be perform'd by Men, because they have no Cattle: The People, who are subject to Russia, pay their Tribute in Furs.

The Customs of these People are very barbarous; if a Mother is brought to bed of two Children the Custom is to stifle one of them as soon as it is born, and the keeping it alive would be accounted a Crime; another Custom, at least as barbarous, is this, when a Father or Mother falls sick, altho' all Sicknesses are not mortal, yet the sick Person is carried into a neighbouring Forest, as well in Winter as Summer, where he is left with Provision indeed for a few Days, but it seems hard for any of them to recover; there are some of them who leave their House if any one happens to die in it; they don't bury their Dead, they only just draw them into the Woods, where their Bodies are devour'd by the Dogs: The Kuriles burn their Dead, and it hath been forbidden hitherto to no purpose.

The Captain, being come down to Low Kamtschatka, found the necessary Timber, which had been drawn thither by Dogs for the building of a Ship, almost ready: The Ship was put upon the Stocks the 4th of April 1728, and finished the 10th of July: As there was no Pitch and Tar, the want of it was supplied by burning a certain Wood call'd Lisnischnik, and extracting its Juice, which was till then unknown to the Inhabitants of this Country: There was made a kind of Aqua Vitae for the intended Sea-Voyage, and Salt of the Sea-Water; the Provisions consisted of Carrots for want of Corn, the Fat of Fish uncured served instead of Butter, and Salt-Fish supplied the place of all other Meats: The Ship was loaded with so great a quantity of this kind of Provision as might be sufficient to maintain forty Men for a whole Year.

The 14th of July we got out of the River of Kamtschatka, that we might fully comply with the Orders of the Court of Russia, and the Instructions of the Czar, Peter the Great, signed by his own Hand.

On the 8th of August we found our selves in 64 Degrees and 30 Minutes of Latitude, and presently eight Men got into a Leather

Bark, quitted the Shore and made towards the Ship; they inquired whence it came, and for what Intent; after which they inform'd us that they were Tzuktschi, which is the Name of a Nation that hath been a pretty while known to the Russians, and who indeed inhabit this Quarter: These Tzuktschis were spoke with several times, and at last one of them was sent off, who came to the Ship floating upon the Skins of the Sea-Dog; but a Moment afterwards the others also came up; they told us that the Sea-shore was full of little Towns of their Nation, and inform'd us that the Terra firma extended towards the West: They shew'd us likewise an Island which was not far off, and which appear'd plainly as we went from thence, but we did not see any one upon this Island, although there appeared some Houses; we gave it the Name of St. Laurence, because this Day was the Festival of this Saint, which is on the 10th of August.

On the 15th of the same Month the Latitude was found to be 67 Degrees, 18 Minutes; this was the Ne plus ultra of Captain Beerings, who thought he had sufficiently executed his Commission, and fulfilled the Orders he had receiv'd; especially, as he could not perceive that the Land kept the same Course to the North, and was also apprehensive that in going further, if he should be overtaken by any contrary Wind, it would be impossible for him to return to Kamtschatka before the end of the Summer, and, alas! how could he think of wintering in such a Climate, in danger of falling among People who were never under any Government, and who have only the

Figure of Men; the whole side of the Land, from the Place of his departure from Kamtschatka, had appeared like a Wall by a continued ridge of Mountains covered with Snow.

On the 20th of August on his Return there came about forty People towards the Ship in four Canoes, they were Tzuktschi as well as those we before spoke of; they brought us some Meat, Fish, and fresh Water; they brought also fifteen Pieces of Furs; they had two sorts, one of which was that of a white Fox; they had besides four Teeth of a Sea-horse; the Captain's Servants had them all for Pins, and Steel to strike Fire with: These Savages inform'd us that their Countrymen went towards the River of Kohlima, which falls into the frozen Sea at the East of the Lena, with Commodities drawn by Rain-Deer; and that they always went by Land and not by Sea: The Russians have been long known to them, and one of them particularly had travell'd to the Fort of Anadirshi.

On the 7th of September we return'd to the Mouth of the Kamtschatka, and winter'd at Low Kamtschatka.

The 5th of June 1729, the Ship being in a Condition to go to Sea again, the Captain went out of the Mouth of the Kamtschatka, making his Course to the East, and this upon the Information the Inhabitants of Kamtschatka had given him; that when the Weather was clear and fair one might at Sea discover Land: But, altho' we at first made more than two hundred Vverstes right forwards in an open Sea, no Land appear'd; for which reason the Course was alter'd, and directed South on the side of Schatzik, (the Narrative does not tell us what it is) in order to double the Point of

Bolschay recki, that is of the Continent of Kamtschatka, of which

we had no Knowledge before that which is here given of it: In

the Course of this Voyage there was deliver'd to the Governors

of Kamtschatka and Bolschayrecski eight hundred Puds weight of

Meal or Oatmeal, and dry'd salt Meat.

From the Mouth of Bolschay they cross'd the Sea to the Mouth

of the Ochota, where they arrived the 23d of July: The Ship, and

all that belong'd to it, was deliver'd to the Governor of that

Fort that is in that Place; after which the Captain took the Road

to Sudoneska kresta, upon Horses, which he hired for that Journey;

after this he made use of flat-bottom'd Boats to go down the

Rivers of Maya and Aldan, quite to the Entrance of the Belaya,

where he took Horse to get to Takutski: This whole Journey from

Ochotski was made from the 23d of July to the 3d of September:

From Takutski he got on board two flat-bottom'd Barks to go up

the River Lena, which was perform'd by the first of October. He

was obliged to stop at the Village of Peledun, where the Ice began

to hinder sailing.

The Snow falling, and the River Lena being froze, on the 2d

of October he set forward for Himski, and from thence to Teniseiski:

On this Road there are Villages and Houses of the Russians: From

Teniseiski he took a different way from that he travelled when he

went out, and came to the City of Tomski by the River Tschulim,

meeting in the Road with Villages of Russians or Tartars newly converted: There were also some of them between Tomski and Tscheuski, which is higher up the Obi: From Tscheuski he took the Road by the Desarts of Barabut, at the going out of which he cross'd the River Irtisch; from whence quite to Tobolsk there were Villages of Russians, or, to speak more properly, almost all Tartars: On the 10th of January 1730, he arriv'd at the Metropolis of Siberia; on the 25th of the same Month he set out for Petersburgh by the same Road he went, and enter'd it the 1st Day of March.

An Account of the Travels of Capt. Beerings, into Siberia.

On February 5, 1725, Captain Beerings received Orders from Count Apraxim, Admiral of Russia, to begin his Journey into Siberia. By his Instructions signed by the Czar he was obliged to inform himself of the North-eastern Frontiers of that Country, in order to discover whether they were contiguous to, or what might be their Distance from, the Continent of North America, and if any Passage could be obtained that Way by Sea. He was permitted as he went thro' the Cities of Siberia to take along with him whatever People he wanted. His own Retinue consisted of 30 Persons, and a Lieutenant was ordered before with 25 Men, and 25 Horses loaded with Baggage and necessary Instruments; with whom the Captain came up at Wologda, and travelling towards Tobolsk passed thro' the Towns Totma, Vstiug welikoi or Great Ustiug, Soli Witziogda, Kaigorod, Solikamski, Verkhoturia, Turinski, or Japantzin, and Tumen. He reached Tobolsk March 16, where he stay'd till May 15, before the Season would allow him to pursue his Journey. Here he took along with him a Monk of the Order of St. Jerome, a Muster-Master, some Subalterns and 37 Soldiers, and fell down the River Irtish to Samarofko Yam with his Retinue and Baggage in four large Barks. A little below this Place they came into the River Obi, and going up it pass'd by Surgut and Narim, and entered the River Keta, which brought them to the Fortress (or as others say the Monastry) of Makofsk. This Country from Tobolsk is inhabited by the Ostiaks, who were formerly Pagans, but lately converted to Christianity by the Care of an Archbishop of Tobolsk. From Makofsk they travell'd by Land to the Town or Fortress of Jenisseiskoy, where he took with him 30 Carpenters and Smiths, and again embark'd in four Vessels. From the River Jenissea they passed into that of Tunguska whose Navigation is both difficult and dangerous, by the frequent Rapidity of the Stream, and three great Cataracts, besides shelving Rocks which don't appear above Water. After much Fatigue they got into the Ilim: But this River having some Falls, and being very shallow, they were obliged to quit their Barks, and put their heaviest Baggage into little Boats, and the rest upon Sledges. When they came to Ilimski, the Captain detach'd a Lieutenant with some Subalterns and 39 Carpenters to the Lena, to build in the Winter-time, 15 Barks to carry his People down that River, and he winter'd with the rest of the Retinue at Ilimski; where and at Irkutski he furnished himself with fresh Provisions and Corn, of which Yakutski, whither he intended to go, produced none. The Governor of Irkutski having travelled that Way, informed the Captain of the Nature of the Country, the Manner of travelling, and of the Road to Okhotski and Kamchatka. At Irkutski the Captain augmented his Company with 18 Smiths and Carpenters, and 2 Coopers. Towards the End of Winter the Captain set out with his Retinue in Sledges to Uskut, and in the Spring 1726, they fell down the Lena in 15 Vessels to Yakutski.

The Country water'd by the Tunguska, Ilim and Lena, as far as the Witim, is inhabited by the Tunguses, who are Heathens, and chiefly subsist by their Rain-deer, but those who have none, live nearer the Rivers, and maintain themselves by Fish. Both Sides of the Lena below the Witim are inhabited by the Yakutes and some Tunguses. The Yakutes are likewise Heathens, and worship the Sun, Moon, and some Birds, such as the Swan, the Eagle, and the Crow. They place a great Confidence in their Shamans or Sorcerers, and keep in their Houses little Images called by them Sheitans. They seem to have the same Origin with the other Tartars, and they abound with Horses and Cattle, which afford them Food and Cloathing, but the poorer Sort live upon Fish.

The Captain having his Retinue augmented on his Arrival at Yakutski, set out from thence for Okhotski Ostrog, with a few of his Attendants on Horseback, and it being impossible in that mountainous and marshy Country, to use Carriages for the Provisions and Baggage, Horses were loaded with about 1600 Puds Weight of them, each Horse carrying 5 Puds, and each Pud weighing about 35 or 40 Pounds. He left a Lieutenant to winter at Yakutski, who was to follow him by Land in the Spring, and ordered another Lieutenant, with the greater Part of His Company, and the heavy Baggage, to go by Water, along the River Lena, to where the Aldan joins it, and up the Aldan, Maya, and Yudoma, thinking to reach Yudomska kresta by this easy Way of travelling. But about the End of December 1726, the Captain having reach'd Okhotski, where he found no more than 10 Russian Families, received Advice from the Lieutenant, that he was surprised by the Ice as he entered the River Gorbea, 450 Werstes, or 108 French Leagues from Yudomska kresta. However on November 4, he set out with his Company on

Foot, having made some little narrow Sledges for carrying the most

necessary Part of the Baggage over the Snow, which is generally,

during 3 or 4 Months in Winter, a Russian Fathom, or 5 1/2 French

Feet deep; these Sledges they were obliged to draw themselves, with

no more upon them than 15 Pounds, and not being able to carry a

sufficient Quantity of Provisions, they were reduced to the greatest

Extremity, and forced to leave their Baggage behind them in three

different Places; the only supply they received was a few dead

Horses, which being worn out with Fatigue, the Captain had left at

Yudomska kresta. What Skins they could find they made Use of to

defend themselves from the excessive Cold; and all the Shelter

they could procure by Night was a Bed dug deep in the Snow. But

at last they arrived at Okhotski, January 1, 1727. In the Beginning

of February, the Captain sent a Lieutenant with 90 Men, and

some Dogs for drawing the Baggage, that was left by the Way, upon

Sledges. They returned in April, but were not able to bring the

whole. Whereupon another Detachment of 27 Men were sent out, who

returned in May.

The Banks of the Aldan and Maya are inhabited by the same

Yakutes already mentioned. But the Country about the River Yudoma

and the Fortress Okhota is possessed by a People called Sea-

Tunguses, or in their own Language, Lamutki. They have Plenty of

Rain-deer, which are their chief Support, but some dwelling near

the Lakes and the Sea, live upon Fish. They are of the same relig-

ion with the Yakutes.

June 30. The Captain sent a Lieutenant, and the Carpenters with Part of the Baggage and Tools in a new built Bark, over from Okhotski Ostrog to the Mouth of the Bolskhaya reka or Great River. The Carpenters were ordered to proceed to Kamchatka to prepare Wood for building a Vessel; and the Lieutenant was to return directly. July 3, the Lieutenant left at Yakutski arrived at Okhotski, and brought with him 2300 Puds of Meal, which, upon the Return of the Bark was put on Board with the Baggage, and the Captain sailed August 21 for the abovesaid River, where, when he arrived, he sent the Baggage to Bolskhay rekski Ostrog, a small Fort, round which are Fourteen Russian Families. From thence the heavy Baggage was carried 120 Werstes up the River, where they took Sledges drawn by great Dogs, and crossed the Country between the Rivers Bolskhaya and Kamchatka. Very furious Hurricanes, called Purgi, sometimes rage in these Parts, which are apt to surprise Travellers, and, before they can shelter themselves, bury them in the Snow. Our Captain, therefore, with his People, took Care to lodge themselves by Night deep in the Snow.

In the Map are set down three distinct Towns, High, Middle, and Low Kamchatka. The first consists of 17, the second, where the Church stands of 15, and the third of 50 Russian Families. The Garrisons of these three Forts amounted to no more than 150 Men, who are placed there only to raise the Taxes, which are paid in Furrs. We gave the People, for the Carriages with which they had supply'd us, 300 Puds Weight of the fat of a Whale, which had been thrown on Shore the preceding Autumn, and a little Chinese Tobacco, with which they were fully satisfied.

In this Country there is neither Corn nor Cattle, except a little of the former, near the Convent of Pakutsiska, about one Werste from the Church of Kamchatka. The Captain sow'd some Rye and Oats, but he never saw the Produce; for besides the early Frost there, they are ignorant of dunging the Ground, and have no Cattle for Tillage. But in the Russian Plantations they have some Hemp and Radishes, and Turneps so very large that six of them weigh a Pud. The Inhabitants live mostly upon Fish, and in Summer they have some Game, also Carrots and Beans. Their Carriages are all drawn by Dogs whose Skins supply them with Cloathing. There is hardly any Religion among the Natives of this Country, and their Language is generally the same. Some of their Customs are extremely barbarous. When a Woman is delivered of two Children, they smother one of them, and its Preservation would be deem'd a Crime. Some forsake their Houses if any happen to die in them; and if even a Father or Mother fall sick, they, without any Regard to the Nature of the Distemper, whether or not it may prove mortal, or to the Season of the Year, carry the sick Person into an adjacent Wood, where he is left, with a few Days Provision, so that hardly any recover. They never bury their Dead, but throw them into the Woods, where the Carcasses are devoured by the Dogs. The Kurile, a Nation South of Kamchatka, burn their Dead, which has been often prohibited, without Effect.

The Captain being arrived at lower Kamchatka, and the Timber for building the Ship being ready, she was put upon the Stocks April 4, and finished July 10. He supplied the Want of Pitch and Tar by extracting with Fire the Pith of a Tree called Lisnishnik; an Art till then unknown in that Country. They loaded their Vessel with a Twelve-months Provision for 40 Men, which consisted of Roots in Place of Corn, the Fat of Fish instead of Butter, and Salt-Fish which supplied the Want of all other Meats. They likewise made a Sort of Aqua-vitae, and Salt of Sea-water. July 14, they sailed from the River Kamchatka, and August 8, found their Lat. 64° 30'. Here they saw 8 Men come from Shore in a Leathern Boat towards the Ship, who enquired whence and for what Design it came; then they told they were Tzukchi, a Nation not unknown to the Russians. They were spoke with frequently, and one of them came floating to the Ship on the Skins of the Sea-dog. They said that they dwelt upon the Shore, and that the Land extended Westward. They shewed our Adventurers an Island at no great Distance, which they approached: but tho' they saw something like Houses, no Inhabitants appeared. They called it St. Laurence, because they discover'd it on August 10, that Saint's Day. On the 15th, their Lat. was 67° 18' and the Captain thought proper not to proceed, as he could not observe that the Land reached further Northwards, and was apprehensive least some contrary Wind might prevent his Return to Kamchatka before the End of Summer. The Ridge of Mountains covered with Snow all along the Coast from Kamchatka to this Place, appeared at Sea like a Wall.

August 20, about 40 Tzukchi came towards the Ship in four Boats.
They brought with them Meat, Fish, and fresh Water, likewise 15
Pieces of Furs, some of them Skins of a white Fox, and four Teeth
of a Sea-horse, all which they gave for Pins, and Steel for striking
Fire. Sept. 7, the Captain re-entered the Mouth of the River Kam-
chatka, and winter'd at lower Kamchatka.

June 5, 1729, the Captain sailed again from the River Kamchatka,
and steer'd Eastward, as he was informed that Land might that Way be
discerned at Sea in clear Weather. But having made 200 Werstes, and
no Land appearing he changed his Course Southwards along the Coast
of Shatzick (of which the Narrative gives no Account) to double the
Point of the Continent of Kamchatka which was before unknown. From
the Mouth of the Bolskhaya he crossed the Sea to Okhotski, where
he arrived July 23, and delivered the Ship with every Thing belonging to it to the Governor of that Fortress. Here the Captain took
Horses for Yudomska kresta; from thence he went down the Maya and
Aldan in flat-bottom'd Boats, till he came to the Belaya; where he
again took Horse for Yakutski, and arrived there September 3. He
went up the Lena in flat-bottom'd Boats, but was stop'd by the Ice
at the Village of Peledun, October 1. The next Day he set out for
Ilimski, and thence to Jenisseiski, and met with several Russian
Villages along the Road. Then went to Tomski by a different Way
from that he came; whence he went to Cheuski, there being Russian
and Tartar Villages by the Road. Then he took his Way thro' the
Desarts of Barabut, and crossing the River Irtish, he reach'd

Tobolsk, passing several Russian and Tartar Villages. He came to
the Capital of Siberia, Jan. 10, and setting out the 25th, he
arrived at Petersburg, March 1.

Bering's "Short Account" edited by John Campbell.

3. It was in the last Year of the Life of Peter the Great,
that Captain Behring received Orders from Count Apraxin, Admiral
of Russia, to traverse the vast Country of Siberia, to penetrate
its utmost Extremities to the East or North-east, in order to obtain a distinct Notion of its Bounds, and of the Distance between
them and the Continent of North America. The better to enable him
to fulfil these Instructions, which were given him in the Month
of February 1725, a Lieutenant was dispatched with twenty-five
Men, and such Baggage and Tools as could be carried upon twenty-
five Horses before him; and as soon as he could make the necessary
Preparations, the Captain followed with a Retinue of about thirty
three Persons. He came up with his Lieutenant at Wologda, and
continued his Journey to Tobolsky, which is looked upon as the
Capital of Siberia, where he arrived on the 16th of March.

The Season being too far advanced for him to make an immediate
Progress, he continued there for two Months, and then having received
a considerable Reinforcement, he proceeded on his Expedition
on the River Irtish till it falls into the River Oby or Obb, and
then remounted that River as far as the Town of Narin. All the
Country through which he passed was inhabited by the Ostiacks,
formerly Pagans, but a little before converted to the Christian
Faith by the Care of the Metropolitan of Tobolsky. He proceeded
from thence to the Monastery of Makofsk, and from thence went by

Land to the City of Jenisciski. He embarked there with thirty
Persons on board of four small Barks, in order to continue his
Voyage on the River Jenisa, and afterwards on that of Tunguska;
from whence with much Difficulty he reached Ilimski.

There he determined to winter, and to send his Lieutenant
to make the necessary Preparations for continuing their Voyage
upon the Lena, directing him to employ his Time in constructing a
small Squadron of Barks for that Purpose. The Captain himself,
during the Winter, took all the Care he could to inform himself
of the Countries that he had still to pass through, before he
reached that which was the proper Object of their Enquiries. And
the Accounts that he received, were such as gave him to understand
that a more difficult Task could scarce be imposed on any Man,
than that which had been lain upon his Shoulders. The Country
where he now was belonged to the Tunguses, a Nation of Pagans,
who lived very miserably along the Sides of the great Rivers,
which they navigated in small Boats, or rather Canoes made of the
Barks of Trees. When the Severity of the Season was a little
over, he resolved to prosecute this tedious and dangerous Expedition with all the Diligence and Caution in his Power.

4. In the Beginning of the Spring he began to descend the
Lena with his small Squadron of fifteen flat-bottom'd Boats, and
arrived safely at Jakutsky. Both Banks of the Lena below the
River Witem, are inhabited by the Jakuts and some few Tunguses.
As for the former, they are well provided with Horses, and have

great Herds of Black Cattle, that is to say, such as are in a tolerable Situation in the World; and as for the poorer Sort, they maintain themselves as well as they can by Fishing. As for their Religion, they are Pagans and gross Idolaters, worshipping the Sun and Moon, and some Kind of Birds, such as the Swan, the Eagle, and the Crow. They are famous for having many Conjurers among them, and for praying to a Sort of diminutive ugly Idols, called in their Language Saitans. In other Respects they reckon themselves, and are esteemed by others, a Tribe of Tartars. Upon his Arrival at Jakutsky the Captain demanded a Reinforcement, and having obtained it, he gave Instructions to a Lieutenant to proceed with the best Part of his Troops and all the heavy Baggage upon the Lena, to its Confluence with the River Aldan, in order by remounting that, and the Rivers Maya and Judoma, to reach Judomska Kresta, that is, the little Fort of Judomska, and by this Route he was in Hopes of lessening the Fatigue of so long and troublesome a Passage.

As for himself, he set out on Horseback, attended by the few People that were left about him, and some Horses laden with Provision, to go by Land to Ochotski, though the Road was very far from being tolerable. The Captain also left a Lieutenant at Jakutski, with Orders to pass the Winter there, and to follow him at the Beginning of the Spring over Land to Ochotski. Upon his arriving in Person at that Fortress, he found it in a very poor Condition, and no more than ten Russian Families residing there or in its Neighbourhood. About the End of the Month of December he received Advice from his first Lieutenant, importing that he had been surprized by the Ice at his Entrance into the River of Gorbea, distant above one hundred Leagues from Judomska; and that this obliged him immediately to construct some long and narrow Sledges for the Carriage of his Provisions and Baggage; but as for himself and his Men, they continued their Route on Foot. Upon receiving this News, the Captain thought proper to advance from Ochotski to receive his Lieutenant, carrying with him a Convoy of Provisions laden upon large Dogs. By this wise Precaution he brought his Lieutenant and the Remainder of his Detachment safe to Ochotski, upon New Year's-Day 1727.

5. The Account which this Officer gave him of the Miseries they sustained in their March was equally melancholy and sincere. They quitted the River of Gorbea on the 4th of November, and not being able to carry with them a sufficient Quantity of Provisions, were very quickly constrained to feed upon the Flesh of their dead Horses. They afterwards burnt off the Hair from their Skins with Lime, and then converted them into Coats and Shoes. They were forced to abandon their Baggage in three different Places, and had certainly perished at Judomska Kresta, if it had not been for a small Quantity of Meal which the Captain had been obliged to leave there by Reason that some of his Horses died. The Nation of Jakuts, who inhabit the Banks of the Lena, dwell also on those of the Rivers Aldan and Maya, but on the Sides of the River Judoma, and

in the Neighbourhood of the Fortress of Ochota, reside the Nation
Lamutki. These People have tame Rain-Deer, which they employ in
drawing their Carriages, as well as to furnish them with Cloaths
and Subsistance. In the Neighbourhood of the Lakes and of the
Sea, dwell the Tunguses, for the Conveniency of Fishing. These
People are as barbarous and as much Idolaters as the Jakuts.

In the Beginning of the Month of February, the Captain dispatched a Lieutenant and 90 Men, with some Dogs, to fetch off the
Baggage that had been abandoned in the Manner before-mentioned;
he returned with a part of it in April; and another Detachment
being order'd on the same Service, they brought the rest back in
May. In this Country the Snow falls in such prodigious Quantities,
that it commonly lies about two Yards thick, and sometimes more,
upon the Ground, which obliges People, for three or four Months,
to travel on Foot, and to drag their Baggage on little Sledges,
which will carry 6 or 700 Weight. In this Manner the Lieutenant
marched that came to Ochotski, and during his whole Passage, the
poor People had no other Relief in the Night-time, or when the
cutting icy Winds blew, than to cover themselves as deep as they
could in the Snow. This is practised on the Coasts of Hudson's-
Bay, and in other cold Countries as well as here; and if Credit
may be given to several Narrations written by those who have
visited these frozen Climates, it is a very convenient and
effectual Screen from the extreme Fury of the Weather, which will
be the less wonder'd at, if we consider, that both Gardiners and

Husbandmen acknowledge very discernable Heat in Snow, by which Corn, Fruit and Flowers, are defended from the Rage of Winter, in the Earth, and are enabled by this kindly Covering to push out and discover that they are alive in the Spring.

On the 30th of June the Captain ordered Lieutenant Spanberg to cross the Gulph to the Mouth of the Balchaia rerca, or Great River; he was to perform this Voyage in a new stout Vessel built by their own Workmen, and had Orders to carry over with him the second Architect, and a sufficient Number of Men to cut down Timber, and to build a new Vessel there, which when they had performed, they were instructed to give the Captain Notice of it at Ochotski. While they were thus employed, the other Lieutenant Crezihoff returned, bringing with him 2300 Poud of Meal, that is about 800 Weight, which was immediately embarked on board the new Vessel that was returned from Kamschatska. The Captain then ordered all the heavy Baggage and Provisions to be embarked without Delay, and on the 21st of August he went on board himself for the Port before-mentioned. He left behind him a Pilot, and a small Number of Persons, with Instructions as to the recovering and securing the Provisions that had been left behind, which they were to bring with them if they could, but if not, they were to deliver them to the Government of Jakutsky, and to take a Discharge for them; after which, the Pilot, and those under his Command, were to join the Captain, and bring with them a small Supply of Provisions, Iron, and Tar. However, he saw nothing of them till the Year 1728.

The Captain being come to the Mouth of Bolchaya rerka, trans-

ported his Provisions and other Necessaries to Bolchay reeski
ostrog, or the Habitation of the great River. The heavy Baggage
was from hence conveyed in small Boats, that were drawn against
the Stream for 120 Wersts, to the higher Settlement in Kamschatska.
This Journey they performed themselves by Land, making use of the
little Sleds before-mentioned, that were drawn by Dogs, for the
Carriage of what was necessary for them during the Journey. On
this Occasion, they had thorough Experience of the extreme Rigour
of the Climate, being obliged to have Recourse to the Method
before-mentioned, that is to say, towards Night, or when-ever they
had a Mind to rest, they ran a very deep Trench or Ditch through
the Snow; at the Entrance of this Trench they hung up Deer Skins,
and then lay down under the Snow, either to sleep or to take Repose.
The Intent of hanging up the Skins, is to prevent those sudden
Storms which are common in these Parts, and to which they give the
Name of Purgi, from being fatal to them, as they often are to less
cautious Passengers, by bringing with them such prodigious Quantities of Snow as bury these unfortunate Victims under it, past all
Possibility of extricating themselves or excaping.

As we have now conducted the Reader into that Country which
is the proper Subject of this Section, and which, for any thing
that is yet known, seems to be the very Extremity of the Continent,
on this Side, tho' there is a very wide Country behind it, extending directly North for above 15° of Latitude. I say, as we
have followed him hither, the next thing is to see what Account

he gives us of this strange Place, which lies so far out of the
Reach of the rest of Mankind, and which could never have been
visited, much less planted and possessed by any but the Russians,
and even these had not been long fixed there at this Time.

The Russians have three Settlements, or to speak with greater
Propriety, have occupied three Posts in this Country. In the
Fortress which is in the upper Kamschatska, there are seventeen,
in the lower Fortress there are about fifty Russian Houses, ex-
clusive of those that are about the Church, which may be about
fifteen in Number. At the Mouth of the River before-mentioned,
there were at this Time fourteen Houses. In these three Posts
there were about 150 Soldiers in Garrison, and the principal Point
aimed at by fixing them here, was to collect the Tribute from the
neighbouring Nations. The Captain, to reward those that had
assisted him in transporting his heavy Baggage, his Stores and
Ammunition, and who had likewise furnished him with Carriages,
gave them about an hundred Weight of Train Oil, which he extracted
from a Whale the Sea left upon the Coast at the warm Season of the
Year; and with this and a little Chinese Tobacco, they were better
contented than if he had given them Money. To the South of this
Country inhabit the Nation of Kuriles, and to the Northward dwell
the Kamtschadales, the Languages spoke by these Nations are so
different, that they hardly understand each other; some of them
are addicted to Idolatry; amongst others there are no apparent
Signs of any Religion; and to say the Truth, hardly any convincing

Tokens of Humanity.

The Russians that are settled in Kamtschatska, as well as the Natives or original Inhabitants, are destitute both of Cattle and Corn; instead of the former they make use of Dogs, which are very large and strong; and by the way, this is likewise the Custom in Groenland, and in the Countries bordering upon Hudson's-Bay. As to Provisions, they live chiefly upon Fish, Roots, and Pears; they have likewise Carrots and Beans, and in some Seasons of the Year tolerable plenty of Wild-fowl. As to their Cloaths, they are made of Dogs-skin; it is however worth observing, that in the Country about the Convent of Pakussiska, which is not far from the Church, they have a little Barley, as also some Hemp and Radishes, and in the Plantations about the Russian Houses, they have Turnips of a prodigious Size, that is to say of five or six Pounds Weight apiece. The Captain, while he was there, caused some Rye and Oats to be sowed, but he did not stay long enough to see whether they came up. The Frost sets in here very early, and the People, who are tributary to the Russians, pay their Taxes in several Sorts of Furs.

The Customs of these People are barbarous in the highest Degree, of which a very few Instances may be sufficient to convince the Reader. If a Woman happens to have two Children at a Birth, one of them is destroyed as soon as it is born, and it would be esteemed a Crime to preserve it. Nor are they cruel only to Children, for if the Father and Mother of a Family happens to fall sick, tho' the Disease does not appear to be mortal, yet they drag them away presently to a Wood, let the Weather be what it will, and there they leave them, not indeed without Provisions, for they commonly carry them as much as will serve them for a few Days, but they very seldom hear any more of them. When People die so suddenly that they cannot be thus removed, they drag the Body into the Woods, and leave it there to be devoured by the Dogs. There seems to be a good deal of Superstition in this, for some of them will quit the Place of their Residence, if a Man happens to breathe his last in it. The Nation of the Koratkes burn their Dead, and though they have been often admonished to leave off this Practice, yet hitherto there has been no breaking them of it.

Since the Time our Author wrote, it appears from several Books that have been published at Petersbourg, that this Country, at least the Russian Settlements in it, have been greatly improv'd; so that in the Latitude of 56, and even higher, they have Barley, Oats, and Rye, in tolerable Plenty. The Number of Houses also are greatly increased, and the Fortresses are in much better Order, which is owing to the Hopes that are still entertained of opening on this Side, some Time or other, a very advantageous Commerce. We have been promised, and were in Hopes of receiving a large and accurate Description of this Country in its present Condition, but as yet it has not been published; many People may possibly think, that considering the Rigour of the Climate, the Barrenness of the Soil, and the Thinness of its Inhabitants, that it is no great Matter whether it be ever published. Yet notwithstanding all this,

it is not impossible, or even improbable, that in Process of Time
Things may change their Face here, for the Country now called
Kamtschatska, is not that vast Northern Continent that extends from
60 to 73 Degrees of North Latitude, which was formerly included
under that Name, but the Peninsula only which extends from the
Latitude of 51 to 60, and lies between 80 and 95 Degrees Longitude
East from Tobolski; so that if a sufficient Number of People were
sent thither to cut down the vast Forests with which it is incum-
ber'd, and enabled to till, manure, and cultivate the Earth, it
might be render'd a Place far enough from being despicable; and
then the great Importance of its Situation would very quickly appear.
But to return to our Narrative.

7. Upon the Captain's Arrival at the lower Fortress, he found
Wood enough cut for the building a Vessel, which was put upon the
Stocks April 4, 1728, and was entirely finished the 10th of July
following. It is certain that a properer Person could not well
have been employed, since he thought nothing a Difficulty, nor was
afraid of any kind of Hardship or Danger that stood in the Way of
the Execution of his Orders, but with infinite Address, and almost
incredible Patience, got over those Difficulties, that to another
Man would have appeared unsurmountable. All the Timber that was
used in Building, was conveyed to the Place where his new Vessel
was constructed, upon Sledges drawn by Dogs, and consequently
with infinite Pains and Trouble. The Supply of Tar he expected
not being arrived, was another great Inconveniency, but the Cap-

tain, who had a Brain very fertile in Expedients, observed a Tree there, called by the Natives Lisnischink, which he fancied would supply them either with Tar, or something like it; accordingly he caused great Quantities of it to be cut and burned, and, as he expected, the resinous Matter that run from it answered the Ends of Tar, if not perfectly, at least tolerably.

The Vessel being built, the next Thing was to victual her, and that for a Voyage, the Length of which was altogether uncertain; and to do this in a Country in a Manner destitute of Provisions, was none of the easiest Undertakings. The Captain however went about it, and, in the first Place, having collected a vast Quantity of Plants and Herbs, he distilled from them a pretty strong Spirit, upon which he was pleased to bestow the Name of Brandy, and of this he laid in a plentiful Stock. Instead of Meal or Corn, he furnished himself with Carrots or other Roots. By boiling the Seawater, he procured as much Salt as he wanted. Fish Oyl served instead of Butter, and dry and wet Salt-fish took the Place of Beef and Pork. These Provisions, such as they were, he embarked in such Quantities as would serve his Crew, consisting of forty Men, for a whole Year.

Thus equipped, he undertook the Execution of the Instructions given him by his Sovereign Peter the Great, under his own Hand, and of which the following is a Copy taken literally from his Journal.

I. You shall cause one or two convenient Vessels to be built at Kamtschatska, or elsewhere.

II. You shall endeavour to discover, by Coasting with these
Vessels, whether the Country towards the North, of which at present
we have no distinct Knowledge, is a Part of America, or not.

III. If it joins to the Continent of America, you shall
endeavour, if possible, to reach some Colony belonging to some
European Power; or in case you meet with any European Ship, you
shall diligently enquire the Name of the Coasts, and such other
Circumstances as it is in your Power to learn; and these you shall
commit to Writing, so that we may have some certain Memoirs by
which a Chart may be constructed.

On the 14th of July, having recommended himself to the Protection of Almighty God, he sailed out of the River of Kamtschatska.
On the 8th of August he found himself in the Latitude of 64 Degrees,
30 Minutes, and being perceived by the Inhabitants on Shore, eight
Men put off in a Boat made of Skins, and came to the Vessel, that
is to say, to the Side of it, where they enquired whence he came,
and to what Purpose. After he had answered them, they acquainted
him in their Turn that they were Tzuktschi, which is the Name of
a Nation with whom the Russians have been for some Years acquainted.
It was with some Difficulty that he got one of them to come to him,
but he was soon followed by the rest. They informed him that the
Coast, for a considerable Extent, was inhabited by their Nation,
and that the Land tended to the West. They likewise gave him
Information of an Island that was not far off, which he accordingly
found on the 10th of August; and as that is the Feast of St.

Lawrence in the Russian Kalendar, he thought fit to bestow that
Name upon the Island. He sent an Officer on board a Shallop of
four Oars thither twice to examine it, but he could not find any
Inhabitants, though there were some Houses upon it; which sufficiently shewed that it was inhabited, though the People, out of Fear,
or from some other Motive, thought proper to conceal themselves.

He continued his Course to the 15th of the same Month, when
he found himself in the Latitude of 67 Degrees 18 Minutes, and
conceiving that he had now fully executed the Emperor's Orders,
as he saw no Land, either to the North or to the East, he resolved
to return, as thinking it to no Purpose to continue his Voyage
towards the West, or to run the Hazard of being driven by a contrary
Wind beyond the Possibility of getting back during the Summer to
Kamschatska, and to winter in a Country where he was sure of
meeting with little or no Wood, and which might very possibly be
inhabited by some Nation, Enemies to the Russians, was, in his
Opinion, running a very great, and, at the same Time, unnecessary
Hazard.

From the Mouth of the River Kamschatska, to the Utmost Point
of their Voyage, they saw nothing upon the Coast but great Ridges
of Rocks, the Tops of which were covered with Snow, though it was
Summer. They traversed, according to their Computation, about ten
Leagues of Latitude, and thirty of Longitude, that is to say, the
farthest they sailed East, was 372 German Leagues. On the 20th of
August, in their Return, they saw forty Persons on board four small

Boats rowing towards them from Shore with all their Force; they lay by for them, and upon their coming near them, they concluded them, from their Appearance, to be of the Nation called Tzuktschi. They had with them a good Quantity of dry'd Flesh, Fish, and Water contain'd in Whales Bladders, 15 Fox Skins, and four Narval's Teeth, which they sold, or rather exchanged for Pins and Needles with the Seamen. These People told them, that their Nation travelled with Rain Deer as far as the River Kohlima, which runs into the North Sea, but that they never had attempted any Passage by Sea. That their Nation inhabited a very long Tract of Country upon that Coast, and had been possessed of it for many Years; one of them particularly said, he had been at the Fortress of Anadirski, where they had traded with, and been very well treated by the Russians. They had very great Hopes of obtaining considerable Intelligence from this Man, but notwithstanding all the Questions they proposed, they could gain from him no more than a Confirmation of what they had formerly learned from the Tzuktschi.

On the 29th of August they met with a great Storm, attended with a thick Fog, by which they were driving upon the Coast of some Country East of Kamschatska, and where they were oblig'd to come to an Anchor. Upon their endeavouring to weigh it the next Day, their Cable broke; however, they were so lucky as to escape with no other Loss than that of their Anchor. On the 2d of September they arrived safely in the Mouth of the River of Kamschatska, where they landed, and having secured their Vessel in a Creek, went to the lower Fortress, where they passed the Winter. There they met with the rest of their Companions, who brought them a considerable Supply of Provisions, which, after the Fatigues they had sustained, were very acceptable. In this Place they spent the Winter, without meeting with any thing worthy of our Notice. On the 5th of June 1729, they repaired their Vessel and put to Sea, steering due East from the Mouth of the River Kamschatska, in Hopes of discovering that Land, which the Inhabitants affirm'd might be seen in a clear Day; which, however, they were not so happy as to meet with, though they continued that Route for 30 Leagues, and then meeting with a Storm at East-North-East they were obliged to return to the Mouth of the Bolschay reeschi, after having passed round the South Point of Kamschatska, which was a Voyage that was never performed before. They went from thence by Sea to the Fortress of Ochotsky, where they delivered up their Stores of Provision, consisting of Flour, dry'd Flesh, and Salt, to the proper Officers. On the 20th of July they arrived at the Mouth of the River Ochota, where they delivered up the Vessel, with the Materials and Tools on board her, to the Governor. The Captain then hired Horses for himself and Company, to go by Land to Judomska kresta; thence they proceeded by Water in small Boats and Rafts, along the River Aldan to the Passage of Beloya, and thence they went on Horseback to Jakutski; all this they performed exactly in a Month, arriving there on the 29th of August.

On the 20th of September they left that Place, and went in two

Vessels up the River Lena, as far as the Village of Peledun, where they arrived on the 10th of October, and there they were obliged to stay for about ten Days, because the Rivers began now to be covered with Ice. The Snow falling in great Quantities, and the River being thoroughly froze, they set out on the 29th of October for Ilimski, and from thence by the Rivers Tungus and Jenesci, which were now covered with Ice, they came to the Town of Jenischiski; from that Town, passing through several Villages of Russians and Tartars newly converted, they reached Tomski, and passing over the great Deserts of Bambinski, they reached Tara, and from thence mounting the River Irtisch, they came to Tobolski, January 10, 1730. In this City they remained till the 25th of the same Month, and then set out by the Road before described, for Petersbourg, where the Captain safely arrived on the first of March following.

The Detail which we have given our Reader, is not barely copied from the Accounts that have been published in German, Low-Dutch, French, and other Languages, but hath been compared with a Copy of Captain Behring's original Journal, which has been of very great Service; we have also examined his Map very carefully, and considered, at the same Time, how far it was consistent with prior and with posterior Discoveries, of which more shall be said hereafter. At present I will crave Leave to add here, from a Manuscript Copy of the Journal, a very curious Table of the Places mentioned therein, with their Latitudes and Longitudes from Tobolski, the rather, because it has never been published, at least so far as I know, and because it will serve as Kind of Test, by which all subsequent Accounts may be tried with respect to their Veracity; for I make no Doubt at all, that this Table was framed with the utmost Care and Circumspection, because I find it was transmitted by the Author to the Russian Court in 1728, immediately after his Return from his Voyage for Discovery, and while he remained at the Lower Fortress of Kamschatska.

It is also necessary to take Notice of the Meaning of the Russian Words made use of in this Table, which, as they are but very few, cannot burthen the Reader's Memory. Krepost signifies a Fortress, Ostrog a little Fort, Slaboda a Borough or Place bigger than a Village, Monasteria, a Convent or Monastery. It is true, we might have avoided these, and have given the Places in plain English, but as the Design of this whole Section is to facilitate the understanding such Accounts as may be hereafter received of the Russian discoveries, I thought proper to preserve the Names for that Reason, as well as because we find them frequently occurring in the Maps. These Points being premised, the following Tables will be very plain and perspicuous.

Relation Du Voyage fait par le Capitaine Beering, au Kamtschatka

depuis 1725 jusqu'en 1730; ou Abrégé de son Journal.

Le 5 Février 1725 je fus dépêché par l'Amiral Général de ce
tems-là, le Comte Apraxin, pour entreprendre une Commission en
Sibérie, & alors on m'ordonna par une Instruction dressée à cette
fin, de m'informer entre autres choses des limites de ce pays, &
particulierement si le coin Oriental de Sibérie se trouvoit séparé
de l'Amérique. On me donna en même tems la liberté de prendre
dans les villes de Sibérie, autant de gens de métiers que j'aurois
besoin, & tout ce que je trouverois nécessaire pour mon voyage;
m'enjoignant aussi d'en faire rapport tous mois au Collége de
l'Amirauté de Sa Majesté Impériale.

Avant que d'obtenir les Instructions susdites, un Lieutenant
fut expédié du Collége de l'Amirauté le 24 Janvier, pour prendre
le devant avec 20 hommes, & 25 chevaux chargés d'outils & des in-
strumens nécessaires en voyage.

Dans tout mon détachement il n'y avoit que 33 personnes, les
subalternes y compris. Je rattrappai celui qui étoit parti avant
moi, à Vologda; d'où nous poursuivîmes notre voyage de S. Petersbourg à Tobolske, passant par les villes Vologda, Totma, Ustiug-
veliki, Solveichégorskaia, Kaygorod, Solkamska, Verkhoturia,
Turinske ou Iepantzine, & Tumene.

Le 15 Mars nous arrivâmes a Tobolske, & nous y demeurâmes
jusqu'au 15 Mai, parce que la saison étoit déja passée pour pouvoir
passer outre. Pendant mon séjour, j'y fis faire les outils

nécessaires pour le succès de ma commission.

Le 15 Mai, je poursuivis mon voyage par eau, descendant la riviere Irtische, de Tobolske à Samaroskoie-Iam, endroit de relais,[1] où je chargeai quatre barques qu'on appelle en Sibérie Doscheniki, & que je remplis du bagage & des outils que j'avois emportés de S. Petersbourg, & de ceux que j'avois fait construire à Tobolske.

On m'avoit donné à Tobolske un Moine de l'Ordre de S. Jérôme, un Commissaire, des bas Officiers, & 27 soldats que j'avois demandés.

De Samaroskoie-Iam j'envoyai devant moi un Garde-marine sur une barque avec les ordres qu'on m'avoit donnés à la Chancellerie de Tobolske, sçavoir, qu'il feroit tenir des barques Sibériennes toutes prêtes à Doschenikoye, à Ieniseiske, à Anskuthe, & qu'ensuite il s'avanceroit vers Iakutske.

Nous montâmes de Samaroskoie-Iam, le fleuve Obi, jusqu'à Surgute, & ensuite à Narime; après quoi nous montâmes la riviere Kete jusqu'à Makostkoie, qui est une espece de forteresse.

Quant aux habitans qui demeurent depuis Tobolske jusqu'à ce dernier lieu, près de la riviere où nous fîmes notre route, ils s'appellent tous Ostiaki: ils étoient il y a peu de tems idolâtres; mais par les soins du Métropolitain de Tobolske, ils ont embrassé la Religion Chrétienne.[2]

De la forteresse de Makostkoie, nous passâmes par terre à Ienisseiske. De cette ville, pour aller à Ilimske, nous montâmes le Ienissea & la Tunguska, dans quatre barques, comme nous avions fait ci-devant.

On trouve dans la Tunguska trois cataractes & d'autres grandes
chûtes d'eau, qui débordent en passant les bords de la riviere.
On y trouve aussi de grands rochers qui sont cachés dans l'eau:
ce qui fait qu'il n'y a qu'un ou deux passages pour les batteaux;
& par rapport aux cataractes, les pierres qui s'y trouvent sont
en si grand nombre, que le passage y est presque impraticable. Mais
la différence qu'il y a entre ces cataractes consiste en ce que
l'eau dans les plus élevées est fort basse pendant presque une
lieue de France. Nous n'avons pu passer dans ces endroits sans
courir de grands dangers, & sans essuyer beaucoup de peines.

Selon les ordres que j'avois reçus de Tobolske, je m'étois
pourvû (à Ieniseiske) de trente hommes, tant charpentiers que
maréchaux.

On ne peut se servir de barques Sibériennes sur la riviere
Ilime, jusqu'à la ville d'Ilimske, parce que dans cette riviere
il y a aussi des cataractes & des eaux basses. C'est pourquoi on
nous envoya de cette ville de petits batteaux dans lesquels nous
transportâmes le plus gros de notre bagage à Ilimske, & le reste
y fut porté sur des traîneaux.

Je dépêchai d'Ilimske le Lieutenant par terre, vers le fleuve
Lena & jusques vers Uskute, avec des subalternes & des charpentiers
au nombre de 39 hommes, pour y bâtir pendant l'hyver 15 barques
pour descendre le Lena à Iakutzke, & y transporter les provisions,
le bagage & tout mon détachement, parce que Uskute, est presque
désert, & qu'il eût été impossible d'aller à Iakutzke en traîneaux

à cause de la grande quantité de neige, du manquement de chevaux,
& du froid excessif; comme aussi des grands déserts qu'il auroit
fallu passer. C'est pourquoi comme il nous falloit beaucoup de
vivres pour une si grande route, la Chancellerie de Tobolske avoit
donné ordre qu'on nous en fournît sufficamment a Irkutzke, & à
Ilimske, parce qu'aux environs de Iakutzke il ne se trouve point
de bled.

Je partis le même hyver d'Ilimske pour Irkutzke, afin de
m'aboucher avec le Voevode ou Gouverneur, qui avoit été ci-devant
Voevode à Iakutzke, & qui par cette raison connoissoit la nature
de ces endroits, & par conséquent la maniere la plus commode d'aller
de Iakutzke à Okhostke & à Kamtschatka; car sans lui personne
n'étoit en état de nous en informer en aucune façon.

Au déclin de l'hyver je poursuivis mon voyage en traîneaux
à Uskute avec tout mon détachement. A Iakoutzke il fut renforcé
par quelques forgerons & quelques charpentiers, qui faisoient
ensemble 20 hommes. Je me fis donner aussi à Ilimske deux tonneliers.

Le long des rivieres Tunguska, Ilim & Lena, jusqu'à celle de
Wittima, se trouve un Nation qu'on appelle Tungusi, qui estiment
fort les Rennes, à cause de l'utilité qu'ils en tirent en voyage.
Ceux qui n'ont point de ces animaux, habitent les bords de ces
rivieres, où ils se nourrissent de poissons seulement, se servant
de barques faites d'écorce de bouleau. Cette Nation est idolâtre.

L'an 1726 au printems, nous descendîmes le Lena à Iakutzke

dans les 15 barques dont j'ai parlé. Aux deux bords de la riviere Wittima, au-dessous de celle de Lena, on trouve un peuple nommé Iakuti, avec une partie de celui qu'on appelle Tungusi qui sont tous sans demeure fixe.

Les Iakutes ont beaucoup de bêtail, comme des chevaux & des bêtes à cornes, dont ils se servent tant pour leur nourriture que pour leur vêtement; mais ceux qui n'en ont pas tant, se nourrissent de poissons. Ils sont tous idolâtres, & adorent le Soleil, la Lune, les oiseaux, comme sont le Cigne, l'Aigle, & les Corbeaux. Ils font grand cas des sorciers, qu'ils nomment en leur langue Schemani.

Ils ont aussi auprès d'eux de petits Bolvan ou des Statues qu'ils nomment en leur langue Scheitan. Au reste il semble que ce peuple est une race Tatare.

A mon arrivée à Iakutzke, je demandai du monde pour faciliter la marche de mon détachement, & dès que j'eus reçu du secours, je descendis le Lena. Un Lieutenant monta les rivieres Aldan, Maia, & Iudoma, avec trois barques construites à Uskute, qui étoient plates au fond, & sur lesquelles on charges les provisions, dont la plus grand partie ne pouvoit pas être traînée ni portée par des chevaux. Je croyois qu'ils pourroient arriver jusqu'à la Iudomska Kresta,[3] & alors ce voyage n'auroit pas tant coûté que par terre. Pour moi avec un petit nombre de mes gens, je pris à cheval le chemin de Iakutzke à Okhotskoi-Ostrog, qui est une forteresse; c'étoit le même été. Quant à notre provision nous la

325

mîmes en paquets & en caisses, & nous fûmes obligés de les charger
sur des chevaux, c'est-à-dire, le poids de 220 livres sur chaque
cheval; car il est de toute impossibilité de se servir dans ce
pays-là d'autre voiture. Je pris donc avec moi pour provisions
1600 pudes[4] pesant.

On ne trouve que dix ménages Russiens auprès de la forteresse
d'Okhotske.

Je laissai à Iakutzke le Lieutenant Tchirikov pendant l'hyver;
avec ordre qu'au printems suivant il continueroit par terre la
même route vers Okhotske.

A la fin de Décembre 1726, le Lieutenant me manda par une
lettre que les barques que j'avois expédiées avec lui, ne pouvoient
avancer jusqu'à Iudiumska, à 450 verstes près, parçe qu'elles avoient
été prises par les glaces dans la riviere Gorbée, & qu'il avoit
fait faire des traîneaux longs, sur lesquels il avoit chargé les
outils, les bagages & les hardes les plus nécessaires, & qu'il
alloit partir à pied avec son détachement, portant avec lui autant
d'ustensiles qu'il pourroit.

J'allai avec mon détachement & avec les Citoyens d'Okhotske,
au-devant du Lieutenant & de sa suite, menant avec nous des chiens
qui portoient une partie des provisions. Ce détachement arriva à
Okhotske, le premier Janvier 1727, après avoir commencé le voyage
de la riviere Gorbée le 4 Novembre 1725. Cependant comme ils ne
purent mener avec eux que très-peu de provision & de bagage, ils
souffrirent une faim si terrible qu'ils furent obligés de manger

des chevaux morts, se servant de toutes les peaux crûes qu'ils pouvoient trouver & qu'ils mettoient dans la chaux chaude, pour s'en couvrir le corps & se garantir les pieds de la rigueur du froid. Ils avoient été obligés de laisser en quatre endroits différens, chemin faisant, le bagage & les outils, parce qu'ils ne trouvoient point d'habitans dans leur route pour les aider. Cependant ils eurent pour subsister une partie de la farine que j'avois été contraint de laisser en chemin, quand je fis le voyage de Iudomska-Kresta, parce que plusieurs chevaux, dont je ne me souviens pas du nombre, y moururent.[5]

Le même Peuple qui demeure près du Léna, s'appelle Iakuti, & habite aussi les environs des rivieres Aldan & Maia; mais les bords de la riviere Iudoma, & les environs de la forteresse d'Okhotske, sont occupés par une Nation qui se nomme Tungusi de mer, ou, selon leur langue, Lamutki; ils ont une grande quantité de Rennes apprivoisées qui leur servent de portefaix. Ces bêtes, aussi bien que les Rennes sauvages, leur fournissent la nourriture & le vêtement. On trouve aussi parmi eux des Tungusi à pied qui demeurent plus près des lacs & des rivieres, parce qu'ils se nourrissent de poissons. Au reste, ils sont tous de la même religion que les Iakuti.

J'envoyai au commencement du mois de Février un Lieutenant, 90 hommes, & quelques chiens, avec des traîneaux, pour rassembler notre bagage, qui avoit été laissé près de la riviere Iudoma.

Le même Lieutenant retourna à Okhotske au commencement d'Avril

& une partie de sa suite au milieu d'Avril, sans qu'elle eût
pu pourtant emporter tout le bagage. C'est pourquoi j'expédiai
encore une fois 27 hommes à Iudoma-Kresta, qui revinrent au mois
de Mai.

Le reste de nos hardes fut amené par des chevaux de Iakutzke
à Okhotske. Vers les autres lieux éloignés on ne pouvoit plus les
transporter par traîneaux, parce que la neige y est trop profonde
& tombe jusqu'à une sagene ou la hauteur d'un homme; & même beaucoup
au-delà dans quelques endroits. Ainsi on est obligé d'aller à pied
pendant 8, 10 & 15 semaines, traînant soi-même le bagage dont on
a besoin, sur des traîneaux chargés de 10 à 15 pudes; & mon détachement fit ainsi depuis la riviere Gorbée jusqu'à Okhotske. Ceux
qui furent obligés de tenir cette route en hyver, furent con-
traints de miner des trous très-profonds dans la neige, où ils se
mettoient pendant la nuit pour être a l'abri du grand froid qui
regne dans ce pays-là, sans quoi ils fussent morts indubitablement.

Le 30 Juin j'envoyai un Lieutenant par eau d'Okhotske, sur
une barque nouvellement construite, avec tout le bagage à l'embouchure de la riviere Bolchaia Reka (ou la grande riviere) & je
lui commandai d'y débarquer nos outils & nos bagages, & de conduire à Kamtschatka le sous-Architecte & les Charpentiers de notre
détachement, pour y tailler le bois nècessaire à la construction
d'un vaisseau; mais que pour lui il ne tardât pas de revenir au
plutôt.

Le Lieutenant Tchirikov arriva le 3 Juillet de Iakutzke,

portant avec lui, selon mes ordres, 2300 pudes[6] de farine.

Le 21 Août, après avoir non-seulement chargé le batteau qui étoit de retour de la Bolchaia-Reka, mais aussi un autre qui arriva du même endroit, de tout le bagage & des provisions dont je viens de parler, je m'en allai par eau d'Okhotskoi-Ostrog à Bolchorêt-koye-Ostrog avec tout mon détachement.[7]

Quant à la partie des provisions qui fut prise par les glaces dans la riviere de Gorbée, j'y laissai un pilote avec un détache-ment pour la garder jusqu'à ce qu'il put la mener vers la riviere Notora[8] pour la livrer à la Chancellerie de Iakutszke, de laquelle il devoit prendre un reconnoissement, & une partie du fer & du goudron qui y étoit, pour nous rejoindre ensuite au Kamtschatka, où il arriva l'an 1728.

Pour nous, en arrivant à l'embouchure de la Bolchaia-Reka, je fis mener notre bagage à Bolchorêtzkoye Ostrog, avec les pro-visions que je fis charger sur de petites barques. Il n'y a auprès de cette forteresse que 4 ménages Russiens, je fis ensuite conduire dans de petites barques, le plus pesant de notre bagage & une partie de nos provisions, jusqu'à la hauteur du haut Kamtschatkoye-Ostrog, 120 verstes près.

Nous poussâmes notre chemin en traîneaux tirés, selon la maniere du pays, par des chiens; voyageant quelquefois en-deçà de la forteresse de Kamtschatka, & quelquefois de l'autre côté. Pendant ce voyage nous nous cachions sous la neige, où nous passions, toutes les nuits, ayant soin de nous bien couvrir par le

haut, parce que ces endroits sont très-exposés au mauvais tems
& aux ouragans, qu'ils nomment en leur langue Purgi. Il arrive
même fort souvent que les voyageurs sont surpris en chemin faisant
par ces ouragans, avant qu'ils puissent achever leur gîte sous la
neige; & alors ils sont accablés d'une si prodigieuse quantité
de neige, qu'ils en meurent sous le poids.

Près du haut de la forteresse, il se trouve 17 familles, en
bas il y en a 50, & plus loin dans un autre endroit, où l'Eglise
est bâtie, il y en a 15.[9]

Pendant notre séjour à Kamtschatka, les garnisons des trois
forteresses ne consistoient qu'en 150 soldats, qui n'y sont que
pour lever les contributions que les habitans payent tous les ans.

Nous donnâmes aux habitans de cet endroit pour le payement
des voitures qu'ils nous avoient fournies depuis Bolchorêtskoye-
Ostrog jusque-là 300 pudes de la graisse d'une baleine qui avoit
été jettée l'automne précédent sur le bord du rivage, & du tabac
Chinois, au lieu de l'argent que nour aurions dû leur donner.

Dans le Kamtschatka du côté du Sud, il y a une Nation qu'on
nomme Kurili. Vers le Nord, il y a parmi les Kamtschadali peu de
monde qui soit idolâtre; le reste est sans religion & infecté de
plusieurs mauvaises coûtumes. Au reste leur langage differe fort
peu l'un de l'autre.

Les Russiens, aussi bien que les Kamtschadali, n'ont ni bled
ni bêtes, excepté des chiens, par lesquels ils menent & trans-
portent selon leur besoin d'un endroit à l'autre; ils s'en servent

aussi pour leur vêtement. Ils se nourrissent de poissons, de carottes & de fêves, de gibier, & en été de ce que la Mer rejette.

Il croît du bled près du couvent nommé Pakut-Siska, qui est à une verste de l'Eglise de Kamtschatkoye-Ostrog: il y vient aussi des raves. Chez les soldats Russiens qui restent en-deçà de ces forteresses, on y trouve quelques années, des navets d'une telle grosseur qu'il n'y en a pas en Russie de pareils, puisque six font quelquefois un pude environ 40 livres.

J'apportai audit couvent du seigle & de l'avoine, qui y fut semé pendant mon séjour, mais je ne sçai s'il devint mur ou non. Au reste, il y gele de bonne heure, & on n'y engraisse pas la terre. Ils n'y ont point de bêtes, & la terre est labourée par les hommes.

Le peuple du Kamtschatka est sous l'obéissance d l'Empereur de Russie: il paye ses contributions en fourrures.[10] Il a la superstition ou la vilaine habitude d'étouffer un enfant sitôt que la femme a mis deux jumeaux au monde, croyant commettre le plus noir de tous les crimes si l'on ne tue pas l'un des deux.

Il a encore une autre mauvaise coûtume, que quand l'un des deux du pere où de la mere devient malade, quand même la maladie ne seroit pas mortelle, de les porter dans une forêt, soit en été, soit en hyver, & de les y laisser avec la provision d'une semaine; de cette maniere il n'y en a guere qui en reviennent. Ils n'enterrent pas leurs morts, mais les donnent aux chiens qui les mangent. Il y en a aussi d'entre eux qui abandonnent leur gîte sitôt que quelques-uns y sont morts.

Les Kurili brûlent leurs morts, malgré la défense qui leur en a été faite; mais aussi le font-ils impunément.

A mon arrivée à Kamtschatskoye-Ostrog l'inférieur ou Niznei je trouvai la plus grande partie du bois dont j'ai parlé entiére- ment prêt pour la construction d'un vaisseau. Le 4 Avril nous en mîmes un sur le chantier, pour y être construit, aussi le fut-il avec l'assistance du bon Dieu le 10 Juillet: les matériaux furent traînés par des chiens. Le goudron y fut brûlé d'une espece de bois qu'on appelle Lisnischnick, parce que nous n'avions point d'autre goudron avec nous. Jusques-là les habitans n'avoient pas connu la propriété de ce bois de leur pays.

Nous brûlâmes de l'eau-de-vie pour notre trajet de Mer, & nous prîmes des carottes & des racines au défaut de bled. Nous fîmes du sel avec de l'eau de la mer; & au défaut de certaines provisions dont nous avions besoin, nous nous servîmes de la graisse crûe de poisson, à la place de beurre, & de poisson salé au lieu de viande.

Ensuite nous chargeâmes le navire d'une si grande quantité deprovisions, que 40 hommes en pouvoient subsister pendant une année entiere; & le 14 dudit mois de Juillet (1728) nous sortîmes de la riviere de Kamtschatka, en poursuivant le voyage, selon l'instruction que Sa Majesté Impériale Pierre le Grand m'avoit donné écrite de sa main, de la maniere que ma Carte le montre.[11]

Le 8 Août nous arrivâmes sous le 64 degré 30 minutes de latitude vers le Nord, & 8 hommes vinrent à nous ramant dans une barque de cuir, & nous demanderent d'où nous venions, & à quel propos nous étions-là. Ils dirent d'eux-mêmes qu'ils s'appelloient Tchuktschi: ces peuples sont connus par les Russes qui habitent aux environs de là. Enfin comme nous les appellions, ils détacherent un homme qui vint à nous nageant sur des peaux de chien marin, remplies de vent. Peu après ils s'approcherent aussi de notre navire; & nous apprirent que tout le rivage de la mer étoit fort peuplé par des Tchuktschi, & que toute la terre ferme qui n'en étoit pas fort éloignée, s'étendoit vers l'Ouest. Ils nous dirent en même tems qu'il y avoit devant nous une petite Isle[12] où nous fûmes ensuite; mais nous ne nous apperçûmes de personne, quoi-qu'il y eût quelque bâtiment; nous surnommâmes cette Isle de S. Laurent, comme ce jour-là en portoit le nom. Quelque démarche que j'ai fait faire, on n'a pu y appercevoir une ame pour nous informer de quelque chose.

Le 15 Août nous arrivâmes sous 67 degrés 18 minutes de latitude; mais nous ne passâmes pas outre, parce qu'il me sembloit avoir satisfait à l'instruction qu'on m'avoit donnée, sur-tout ne pouvant découvrir aucune terre du côté du Nord ni du côté de l'Orient des Tchuktschi.[13] D'ailleurs si nous eussions fait voile plus loin & trouvé ensuite un vent contraire, il nous auroit été impossible de retourner le même été à Kamtschatka, & nous eussions trop hazardé de passer l'hyver dans un pays où il ne se trouve pas de bois, & au milieu d'un peuple qui ne connoît aucune domination.

On apperçoit depuis l'embouchure de la riviere Kamtschatka jusqu'à l'endroit d'où nous retournâmes, des rivages élevés comme de hautes murailles par une longue chaîne de montagnes, hyver & été couvertes de neige.

A notre retour, le 20 Août, environ 40 hommes vinrent à nous dans 4 barques. C'ètoit des gens de la même nation que celle dont j'ai parlè ci-devant. Ils apporterent avec eux de la viande, du poisson, & de l'eau fraîche a vendre, avec deux sortes de pelleteries, l'une de renard blanc, & l'autre de renard ordinaire, au nombre de 15 pieces, avec 4 pieces de Morschovi, ou des dents marines, que mes gens troquerent pour des épingles & du fer à feu.

Ils nous dirent que leurs parens alloient par terre avec des marchandises menées par des Rennes, du côté de la riviere de Kolyma, où ils n'avoient jamais été par eau, & que plusieurs de leur Nation habitoient le long du rivage: qu'ils avoient oui parler des Russes, & qu'ils en avoient connu, un d'entre eux ayant commercé près d'Anadyrskoye-Ostrog, où il avoit apporté des marchandises. Au reste leur rapport s'accorde avec ceux des habitans Tchuktschi.

Le 8 Septembre nous arrivâmes à l'embouchure de la riviere Kamtschatka, & nous passâmes l'hyver à Kamtschatskoye-Ostrog, l'inférieure.

Le 5 Juin 1729, après avoir raccommodé notre navire, avec tout ce qui y appartient, nous sortîmes de l'embouchure du Kamt-

schatka en mer, tirant du côté de l'Orient, parce que les Kamtschadali nous avoient dit, que quand il faisoit un tems serein, on
pouvoit y découvrir quelque terre. Voyant que nous n'appercevions-
rien, nous nous avançâmes encore au-delà de 200 verstes, pour
sçavoir si ce qu'on nous disoit étoit réel; mais enfin n'y ayant
rien de vraisemblable,[14] nous dressâmes notre route du côté du
Midi ou du Sud, autour de la pointe de Bolscharetsk, selon le
dessein que j'ai fait des bouts de cette grande pointe du Continent jusqu'ici inconnue.[15]

De l'embouchure de Bolcharetsk, nous passâmes la mer à
Okhotskoye-Ostrog.

En-deçà de la forteresse de Kamtschatka & Bolcharetsk, nous
livrâmes au Voevode ou Gouverneur qui étoit alors en place, de la
farine, du gruau, de la viande seche & salée, la valeur de 800
pudes pesant.

Le 23 Juillet nous arrivâmes à l'embouchure d'Okhota; & nous
y livrâmes au Gouverneur le navire, avec tous les matériaux;
après quoi je pris mon chemin avec mon détachement sur des chevaux
de louage, pour aller à Iudomska-kresta; de là nous reprîmes notre
route par eau, sur des barques & batteaux plats, descendant la
riviere Aldan, pour nous rendre à Bilscha [ou la riviere de
Bielaia.] De-là nous poursuivîmes notre voyage à cheval, jusqu'à
Iakutzke. Je fis le voyage d'Okhota à Iakutzke, depuis le 29
Juillet jusqu'au 3 Septembre.

Depuis Iakutzke nous remontâmes le Léna, dans deux barques

plates; ce trajet dura jusqu'au premier Octobre. Il nous fallut séjourner dans le village Peledue, parce que les glaces nous boucherent le chemin que nous avions pris.

Le 2 Octobre nous allâmes à Ilinske sur la riviere Lena, qui s'étoit glacée par la quantité de neige qu'il tomba. Ensuite nous allâmes à Ienisseiske sur les rivieres Tunguska & Ienissea, passant par des villages Russiens.

Par la riviere Tchulim, nous allâmes de Ienisseiske à Tomske, passant par des villages habités par des Russes & par des Tatars nouvellement convertis.

De Tomske à Tchauskoye-Ostrog, nous avons toujours passé par des villages Russiens. De Tchausk vers les déserts des Barabinski.[16] De Tara-Barabinsk, à Tobolske, passant la riviere Irtische, & par des villages Tatars, nous arrivâmes à Tobolske le 10 Janvier 1730.

De Tobolske nous reprîmes notre voyage vers S. Petersbourg, le 25 Janvier, en prenant le même chemin que j'ai déja dit. Le premier de Mars nous arrivâmes à S. Petersbourg.

Je suis en état de donner une Relation plus circonstanciée de ce voyage, sitôt que l'on voudra me l'ordonner.

Voici la spécification des villes & des places les plus connues en Sibérie, & marquées dans la Carte, par lesquelles nous avons fait notre voyage, & sous quels degrés de longitude & de latitude elles sont situées, en comptant la longitude de Tobolske.

Noms des Villes & Places les plus remarquables.	Latitude	Longit. de Tobolske vers l'Ouest.
	De.Mi.	De.Mi.
La Ville de Tobolske.	50. 5	
Samaroskoye-Iam, Auberge.	60.17	
Surgut, petite Ville.	60.51	5.18
Narime, petite Ville.	58.48	14.36
Ketskoi-Ostrog.	58.19	
Losino-Boiskoi, Monastere.	58.17	23.13
Samachina, Village.	57.25	35.16
La Ville de Ieniseisk.	58.20	25.12
Cachin, Cloître.	58.32	32.
Ilimske.	56.40	36.44
Uskutskoi-Ostrog.	56.40	38.26
Nirimskoi-Ostrog.	57.50	41. 1
Iakustke, Ville.	62. 8	57.53
Okotskoi-Ostrog.	59.13	76. 7
Embouchure de la Riviere Bolchaia.	52.48	89.51
Verschnei Kamtchatkoi Ostrog. (ou le haut.)	54.48	
Niznei Kamtchatkoi Ostrog. (ou le bas.)	56.11	
Embouchure de la Riviere Kamtchatka.	56. 3	96.10
Coin (ou Pointe) de S. Thadee. (à l'embouchure de l'Anadir.)	60.20	111.33
Golfe de la Ste. Croix, à l'Ouest.	65.35	115.37
Coin vers l'Orient.	65.28	115.37
Golfe Preobasenskoi, ou de la Transfiguration.	65.28	180.30
Coin de de Tchukotz, vers l'Orient.	64.25	122.55
Isle de Saint-Diomide.	66.	125.44
L'endroit d'ou nous retournâmes.	67.18	126. 7
Coin de la Terre de Kamtchatka. (ou Pointe du midi.)	51.10	89.51

1. Iam signifie une poste où l'on prend des relais de chevaux ou de chiens: dans la plus grande partie de la Sibérie on se sert beaucoup pour les traîneaux de ces derniers animaux, qui y sont forts & vigoureux.

2. Ils n'ont point de demeures fixes, & ils sont de différentes langues (Razneikche Iazeikove :) quelques-uns sont encore Payens.

3. C'est-à-dire, la Croix de la Iudoma, Riviere qui tombe dans l'Aldan de l'Est.

4. Le Pude Russe est de 40. livres.

5. Cet endroit est si froid même en été, selon M. Gmelin (Flor. Sib. Praefat. pag. 47.) que les Russes l'ont appellé la Fontaine de glaces (Nakipuoi led) & les Iakuti Buss-col, lac de glaces: il est environ à moitié chemin d'Iakutsk & d'Okhotsk.

6. C'est-à-dire, 92000 liv. de France.

7. Cette partie de mer que Beering traversa est appellée sur sa Carte More Pentzinskoe, à cause de la riviere Pentzina ou Pentchina, qui y tombe du Nord-Est: c'est la même chose que le Golfe de Lama & de Kamtschatka.

8. Elle tombe dans l'Aldan de l'Ouest.

9. Entre le haut & le bas Kamtschatkoye, il y en a un autre au milieu, marqué sur la Carte.

10. Au Nord du Kamtschatka, & du Golfe qui le sépare du pays

d'Okhota, sont les Kariaki ou Koraeiki, qui sont appellés
Iasacheni, c'est-à-dire, tributaires; ils n'ont point de
demeure fixe, & sont vagabonds.

11. C'est-à-dire, en suivant les côtes Orientales du Kamtschatka,
& montant au Nord, dans ce que les Russiens appellent Tchaste
(partie) Moria (de la Mer) Tichova (Pacifique).

12. Elle est vis-à-vis la pointe méridionale du Cap Tschutskoi,
& a l'Est du Golfe Préobasinskoi ou de la Transfiguration.

13. M. de l'Isle, l'Astronome, ajoûte dans son Memoire de 1752
(ou il donne un abrégé de cette Navigation de Beering & des
autres qui l'ont suivie) que ce Capitaine en cet endroit
trouva la Mer libre au Nord & a l'Est: il n'en est pas de
même à l'Ouest, parce qu'elle est fort embarrassée de glaces
autour du grand Cap Tschalaginskoi. Cela n'empêche pas que
la mer Glaciale ne puisse étre traversée, comme M. Buache
l'a prouvé dans un Mémoire fort curieux, qui est parmi ceux
de l'Académie des Sciences de l'année 1754.

14. Il falloît apparemment prendre plus haut pour trouver cette
terre; car M. de l'Isle l'Astronome rapporte dans son Mémoire
de 1752, (& l'Officier de la Marine Russienne en convient)
que M. Beering lui a dit, qu'entre 50 & 60 de latitude, il
avoit eu tous les indices possibles d'une côte ou d'une
terre à l'Est; parce que 1°. il n'avoit trouvé en s'éloignant
du rivage que peu de profondeur & des vagues basses, telles
qu'on les trouve ordinairement dans les détroits ou bras de

Mer, bien différentes des hautes vagues que l'on éprouve
sur les côtes exposées à une Mer fort étendue: 2°. Parce
qu'il avoit trouvé des pins & autres arbres déracinés, amenés
par le vent d'Est, au lieu qu'il n'en croît point de tels
dans le Kamtschatka: 3°. Parce que les gens du pays lui
avoient appris que le vent d'Est amene les glaces en deux ou
trois jours, au lieu qu'il en faut 4 ou 5 à celui d'Ouest
pour les emporter: 4°. Parce que de certains oiseaux viennent
réguliérement tous les ans du côté de l'Est, & qu'après avoir
passé quelques mois sur les côtes de l'Asie, ils s'en re-
tournent aussi réguliérement dans la même saison. Au reste
le voyage de 1741 dont on verra dans un moment la Relation,
& ce qui a été rapporté ci-devant de la terre vûe en 1730 ou
1731 à l'Est, prouve la vérité de la conjecture dont il est
ici question.

15. Si nous ne le connoissions pas, les Chinois & les Japonnois
le connoissoient depuis long-tems, comme M. Buache l'a
prouvé dans ses Considerations.

16. Ils prennent leur nom d'une espece de Tatars qui habitent
aux environs, sans demeure fixe, & qui sont tous Payens: il
en a été parlé ci-devant pag. 157; mais on ajoûtera ici que
comme ils font grand usage de tambours dans leurs cérémonies
superstitieuses, il se pourroit que leur nom en vint; car des
joueurs de tambour sont appellés en Russien Barabanski.

Bibliography

<u>An</u> <u>Account</u> <u>of</u> <u>several</u> <u>late</u> <u>Voyages</u> & <u>Discoveries</u> <u>to</u> <u>the</u> <u>South</u> <u>and</u> <u>North</u>. . . London: S. Smith and B. Walford, 1694.

Akademiia nauk SSSR. Institut istorii estestvoznaniia i tekhniki. <u>Istoriia</u> <u>akademii</u> <u>nauk</u> <u>SSSR</u>. Vol. I. Moscow, Leningrad: AN SSSR, 1958.

Anderson, Matthew Smith. <u>Britain's</u> <u>Discovery</u> <u>of</u> <u>Russia,</u> <u>1553-1815</u>. London: St. Martin's Press, 1958.

Andreev, Aleksandr I. "Ekspeditsii V. Beringa." <u>Izvestiia,</u> <u>VGO</u>, 75:2 (March-April, 1943), 3-44.

----------. <u>Ocherki</u> <u>po</u> istochnikovedeniiu Sibiri. 2d ed. Vol. I. Moscow, Leningrad: AN SSSR, 1960.

----------. "Osnovanie akademii nauk v Peterburge." In <u>Petr</u> <u>Velikii</u>: Sbornik statei. Ed. A. I. Andreev. Moscow, Leningrad: AN SSSR, 1947, I:283-333.

----------. "Pervaia russkaia ekspeditsiia XVIII v. v severnom okeane." <u>Izvestiia,</u> <u>VGO</u>, 75:2 (March-April, 1943), 57-58.

----------. "Russkie otkrytiia v tikhom okeane v pervoi polovine XVIII veka." <u>Izvestiia,</u> <u>VGO</u>, 75:3 (May-June, 1943), 35-52.

----------. "Trudy G. F. Millera o vtoroi kamchatskoi ekspeditsii." <u>Izvestiia,</u> <u>VGO</u>, XCI:1 (January-February, 1959), 3-16.

Anville, Jean Baptiste Bourguignon d'. <u>Nouvel</u> <u>atlas</u> <u>de</u> <u>la</u> <u>Chine</u>. La Haye: H. Scheurleer, 1737.

Armstrong, Terence, ed. <u>Yermak's</u> <u>Campaign</u> <u>in</u> <u>Siberia</u>: <u>A</u> <u>Collection</u> <u>of</u> <u>Documents</u>. Hakluyt Society, <u>Works</u>, 2d series, CXLVI. London: Hakluyt Society, 1975.

Arnold, Christoph. <u>Wahrhaftige</u> <u>Beschreibungen</u> <u>dreyer</u> <u>mächtigen</u> <u>Königreiche,</u> <u>Japan,</u> <u>Siam,</u> <u>und</u> <u>Corea</u>. Nuremberg: M. und J. F. Endters, 1672.

<u>Atlas</u> <u>geograficheskikh</u> <u>otkrytii</u> <u>v</u> <u>Sibiri</u> <u>i</u> <u>v</u> <u>severo-zapadnoi</u> <u>Amerike</u>. Ed. A. V. Efimov. Moscow: Nauka, 1964.

Avril, Philippe. <u>Travels</u> <u>into</u> <u>Divers</u> <u>Parts</u> <u>of</u> <u>Europe</u> <u>and</u> <u>Asia,</u> <u>Undertaken</u>. . . <u>to</u> <u>Discover</u> <u>a</u> <u>New</u> <u>Way</u> <u>by</u> <u>Land</u> <u>into</u> <u>China</u>. London: T. Goodwin, 1693.

----------. Voyage en divers etats d'Europe et d'Asie, entrepris pour decouvrir un nouveau chemin à la Chine. Paris: C. Barbin [etc.] 1692.

Baer, Karl E. Von. Peters des grossen Verdienste um die Erweiterung der geographischen Kenntnisse. In Beiträge zur Kenntniss des russischen Reiches und der angrenzenden Länder Asiens, XVI (1872).

Bagrow, Leo. "The First Russian Maps of Siberia and Their Influence on the West-European Cartography of N. E. Asia." Imago Mundi, IX (1952), 83-93.

----------. A History of Russian Cartography up to 1800. Ed. Henry W. Castner. Wolfe Island, Ontario: The Walker Press, 1975.

----------. "Ivan Kirilov, Compiler of the First Russian Atlas, 1689-1737." Imago Mundi, II (1938), 78-82.

----------. "The Vitus Bering First Voyage Maps." Geografisk Tidsskrift, XLIX (1948-49), 32-40.

Baklanova, N. A. "Velikoe posol'stvo za granitsei v 1697-98 gg." In Petr Velikii: Sbornik statei. Ed. A. I. Andreev. Moscow, Leningrad: AN SSSR, 1947. I:3-62.

Barratt, Glynn. Russia in Pacific Waters, 1715-1825: A Survey of the Origins of Russia's Naval Presence in the North and South Pacific. Vancouver: University of British Columbia Press, 1981.

Belov, Mikhail I. Arkticheskoe moreplavanie s drevneishikh vremen do serediny XIX veka. In Istoriia otkrytiia i osvoeniia severnogo morskogo puti. Ed. Ia. Ia. Gakkel', A. P. Okladnikova, and M. B. Chernenko. Vol. I. Moscow: Morskoi transport, 1956.

Berg, Lev S. Geschichte der russischen geographischen Entdeckungen. Leipzig: Bibliographisches Institut, 1954. (A translation of Ocherki po istorii russkikh otkrytii).

----------. Otkrytie Kamchatki i ekspeditsii Beringa, 1725-41. 3rd ed. Moscow, Leningrad: AN SSSR, 1946.

Bering, Vitus. See entries for Dall, Du Halde, Strahlenberg.

Berkh, Vasilii N. Pervoe morskoe puteshestvie rossiian, predpriniatoe dlia resheniia geograficheskoi zadachi: Soediniaetsia li Aziia s Amerikoiu? St. Petersburg: Imperatorskaia akademiia nauk, 1823.

Bernard, Jean Frederic. Recueil de voyages au nord. 10 vols.
Amsterdam: J. F. Bernard, 1725-38.

Bettany, G. T. "Richard Brookes." Dictionary of National Biography,
VI (1886), 436.

Beuchot, A. J. Q. "Jean Louis Barbeau-de-la-Bruyère." Biographie
universelle, ancienne, et moderne, III (1811), 335-36.

Biographia Britannica, 2d ed., 5 vols. London, 1778-93.

Bion, Nicolas. l'Usage des globes celeste et terrestre. Paris:
Michel Brunet [etc.] 1728.

Birket-Smit, Kaj. "Morten Spangberg." Dansk Biografisk Leksikon,
XXII (1942), 329-30.

Boss, Valentin. Newton and Russia: The Early Influence, 1698-1796.
Cambridge: Harvard University Press, 1972.

[Bouillet.] Traite des moyens de rendre les rivieres navigable.
Paris: E. Michallet, 1693.

Brand, Adam. Beschreibung der chinesischen Reise. Hamburg: F. C.
Greflingern, 1698.

----------. A Journal of an Embassy from their Majesties John
and Peter Alexowits, Emperors of Muscovy, &c. into China.
London: D. Brown and T. Goodwin, 1698.

----------. Relation du voyage de Mr Evert Isbrand. . . a l'empereur
de la Chine. Amsterdam: J. L. de Lorme, 1699.

----------. Seer aenmercklijcke land- en water-reyse. . . uyt
Muscouw na China. Tyel: Jan van Leeuwen, 1699.

Brecher. "Johann Baptist Homann." Allgemeine deutsche Biographie,
XIII (1881), 35-38.

Brown, Lloyd A. Jean Domenique Cassini and His World Map of 1696.
Ann Arbor: University of Michigan Press, 1941.

Bruce, Peter Henry. Memoirs of Peter Henry Bruce, Esq. London:
For the Author's Widow, 1782.

Bruyn, Cornelis de. Voyages de Corneille Le Brun par la Moscovie,
en Perse, et aux Indes Orientales. Amsterdam: Freres Wetstein,
1718.

Burney, James. A Chronological History of North-Eastern Voyages of Discovery: And of the Early Eastern Navigations of the Russians. London: Payne and Foss, 1819.

Cahen, Gaston. Les cartes de la Sibérie. Essai de bibliographie critique. Paris: Imprimerie nationale, 1911. In Nouvelles archives des missions scientifiques et littéraires, nouvelle série, fasc. 1, XIX (1911), 1-544.

Carlson, C. Lennart. The First Magazine: A History of the Gentleman's Magazine. Providence: Brown University, 1938.

Chapin, Seymour L. "Joseph Nicolas Delisle." The Dictionary of Scientific Biography, IV (1971), 22-25.

Churkin, V. G. "Atlas Cartography in Prerevolutionary Russia." Trans. James R. Gibson. The Canadian Cartographer, XII:1 (June, 1975), 1-20.

Cook, Warren L. Flood Tide of Empire: Spain and the Pacific Northwest, 1543-1819. New Haven: Yale University Press, 1973.

Coronelli, Vincenzo. Epitome cosmografica, o compendiosa introduttione all'astronomia, geografia, & idrografia. Cologne, 1693.

Cross, Samuel H. "The Contribution of Gerhard Friedrich Müller to Russian Historiography, with some consideration of August Ludwig Schloezer." Ph. D. dissertation. Harvard University, 1916.

Crull, Jodocus. The Antient and Present State of Muscovy. 2 vols. London: A. Roper and A. Bosvile, 1698.

Cruys, Cornelius. Nieuw pas-kaart boek. . . Amsterdam: H. Doncker ⌈1704⌉.

Dall, William H. "A Critical Review of Bering's First Expedition, 1725-30, Together with a Translation of his Original Report on it." The National Geographic Magazine, II (1890), 111-67.

----------. "Notes on an Original Manuscript Chart of Bering's Expedition of 1725-1730, and on an Original Manuscript Chart of his Second Expedition; Together with a Summary of a Journal of the First Expedition, kept by Peter Chaplin, and Now First Rendered into English from Bergh's Russian Version." Report of the Superintendent of the U.S. Coast and Geodetic Survey Showing the Progress of the Work during the Fiscal Year Ending

with June, 1890. Appendix no. 19. Washington: Government
Printing Office, 1890.

Delisle, Guillaume. Atlas nouveau, contenant toutes les parties
du monde. Amsterdam: J. Covens & C. Mortier ₍1741₎.

----------. "Determination geographique de la situation & de
l'éntendue des differentes parties de la terre." Académie
des Sciences, Paris. Histoire de l'Académie royale des
sciences. Année MDCCXX. Amsterdam: Pierre de Coup, 1724,
473-98.

Delisle, Joseph Nicolas. Explication de la carte des nouvelles
decouvertes au nord de la Mer du Sud. Paris: Desaint et
Saillant, 1752.

----------. Nouvelles cartes des decouvertes de l'Amiral de Fonte,
et autres navigateurs. . . dans les mers septentrionales.
Paris, 1753.

Divin, Vasilii A. Russkie moreplavaniia na tikhom okeane v XVIII
veke. Moscow: Mysl', 1971.

Dobbs, Arthur. Observations upon the Russian Discoveries. London:
A. Linde, 1754.

Dodge, Ernest S. Northwest by Sea. New York: Oxford University
Press, 1961

Du Halde, Jean Baptiste. Ausführliche Beschreibung des chinesischen
Reichs und der grossen Tartarey. 4 vols. Rostock: Johann
Christian Koppe, 1747-49.

----------. Description geographique, historique, chronologique,
politique et physique de l'empire de la Chine et de la Tartarie
chinoise. 4 vols. Paris: P.G. Mercier, 1735.

----------. A Description of the Empire of China and Chinese-
Tartary. 2 vols. London: T. Gardner, 1738-41.

----------. The General History of China. 4 vols. London: J.
Watts, 1736.

Ebülgâzî Bahadir Han. A General History of the Turks, Mongols,
and Tatars, vulgarly called Tartars. 2 vols. London: J. and
J. Knapton, 1729-30.

----------. Histoire genéalogique des Tartars. 2 vols. Leiden:
A. Kalewier, 1726.

Efimov, Aleksei V. Iz istorii russkikh ekspeditsii na tikhom okeane. Moscow, 1948.

----------. Iz istorii velikikh russkikh geograficheskikh otkrytii. Moscow: Nauka, 1971.

Eichhorn, Carl. Die Geschichte der "St. Petersburger Zeitung" 1727-1902. St. Petersburg: Buchdruckerei der St. Petersburger Zeitung, 1902.

Euler, Leonhard. Die Berliner und die Petersburger Akademie der Wissenschaften im Briefwechsel Leonhard Eulers. 3 vols. Berlin: Akademie-Verlag, 1959-76.

Eyriès. "Jean-Baptiste Du Halde." Biographie universelle ancienne et moderne, XII (1814), 182-83.

Fisher, Raymond H. Bering's Voyages: Whither and Why. Seattle and London, University of Washington Press, 1977.

----------. "Dezhnev's Voyage of 1648 in the Light of Soviet Scholarship." Terrae Incognitae, V (1973), 7-26.

----------. The Russian Fur Trade, 1550-1700. Berkeley and Los Angeles: University of California Press, 1943.

Fontenelle, Bernard le Bovier de. "Eloge du Czar Pierre I." Académie des sciences, Paris. Histoire de l'Académie royale des sciences. Année MDCCXXV. Amsterdam: Pierre Mortier, 1732.

Foust, Clifford M. Muscovite and Mandarin: Russia's Trade with China and Its Setting, 1727-1805. Chapel Hill: University of North Carolina Press, 1969.

The Gentleman's Magazine: For March 1737. VII, 150 [Note on Cave's edition of Du Halde's work on China.]

----------: For June 1737. VII, 366-67. [Commentary on Watts' translation of Du Halde's work on China.]

----------: For February 1740. X, 95. [Notice on Spanberg.]

----------: For April 1740. X, 205. [Extract from a letter of Spanberg.]

----------: For October 1743. XIII, 552. "Extract of a Letter from Petersburg."

Gibson, James R. Feeding the Russian Fur Trade: Provisionment of the Okhotsk Seaboard and the Kamchatka Peninsula, 1639-1856. Madison: University of Wisconsin Press, 1969.

Gmelin, Johann Georg. Reise durch Sibirien. 4 vols. in 2. Göttingen: Abram Vandenhoecks seel. Wittwe, 1751-52.

----------. Reize door Siberiën naar Kamtschatka. 4 vols. Haarlem: Izaak en Johannes Enschede, 1752-57.

Gmelin, M. "Johann Georg Gmelin." Allgemeine deutsche Biographie, IX (1879), 269-70.

Gnucheva, Vera F., ed. Materialy dlia istorii ekspeditsii Akademii nauk v XVIII i XIX vekakh. Moscow, Leningrad: AN SSSR, 1940.

----------. Geograficheski departament Akademii nauk XVIII veka. Moscow, Leningrad: AN SSSR, 1946.

Golder, Frank A. Bering's Voyages: An Account of the Efforts of the Russians to Determine the Relation of Asia and America. 2 vols. New York: American Geographical Society, 1922.

----------. Russian Expansion on the Pacific, 1641-1850. Cleveland: The Arthur H. Clark Company, 1914.

Greely, A. W. "The Cartography and Observations of Bering's First Voyage." The National Geographic Magazine, III (1892), 205-30.

Grekov, Vadim I. "Naibolee rannee pechatnoe izvestie o pervoe kamchatskoi ekspeditsii (1725-30 gg.)" Izvestiia AN SSSR, seriia geograficheskaia (Moscow) no. 6 (November-December, 1956), 108-12.

----------. Ocherki iz istorii russkikh geograficheskikh issledovanii v 1725-65 gg. Moscow: AN SSSR, 1960.

Grunwald, Constantin de. La Russie de Pierre le Grand. Paris: Hachette, 1953.

Hakluyt, Richard. Voyages. Vol. I. London: J. M. Dent, 1907.

Hanway, Jonas. An Historical Account of the British Trade over the Caspian Sea. 4 vols. London: Mr. Dodsley [etc.] 1753.

Harris, John. Navigantium atque Itinerantium Bibliotheca: Or, A Compleat Collection of Voyages and Travels. 2 vols. London: Thomas Bennet [etc.] 1705.

----------. Navigantium atque Itinerarium Bibliotheca. Or, A
     Complete Collection of Voyages and Travels. Ed. John Camp-
     bell. 2 vols. London: T. Woodward [etc.] 1744-48.

Harrison, John A. The Founding of the Russian Empire in Asia
     and America. Coral Gables: University of Miami Press, 1951.

Harrisse, Henry. John Cabot, the Discoverer of North-America,
     and Sebastian, his Son. London: B. F. Stevens, 1896.

Haven, Peder von. Nye og forbedrede Efterraetningar om det
     Russiske Riga. Copenhagen: Paa Autors egen Bekostning, 1747.

----------. Reise in Russland. Copenhagen: Gabriel Christian
     Rothe, 1744.

----------. Reise udi Rusland. Soroe: Jonas Lindgren, 1757.

Herberstein, Sigismund von. Notes upon Russia. Trans. and ed.
     R. H. Major. 2 vols. Hakluyt Society, Works, 1st ser.
     X, XII. London: Hakluyt Society, 1851-52.

The Historical Register for the Year 1730. XV:60 (1730), 291.

Homann, Johann Baptist. Grosser Atlas über die gantze Welt.
     Nuremberg: J. E. Adelbulner, 1725.

Ides, Evert Ysbrandszoon. Drei-jarige reize naar China. Amster-
     dam: F. Halma, 1704.

----------. Dreyjährige Reise nach China von Moscau ab zu lande
     durch gros Ustiga, Siriania, Permia Daour und die grosse
     Tartarey. Frankfurt: T. Fritsch, 1707.

----------. Three Years Travels from Moscow Over-land to China.
     London: W. Freeman [etc.] 1706.

Isnard, Albert. "Joseph-Nicolas Delisle, sa biographie et sa
     collection de cartes géographiques à la Bibliothèque nationale."
     Comité des travaux historique et scientifique. Bulletin de
     la Section de Géographie, XXX (1915), 34-164.

James Ford Bell Library. An Annotated Catalog of Original Source
     Materials Relating to the History of European Expansion,
     1400-1800. Boston: G. K. Hall & Co., 1981.

Keuning Johannes. "Nicolaas Witsen as a Cartographer." Imago
     Mundi, XI (1954), 95-110.

Kish, George. "Guillaume Delisle." Dictionary of Scientific
    Biography, IV (1971), 22-25.

Köhler, Johann David. Schul- und reisen Atlas. . . Nuremberg:
    J. E. Adelbulnern, 1719.

Kornerup, Bjørn (A. Jantzen). "Peder v. Haven." Dansk Biogra-
    fisk Leksikon, IX (1936), 478.

Korsakova, V. "Matvei Stephanovich Pushkin." Russkii biogra-
    ficheskii slovar, XV (1910), 318-19.

Krasheninnikov, Stepan Petrovich. Exploration of Kamchatka:
    North Pacific Scimitar. Trans. E. A. P. Crownhart-Vaughan.
    Portland: Oregon Historical Society, 1972.

----------. Opisanie zemli Kamchatki. 2 vols. St. Petersburg:
    Imp. akademii nauk, 1755.

Kruta, Vladislav. "Johann Georg Gmelin." Dictionary of Scien-
    tific Biography, V (1972), 427-29.

Kushnarev, Evgenii V. V Poiskakh proliva: Pervaia kamchatskaia
    ekspeditsiia, 1725-30. Leningrad: Gidrometeoizdat, 1976.

Lada-Mocarski, Valerian. Bibliography of Books on Alaska published
    before 1868. New Haven and London: Yale University Press,
    1969.

La Mottraye, Aubry de. Travels through Europe, Asia, and into
    Parts of Africa. 3 vols. London: For the Author, 1723-32.

Lantzeff, George V. and Richard A. Pierce. Eastward to Empire:
    Explorations and Conquest on the Russian Open Frontier, to
    1750. Montreal: McGill-Queen's University Press, 1973.

Lauridsen, Peter. Vitus Bering: The Discoverer of Bering Strait.
    Trans. Julius E. Olson. Freeport: Books for Libraries Press,
    1969; reprinted from the original edition of 1889.

Lebedev, Dmitrii M. Geografiia v Rossii petrovskogo vremeni.
    Moscow, Leningrad: AN SSSR, 1950.

Lensen, George Alexander. The Russian Push toward Japan: Russo-
    Japanese Relations, 1697-1875. Princeton: Princeton Univer-
    sity Press, 1959.

Liashchenko, Peter I. History of the National Economy of Russia
    to the 1917 Revolution. Trans. L. M. Herman. New York:
    Macmillan Company, 1949.

The London Magazine, IX (1740), 155.

Lower, J. Arthur. Ocean of Destiny: A Concise History of the
North Pacific, 1500-1978. Vancouver: University of British
Columbia Press, 1978.

Maier, Lothar A. "Die Krise der St. Petersburger Akademie der
Wissenschaften nach der Thronbesteigung Elisabeth Petrovnas
und die 'Affäre Gmelin.'" Jahrbücher für Geschichte Osteuropas, neue Folge, XXVII:3 (1979), 353-73.

Makarovna, Raisa Vsevolodovna. Russians on the Pacific, 1743-
1799. Trans. Richard A. Pierce and Alton S. Donnelly.
Kingston: The Limestone Press, 1975.

----------. Russkie na tikhom okeane vo vtoroi polovine XVIII
v. Moscow: Nauka, 1968.

Massie, Robert K. Peter the Great: His Life and World. New York:
Alfred A. Knopf, 1980.

Materialy dlia istorii imperatorskoi akademiia nauk. Ed. M. I.
Sukhomlinov. 10 vols. St. Petersburg: 1885-1900.

Medushevskaya, O.M. "Cartographic Sources for the History of
Russian Geographical Discoveries in the Pacific Ocean in the
Second Half of the 18th Century." Trans. James R. Gibson
The Canadian Cartographer, IX:2 (December, 1972), 99-121.

Moriarty, G. P. "John Perry." Dictionary of National Biography,
XLV (1896), 35-36.

Moxon, Joseph. A Briefe Discourse of a Passage by the North-Pole
to Japan, China, &c. . . London: J. Moxon, 1674.

----------. Ein kurtzer Discours von der Schiff-Fahrt bey dem
Nord-Pol nach Japan, China, und so weiter. Hamburg: Johan
Nauman und Georg Wolff, 1676.

Müller, Gerhard Friedrich. Lettre d'un officier de la marine
russienne a un seigneur de la cour concernant la carte des
nouvelles decouvertes au nord de la mer du sud. Berlin:
Haude and Spener, 1753.

----------. A Letter from a Russian Sea-Officer, to a Person of
Distinction at the Court of St. Petersburgh. London: A.
Linde [etc.] 1754.

----------. Nachrichten von Seereisen, und zur See gemachten Entdeckungen, die von Russland aus längst den Küsten des Eismeeres und auf dem östlichen Weltmeere gegen Japon und America geschehen sind. St. Petersburg: Kaiserliche Akademie der Wissenschaften, 1758. (Sammlung russischer Geschichte, III).

----------. Nouvelle carte des decouvertes faites par les vaisseaux russes aux cotes inconnues de l'Amerique Septentrionale avec les pais adjacentes. . . St. Petersburg: l'Academie Imperiale des Sciences, 1754.

----------. "Opisanie morskikh puteshestvii po ledovitomu i po vostochnomu moriu s rossiiskoi storony uchenennykh." Sochineniia i perevody, k pol'ze i uveseleniiu sluzhashchiia, VII (January, 1758), 3-27; (February), 99-120; (March), 195-212; (April), 291-325; (May), 387-409; VIII (July), 9-32; (August), 99-129; (September), 195-232; (October), 309-36; (November), 394-424.

----------. Voyages from Asia to America, for completing the Discoveries of the North West Coast of America. London: T. Jefferys, 1761.

----------. Voyages et découvertes faites par les Russes le long des côtes de la mer Glaciale & sur l'ocean Oriental, tant vers le Japon que vers l'Amerique. 2 vols. Amsterdam: M. M. Rey, 1766.

"A Narrative of some Observations made upon several Voyages, Undertaken to Find a Way for Sailing about the North to the East-Indies, and for Returning the same Way from thence Hither; Together with Instructions Given by the Dutch East-India Company for the Discovery of the Famous Land of Jesso near Japan." Philosophical Transactions X:109 (London, 1674), 197-207.

Nichols, John. Literary Anecdotes of the Eighteenth Century. 6 vols. London: 1812-16.

Nierop, Dirck Rembrantsz van. Tweede deel van Enige Oefeningen. . . Amsterdam: A. S. van der Storck, 1674.

Nordenskiöld, Nils Adolf Erik. The Voyage of the Vega round Asia and Europe. Trans. Alexander Leslie. New York: Macmillan and Co., 1882.

Novlianskaia, Mariia G. Filip Ioann Strahlenberg: ego raboty po issledovaniiu. Moscow: Nauka, 1966.

----------. Ivan Kirilovich Kirilov: geograf XVIII veka. Leningrad: Nauka, 1966.

Omont, M. H. "Lettres de J.-N. Delisle au Comte de Maurepas et à l'Abbé Bignon sur ses travaux géographiques en Russie (1726-1730)." Comité des travaux historique et scientifique. Bulletin de la Section de Geographie, III (1915), 130-164.

Overton, The Rev. Canon. "Edward Cave." Dictionary of National Biography, IX (1887), 338-40.

Pallas, Peter Simon. A Naturalist in Russia: Letters from Peter Simon Pallas to Thomas Pennant. Ed. Carol Urness. Minneapolis: University of Minnesota Press, 1967.

Parker, John. The Strait of Anian: An Exhibit of Three Maps in the James Ford Bell Library at the University of Minnesota, Portraying Sixteenth and Eighteenth Century Concepts of the Waterway between Asia and America, which is now known as the Bering Strait. Minneapolis: The James F. Bell Book Trust, 1956.

Payen, Jacques. "Nicolas Bion." Dictionary of Scientific Biography, II (1972), 132-33.

Pekarskii, Petr Petrovich. Istoriia imperatorskoi akademiia nauk v Peterburge. 2 vols. St. Petersburg: Imperatorskaia akademiia nauk, 1870-73.

Perry, John. The State of Russia, under the Present Czar. London: Benjamin Tooke, 1716.

Pierce, Richard A. "Vitus Jonassen Bering." In The Discoverers: An Encyclopedia of Explorers and Exploration. Ed. Helen Delpar. New York: McGraw-Hill, 1980.

Pokrovskii, A. A., ed. Ekspeditsiia Beringa: Sbornik dokumentov. Moscow: Glavnoe arkhivnoe upravlenie NKVD SSSR, 1941.

Polevoi, Boris P. "Iz istorii otkrytiia severo-zapadnoi chasti Ameriki." In Ot Aliaski do ognennoi zemli. Ed. I. R. Grigulevich. Moscow: Nauka, 1967. pp. 107-20.

----------. "O kartax severnoi Azii N. K. Vitsena." Izvestiia AN SSSR, Seriia geograficheskaia, no. 2 (1973), 124-33.

----------. "O karte 'Kamchadalii' I. B. Gomana." Izvestiia AN SSSR, Seriia geograficheskaia, no. 1 (1970), 99-105.

----------. "Petr Pervyi, Nikolai Vitsen i problema 'soshlasia li Amerika s Asiei.'" Strany i narody vostoka, vypusk VII, Strany i narody basseina tikhogo okeana, kniga 3. Comp. and ed. Y. V. Maretin. Moscow: AN SSSR, 1975.

----------. "Vodnyi put' iz ledovitogo okeana v tikhii; zabytyi
nakaz A. A. Vinius 1697 goda." Priroda, V (1965), 94.

Polnoe sobranie zakonov rossiiskoi imperii, s 1649 goda. 1st
ser., III:4649. St. Petersburg, 1830.

Polonskii, Aleksandr S. "Pervaia kamchatskaia ekspeditsii Beringa,
1725-29 goda." Zapiski Gidrograficheskago departamenta,
Morskoe ministerstvo, St. Petersburg. VIII, (1850) 4:535-56.

Polo, Marco. The Travels of Marco Polo. Trans. Ronald Latham.
London: Folio Society, 1968.

Pritsak, Omeljan. "The Origin of Rus." The Russian Review,
XXXVI:3 (July, 1977), 249-73.

Raeff, Marc, ed. Plans for Political Reform in Imperial Russia,
1730-1905. Englewood Cliffs: Prentice-Hall, 1966.

Ratzel, Friedrich. "Evert Ysbrants Ides." Allgemeine deutsche
Biographie, XIII (1881), 747-49.

"Relation succinte ou abbregé de notre voiage pendant notre commission en Siberie." Manuscript. "Traduit du Suedois a
Stockholm le 5 fevrier 1733." Courtesy of the Bibliothèque
nationale, Paris.

Reynolds, Robert L. Europe Emerges: Transition toward an Indus-
trial World-wide Society, 600-1750. Madison: University of
Wisconsin Press, 1961.

Rich, E. E. "Russia and the Colonial Fur Trade." The Economic
History Review, 2d series, VII:3 (April, 1955), 307-28.

Russkoe istoricheskoe obshchestvo, Leningrad. Sbornik, CIII.
St. Petersburg, 1897.

Rossel. "Jean Baptiste Bourguignon d'Anville." Biographie universelle ancienne et moderne, II (1811), 296-98.

Sadyrev, Anatoli. "The Russian Columbus." Soviet Life, VIII:299
(August, 1981), 34.

Sandler, Christian. Johann Baptista Homann, Matthäus Seutter und
ihre Landkarten: Ein Beitrag zur Geschichte der Kartographie.
Amsterdam: Meridian Publishing Co. [196-]. Reprinted from
Gesellschaft für Erdkunde zu Berlin, Zeitschrift. Ser. 3,
XXI (1886), 328-84.

Sanson, Nicolas. l'Europe en plusieurs cartes, et en divers traittés de geographie et d'histoire. Paris: Chez l'Autheur, 1683.

Semenov, Iurii. Siberia: Its Conquest and Development. Trans. J. F. Foster. Baltimore: Helicon Press, 1963.

Smith, Thomas R. and Bradford L. Thomas. Maps of the 16th to 19th Centuries in the University of Kansas Libraries. Lawrence: The University of Kansas Libraries, 1963.

Sokolov, Innokentii. "Petr Avraamovich Chaplin." Russkii bio-graficheskii slovar, XXII (1905), 25-26.

Solov'ev, Sergei M. Istoriia Rossii s drevneishikh vremen, IX, X, XI. Moscow: Sotialno-ekonomicheskoi literatury, 1963.

Spate, O. H. K. The Spanish Lake. Minneapolis: University of Minnesota Press, 1979.

Stejneger, Leonhard. "An Early Account of Bering's Voyages." The Geographical Review, XXIV:4 (October, 1934), 638-42.

----------. Georg Wilhelm Steller: The Pioneer of Alaskan Natural History. Cambridge: Harvard University Press, 1936.

Steller, Augustin. "Zuverlässige Nachricht von dem merkwürdigen Leben und Reisen Herrn Georg Wilhelm Stöller." In Ergetzungen der Vernünftigen Seele. Ed. Johann Heinrich Gottlob von Justi. V (1747), 362-84.

Steller, Georg Wilhelm. Beschreibung von dem Lande Kamtschatka. Ed. J. B. S[cherer]. Frankfurt, Leipzig: J. G. Fleischer, 1774.

----------. Reise von Kamtschatka nach Amerika mit dem Commandeur-Capitän Bering. Ed. Peter Simon Pallas. St. Petersburg: J. Z. Logan, 1793.

Stieda. "Gerhard Friedrich Müller." Allgemeine deutsche Biographie, XXXII (1917), 547-53.

Strahlenberg, Philip Johann Tabbert von. Description historique de l'empire russien. 2 vols. Amsterdam: Chez Desaint & Saillant, 1757.

----------. An Historico-geographical Description of the North and Eastern Parts of Europe and Asia. London: J. Brotherton [etc.] 1738.

----------. Das Nord- und ostliche Theil von Europa und Asia. Stockholm: In Verlegung des Autoris, 1730.

----------. Vorbericht eines zum Druck verfertigten Werckes von der Grossen Tartarey und dem Königreiche Siberien, mit einem Anhang von Gross-Rusland. Stockholm: B.G. Schneider, 1726.

Sumner, Basil H. Peter the Great and the Ottoman Empire. London: Basil Blackwell & Mott, Ltd., 1949.

Svodnyi katalog russkoi knigi grazdanskoi pechati vosemnadtsatogo veka 1725-1800. 5 vols. Moscow, 1963-66.

Sykes, Godfrey. "The Mythical Straits of Anian." Bulletin of the American Geographical Society, XLVII:3 (1915), 167-71.

Thévenot, Melchisedech. Relations de divers voyages curieux. 2 vols. Paris: T. Moette, 1696.

Tompkins, Stuart Ramsay. Alaska: Promyshlennik and Sourdough. Norman: University of Oklahoma Press, 1945.

Tooley, R. V. Maps and Mapmakers. New York: Bonanza Books, 1962.

Topsøe-Jensen (C. F. Bricka). "Peter Christian Bredal." Dansk Biografisk Leksikon, IV (1934), 48-49.

Towle, E. L. "The Myth of the Open North Polar Sea." Actes du Dixième Congrès Internationale d'Histoire des Sciences, II (1964), 1037-41.

Tracy, James D., ed. True Ocean Found: Paludanus's Letters on Dutch Voyages to the Kara Sea, 1595-1596. Minneapolis: University of Minnesota Press, 1980.

Vakhtin, Vasilii V. Russkie truzheniki moria. Pervaia morskaia ekspeditsiia Beringa dlia resheniia voprosa, soediniaetsia li Aziia s Amerikoi. St. Petersburg: Morskoe ministerstvo, 1890.

Veer, Gerrit de. The Three Voyages of William Barentz to the Arctic Regions (1594, 1595, 1596). Hakluyt Society, Works, 1st ser., LIV. London: Hakluyt Society, 1876.

Vucinich, Alexander. Science in Russian Culture: A History to 1860. Stanford: Stanford University Press, 1963.

Wagner, Henry R. The Cartography of the Northwest Coast of America to the Year 1800. 2 vols. Berkeley: University of California Press, 1937.

Warep, Endel. "Über einige Karten Russlands in J. B. Homanns Atlas vom Jahre 1725." Petermanns geographische Mitteilungen, CVII:4 (1963), 308-11.

Waxell, Sven. The American Expedition. Trans. M. A. Michael. London: Hodge and Company, 1952.

Weber, Friedrich Christian. Memoires pour servir a l'histoire de l'empire russien. 2 vols. The Hague: T. Johnson and J. van Duren, 1725.

----------. The Present State of Russia. 2 vols. London: W. Taylor, 1723.

----------. Das veränderte Russland. 2 vols. Frankfurt: N. Förster, 1721.

----------. Das veränderte Russland. 3 vols. in 1. Frankfurt, Leipzig: Nicolai Försters und Sohnes seel. Erben, 1744.

Whitworth, Charles. An Account of Russia as It was in the Year 1710. n.p.: Strawberry Hill, 1758.

Willan, Thomas Stuart. The Early History of the Russia Company, 1553-1603. Manchester: Manchester University Press, 1956.

Williams, Glyndwr. The British Search for the Northwest Passage in the Eighteenth Century. London: Longmans, 1962.

Williamson, James A. The Cabot Voyages and Bristol Discovery under Henry VII. Hakluyt Society, Works, 2d series, CXX. London: Hakluyt Society, 1962.

Wise, Terence. Polar Exploration. London: Almark Publishing Co., 1973.

Witsen, Nicolaas Corneliszoon. Aeloude & hedendaegsche scheepsbouw en bestier. Amsterdam: Casparus Commelijn, 1671.

----------. "A Letter, not long since written to the Publisher by an Experienced Person residing at Amsterdam, containing a true Description of Nova Zembla, together with an Intimation of the Advantages of its Shape and Position." Philosophical Transactions, X:101 (1694), p. 3.

----------. ₂Letter to Robert Southwell, president of the Royal Society.₃ Philosophical Transactions, XVII:193 (1691), 492-94.

----------. Nieuwe lantkaarte van het noorder en ooster deel van Asia en Europa strekkende van Nova Zemla tot China. n.p.: 1687.

----------. Noord en oost Tartarye. 2 vols. Amsterdam: 1692.

----------. Noord en oost Tartaryen. 2 vols. Amsterdam: M. Schalekamp, 1785.

----------. "A Summary Relation of what hath been hitherto discovered in the Matter of the North-East Passage; Communicated by a good Hand." Philosophical Transactions, XI:118 (1675), 418-19.

Wittram, Reinhard. Peter I: Czar und Kaiser. 2 vols. Göttingen: Vandenhoeck & Ruprecht [1964].

----------. "Peters des Grossen erste Reise in den Westen." Jahrbücher für Geschichte Osteuropas, neue Folge, III:4 (1955), 373-403.

Wright, John K. "The Open Polar Sea." Geographical Review, XLIII (1953), 338-65.

Wroth, Lawrence C. "The Early Cartography of the Pacific." The Papers of the Bibliographical Society of America, XXXVIII:2 (1944), 85-268.

Yule, Sir Henry, ed. The Book of Ser Marco Polo. 2 vols. London: John Murray, 1926.